# ARE YOU GETTING ENLIGHTENED OR LOSING YOUR MIND?

*How to Master Everyday and Extraordinary Spiritual Experiences*

DENNIS GERSTEN, M.D.

*Three Rivers Press/New York*

Published by Three Rivers Press, a division of Crown Publishers,
Inc., 201 East 50th Street, New York, New York 10022. Member
of the Crown Publishing Group.

Originally published in hardcover by Harmony Books in 1997.
First paperback edition printed in 1998.

Random House, Inc. New York, Toronto, London, Sydney,
Auckland
www.randomhouse.com

THREE RIVERS PRESS is a trademark of Crown Publishers, Inc.

Printed in the United States of America

Design by June Bennett-Tantillo

Library of Congress Cataloging-in-Publication Data
Gersten, Dennis.
Are you getting enlightened or losing your mind? / by Dennis
Gersten.—1st ed.
p.      cm.
Includes bibliographical references and index.
1. Mental health.   2. Spiritual life.   3. Parapsychology.   I. Title.
RC489.R46G47       1997
131—dc21       97-5577
ISBN: 0-609-80200-3

10 9 8 7 6 5 4 3 2 1

First Paperback Edition

Praise for *Are You Getting Enlightened or Losing Your Mind?*

"I was enthralled with *Are You Getting Enlightened or Losing Your Mind?* Dr. Gersten's courageous, heartfelt, and practical look at the interface between enlightenment and mental distress is inspiring, authentic, and life-changing. I couldn't put it down. The deep understanding and healing that Dr. Gersten brings to his psychiatric patients is available, through this book, to each of us—regardless of our current state of health."

—Christiane Northrup, M.D., author of *Women's Bodies, Women's Wisdom*

"A psychiatrist openly and honestly shares his life's experience. Read what he has lived and learned so that you can liberate yourself and live fully."

—Bernie Siegel, M.D., author of *Love, Medicine & Miracles*

"Dr. Gersten masterfully moves readers straight into the day-to-day arena of spiritual transformation. This is a profound guide that spiritual seekers will celebrate."

—Bradford Keeney, Ph.D., author of *Everyday Soul: Awakening the Spirit in Daily Life*

"Some very simple truths and techniques from a caring author. Dennis steps in and out of 'reality' with ease. A brave, courageous book that challenges our assumptions and teaches in the same breath. Wonderfully cluttered with techniques, anecdotes, and stories."

—Peter Jensen, author of *The Inside Edge: High Performance Through Mental Fitness*

"In this comprehensive and highly accessible book, Dr. Gersten shares his passion for the healing potential inherent in a spiritual orientation to life. His twenty years of experience . . . have taught him that both mystical experiences and mental illness are real . . . and, most importantly, discernible even to the average lay person. . . His 'Mental Fitness Techniques' and program are practical, easily learned tools. They can change your life."

—Janet Quinn, Ph.D., R.N.

"The current medical industry has no models to aid a clinician in distinguishing, assessing, and helping patients with spiritual experiences. By speaking out and providing integrative language, Dr. Gersten is helping to transform the excesses of an exclusive, narrow, biological model."

—Scott Walker, M.D., Assistant Professor of Psychiatry, College of Medicine, University of New Mexico

*I dedicate this book to the memory of my father,
Dr. Jerome Gersten, a true healer, a physician who was
the embodiment of brilliance, compassion, and humility . . .
and to Sri Sathya Sai Baba, my spiritual teacher, the
embodiment of full consciousness, for whom no challenge
is too great and no person too unworthy to shower love
upon in abundance.*

# Contents

FOREWORD by Larry Dossey, M.D.                                    x

INTRODUCTION                                                     xiii

   Experiences of Spirit in a Secular World                    xvi

   Finding Meaning in Your Own Miracle                         xxii


## Part I: Opening the Mind to Spirit

1   OPENING TO THE POSSIBILITIES                              3

    A Powerful Mystical Experience                          4

    Psychic Beginnings                                      8

    A Spiritual Teacher Remakes a Psychiatrist             10

    Illness: A Doctor Learns Compassion the
    Hard Way                                               12

2   TWENTY-FIVE SPIRITUAL QUESTIONS PSYCHIATRISTS
    ARE AFRAID TO ASK                                      16

3   A DAY IN THE LIFE OF A SPIRITUAL PSYCHIATRIST          25

    Guided Imagery                                         37

**4 THE HEALING POWER OF HUMAN VALUES** 42

Psycho-Spiritual Assessment 48

**5 YOUR MENTAL FITNESS PROGRAM** 56

**6 BELIEF MEDICINE** 86

Shamanism and Sorcery 87

Eastern Healing Systems 90

Universal Healing Principles 92

Folk Medicine of the American Tribe 93

Mixed Messages About Healing 97

**7 GETTING CONSCIOUS ABOUT CONSCIOUSNESS** 101

The Language of Consciousness 108

Kundalini: A Great Masquerader 110

*Part II: The Lost Mind*

**8 WHAT IS THE MIND?** 121

Organic Brain Syndromes: When the Chemistry
Isn't Right 125

Schizophrenia: When the Brain and Mind Drive
Each Other Crazy 127

Mania: When the Brain Goes on Overdrive 133

Borderline Personality Disorder: When Spirit
and Mind Collide 138

Multiple Personality Disorder: When Dividing Is
Surviving 146

**9 WHEN THE SPIRIT CAN HELP THE MIND** 151

Depression: When the Past Won't Let Go 151

Anxiety Disorders: When the Future Takes Over 158

Neurosis and Suffering: When the Same Troubles
Haunt You 165

## Part III: Getting Enlightened

10 **HIGHER STATES OF CONSCIOUSNESS**　　179
　　Out-of-Body Experiences　　180
　　Deathbed Experiences　　183
　　Healing Trances　　184
　　Identity Transformations　　187
　　Nirvana　　188

11 **VISUAL PARANORMAL EXPERIENCES**　　191
　　Visions Versus Hallucinations　　192
　　Angels　　197
　　Visions of the Departed　　202
　　Ghosts and Hauntings　　204
　　Psychic Attack and Spirit Possession　　209
　　Thought-Forms　　213
　　Artistic Hallucinations　　216
　　The Human Aura　　218

12 **EXTRASENSORY PERCEPTION**　　223
　　ESP of Sound　　223
　　ESP of Smell　　226
　　ESP of Empathy　　227

13 **MIRACLES**　　231
　　Mind-Body Miracles　　232
　　The Power of Prayer　　233
　　God's Invisible Hand　　234

## Part IV: Tools for Transformation: Making Your Own Miracles

14 **SPIRITUAL FIRST AID**　　247
　　How to Recognize the Real Inner Voice　　248
　　How to Diagnose Your Own Miracles　　249
　　Practicing Forgiveness　　261

15  SPIRITUAL EMERGENCY: OPENING THE DOOR
    TO CHANGE                                              266

    Anxiety as Spiritual Emergency                        266

    Depression as Spiritual Emergency                     268

    Pain as Spiritual Emergency                           269

    Marital Problems as Spiritual Emergency               270

    Confusion and Panic as Spiritual Emergency            271

    Crisis in Faith as Spiritual Emergency                272

16  FACING THE VOID: HOW PROFOUND EMPTINESS IS
    CURED                                                  274

    Exploring the Void                                     275

    Divine Assistance                                      276

    Reaching the Bottom of the Void                        277

    Transforming the Bottom of the Void                    278

    The Inner Abuser                                       280

APPENDIX A: MENTAL FITNESS TECHNIQUES                      283

    MFT Listing                                            283

    MFT by Human Values                                    284

APPENDIX B: RESOURCES                                      287

    Recommended Reading                                    287

    Cutting the Ties: The Work of Phyllis Krystal          290

    Academy for Guided Imagery (AGI)                       290

    *Atlantis: The Imagery Newsletter*                     291

NOTES                                                      293

INDEX                                                      298

ACKNOWLEDGMENTS                                            309

# Foreword

"The deepest passion of the western world is to reunite with the ground of its being," wrote Richard Tarnas in his 1991 book *The Passion of the Western Mind*. This unquenchable desire to touch the Divine is universal. It is the source of the most sublime music, art, literature, and architecture of every culture.

But if our most intense drives are toward the transcendent, why do references to "the spiritual" create such emotional and intellectual indigestion in modern medicine and psychiatry? In our century, health care professionals have avoided religion and spirituality like the plague. This has created problems not only for patients but for physicians as well. As a result of this avoidance, medicine has become one of the most spiritually malnourished professions in our culture.

The reasons why the healing profession has avoided spiritual issues is rooted in the history of science. Only through great struggle did science finally escape the constraints and confines of the Church. Scientists discovered early on that a hands-off approach to religion worked best for both sides. They learned to leave "the spiritual" to religion as they claimed "the physical" for themselves.

This separation has been disastrous. It has led to the belief that there are basically two ways in which we can live our lives. We may, on the one hand, choose to be rational, intellectual, analytical, and scientific. On the other hand, we can choose the path of intuition, religion, and spirituality.

These paths are divergent; they cannot possibly be brought together. The failure to harmonize these two vectors in the human psyche has created immense emotional pain for millions of people in our culture, as they have attempted the unhealthy task of dividing their minds. Dr. Dennis Gersten shows that this choice is false and artificial. We *can* have it both ways; we can honor both our spiritual and intellectual impulses and heal the hurt that so many feel.

There are pitfalls, to be sure, as Gersten points out. Madness is real, and not every vision of God or Goddess is authentic. Self-deception is alive and well, as it has always been. Gersten makes clear that the path toward transcendence is not easy; the spiritual path is not for wimps. But many have gone before us and the path is well described. Through this book, Gersten becomes a guide.

Medicine and psychiatry are changing. We are gradually learning to lighten up where spiritual issues are concerned. The pressure to do so comes not just from patients, who are hungry for a spiritual spark in healing, but from science itself. For example, there are currently over 130 controlled experimental studies examining the effect of prayer and the ability of an empathic, caring, loving person to intervene in the function of a distant, living being; over half of these studies show statistically that prayer works. In addition, more than 250 studies reveal that religious practices, including prayer, are correlated with better health and a lower incidence of a broad variety of diseases. We need to admit what our research shows: that spiritual practice is *good* for health, both physical and mental. Today we can say that it isn't just nice or humane to include spiritual concepts in medicine and psychiatry; it's bad science *not* to do so.

Gentle rains have begun to fall on some of the spiritual deserts of medicine. The Office of Alternative Medicine, established in 1992 within the National Institutes of Health, has funded a study testing the effectiveness of distant, intercessory prayer in a program of drug and alcohol rehabilitation. A few years ago this study would have been unthinkable.

Not everybody agrees that these developments are a good thing. There are skeptics and cynics who believe that spirituality is ruinous for the human race, and that our best hope is to pull ourselves up by our intellectual bootstraps. While we can honor these opinions, we can observe nonetheless that this is the old-style thinking that creates deep and painful divisions in the lives of human beings. We must honor *all* we are, not just isolated parts, and we must learn to harmonize, not fragment, our psyche. The fact is, most people do not function well when they are deprived of spiritual experiences. There are spiritual-deficiency syndromes, just like vitamin and mineral deficiencies.

André Malraux, France's great novelist and former minister of culture, said, "The twenty-first century will be spiritual or it will not be at all." There is urgency in the spiritualization of modern life; time may *not* be on our side. But the movement has begun.

It gives me great personal pleasure that a physician has written this book, because it tells me there still are physicians who deeply sense the spiritual dimension of healing. Dr. Dennis Gersten is a healer in the highest sense of the word. He has supplemented his technical skills with uncommon wisdom, compassion, and love, which shine through on every page. It is an honor to add my endorsement to his vision.

—Larry Dossey, M.D.
Author of *Healing Words:*
*The Power of Prayer and the Practice of Medicine*

# Introduction

Samantha had not always been joyous. Her mother suffered from manic-depressive illness and kept Samantha's younger brother locked in a room with the windows painted black so that he wouldn't know if it was day or night. Eventually her mother murdered Samantha's father, for which she was put in a psychiatric hospital. Samantha had every reason to be as psychotic as her mother—but she wasn't.

Samantha traces the reason for her happiness and mental stability to something that happened one day when she was fourteen. The agony of her home life had brought her to the edge of suicide. She could find no point in living. But before she could kill herself, an inexplicable urge tugged at her to leave the house—and sit on the front lawn. Suddenly Samantha felt immersed in a state of complete bliss and extraordinary peace, as if she were one with all of Nature. She knew with certainty that there was a reason and a purpose to her life; a God without a name, a loving force that chose to remain anonymous, had completely and instantly pulled her out of her suicidal state and given her joy, which has been a part of her nature ever since.

Pamela, another patient, was hospitalized after making a very serious suicide attempt. One evening one of the nurses in the hospital called me and said, "Pam is hallucinating. She claims to be seeing auras around us." I replied, "She probably is! Don't give her any more medication." Pamela had other experiences that fell beyond the traditional reach of psy-

chiatry as well. One night immediately after her mother died, Pamela's bedroom windows were violently shaking. She became terrified that a "huge,
dark, menacing, terrifying force or being" was trying to break through
them. She feared that it was her mother, with whom she had been on very
bad terms and who she now thought had come back to menace, harm, or
haunt her. Pamela's interpretation of this experience would be strange and
perhaps totally unbelievable, except that that same night Pamela's brother,
who lived in another city, had the identical experience. Perhaps the
mother's spirit needed to get in one good last scare before moving on to
a more peaceful afterlife.

James, a 25-year-old, had been schizophrenic for many years before
I first met him in a VA clinic. The drug Stelazine made it easier for him to
cope with the world, allowed him to think more clearly, and cut down on
the number of auditory hallucinations he had. I was seeing James every
few months to reevaluate his medication needs—until he came in one day
and looked totally different. "What's going on, James? I've never seen you
look so good." He said, "I started meditating, joined a spiritual organization called Self-Realization Fellowship, and quit taking my medicine. I
feel great." Schizophrenics aren't supposed to do that—suddenly recover—
because schizophrenia is a nasty brain disorder with serious biochemical
imbalances. Almost invariably, schizophrenics live a life of torment—
hearing voices and having periodic paranoid episodes in which they completely lose touch with reality and sometimes have to be hospitalized. I
continued to see James every few months to see how his meditation was
going. For about a decade he continued to blossom and seemed to have
no need of medication. Although I never suggested that James discontinue
his medication and in fact disagreed with his decision to do so, I was happy
for him, but I remained cautious.

Sometime in the last ten years, many years after I had stopped working at the VA clinic, James went back on his medication. Recently, his
brother phoned me to tell me that James wasn't doing so well—he'd "gone
off his medication again." I felt as if the universe were telling me something. "Get James's story straight," I said to myself. "The meditation and
spiritual path helped, but he's not cured. Don't glorify the situation. He's
schizophrenic and needs medication. Meditation is not enough." James's
decade of wellness had been miraculous, but people with schizophrenia
almost always require medication. The ideal treatment would have been
a combination of medication and meditation.

A friend of mine, Norma, walked into church one day and saw
"golden rain" falling through the air. The sight filled her with awe, rev-

erence, and extraordinary happiness. Her priest told her that she was blessed to have had such an experience—it was a rare spiritual experience, one recognized and acknowledged by the Roman Catholic Church. Norma herself still had doubts about the reality of the "golden rain," though, so she visited a psychiatrist who had treated her in the past for depression. Now he wanted to send her into a psychiatric hospital immediately and put her on antipsychotic medication to help her get rid of the "hallucination." This psychiatrist was unable to consider the medically taboo possibilities about God, spirituality, visions, and higher states of consciousness that Norma's experience may have reflected. Thankfully, her priest was able to reassure her that she was not losing her mind.

Pepe Romero, widely regarded as the greatest living classical guitarist, says that "God plays most of my concerts. When he does that, I am in a state of total and complete ecstasy. I am one with the audience. There is not an audience *and* me. There is only one."

I have been fortunate to share in a few special synchronistic experiences with Pepe. On one occasion, upon returning from Vienna, he told me he knew how Mozart had written *The Magic Flute*. Pepe had stood in Mozart's studio and heard birds singing, and he recognized the melody of the birds to be that of *The Magic Flute*. This in itself is not a stunning revelation, since Mozart himself wrote about how he used bird songs. Yet as we talked in Pepe's backyard in Del Mar, I jokingly said, "I wonder if Vivaldi's guitar quartet was inspired by the birds." At that moment a bird in a tree overhead began singing the exact melody of Vivaldi's quartet. Granted, it was only one bird—we didn't hear the full orchestration of four birds singing all four of the guitar parts!

What do these people, these experiences, have in common? They all share a quality that some might call "spiritual," illustrating miracles and madness, grace, and skepticism. But others would call them "crazy" or dismiss them as mere coincidence. Many medical doctors and scientists would agree with Karl Marx that "religion is the opiate of the masses" and with Sigmund Freud, who regarded religion as a crutch. Recently, Freud's attitude was reaffirmed by the American Psychiatric Association (APA) as a necessary "scientific pessimism." This reaffirmation reflects a dim view of human nature, one that excludes not only spirituality and religion but all higher instincts, let alone altruism. An APA panel in 1991 agreed that people have an "innate tribalism and need for conflict." It warned that "there will always be enemies. For there to be 'us' and 'them' is human nature."

As a psychiatrist, I am embarrassed by the APA statement and its general mind-set. How arrogant for a profession that is less than a century old to make such sweeping statements about human nature! If we can attain happiness only by fulfilling our personal desires, and if we are motivated only by finding and defeating an appropriate enemy, then surely we are doomed.

Yet history is replete with examples of heroes who disregarded their own self-interest and were willing to surrender even their lives for the good of others. Mother Teresa is one, so is Boris Yeltsin, who stood on top of a tank to make one of the boldest statements of the twentieth century: "I will give up my life rather than allow Communism to stand." The lone man in Tienanmen Square in Beijing, who stood in front of a brigade of tanks for freedom, is another example. Thousands of unknown people rise above their own needs for a greater cause every day—just watch *Rescue 911* on television to see people who risk their lives to help total strangers. In the average family anywhere in the world, parents risk their lives for their children. Call it love, call it spirit, or call it courage, but there is no doubt that the urge to rise to something higher, to follow a higher cause, is inherent in humankind.

The world's great teachers, throughout history, have all taught that we do not need enemies. Only limited minds need enemies. Nor will every psychological problem be solved by finding new drugs to "fix" the brain's various moods and organic problems. The saints, sages, and wise men and women throughout history have experienced, lived, and taught that we have a need for a higher vision. They have taught that love, truth, peace, nonviolence, faith, and moral conduct are the guideposts to human life . . . that all of life is one . . . and that the physical, mental, and spiritual universes are all one interwoven tapestry. They have taught that life has a purpose—to love all and serve all.

## EXPERIENCES OF SPIRIT IN A SECULAR WORLD

Theresa was a beautiful, gregarious Catholic girl and a brilliant student. By the time she was a teenager, she was so popular, she could have had her own fan club. Her parents adored her, and she was her teacher's pet. Her vivacious personality, her curly dark hair, and her pitch-black eyes made her the dream of many young men's imaginations. She had a zest for life and an extraordinary exuberance, and she could throw herself into any activity with complete abandon.

Theresa's carefree life suddenly changed at the age of sixteen, when she began to receive love letters from her cousin. Part of her was falling in love with him too, but another part was wracked with guilt. Finally, after resisting his advances for some time, she confided her problem to her father, who promptly sent her away to a convent for one year. Although Theresa was quite religious, a life of disciplined prayer was not what she had had in mind for herself. Nonetheless, she spent the next year trying to respect her father's wish that she be a responsible member of the convent. She fit in quickly, as she had previously adapted to every other situation in her life, but she was unhappy.

Theresa eagerly awaited the end of her year of "confinement." But just prior to leaving for home, she suffered an attack of severe weakness, followed by agonizing pains. They started in her chest and abdomen, then filled her entire body. Her face, which had always been cheerful and upbeat, became flaming red and took on the look of someone who fears imminent death. The attack subsided, but later such attacks of pain and weakness returned over and over again, leaving her with an intense fear of them.

Theresa's interest in boys vanished, as did every other "normal" desire. She craved God alone and focused all her energies on "pleasing the Lord." She prayed incessantly. Then she began to hear voices and experience visions. At first, she felt a "presence" around her, which she "knew" to be God. Then began a lifetime of experiences similar to one Theresa described this way: "One feels that one has been wholly transported into another and a very different region from that in which we live, where a light so unearthly is shown that if during one's whole lifetime one would be trying to picture it and the wonders seen, one should not possibly be able to succeed." Theresa experienced ecstasies: "An upward flight takes place in the interior of the soul, and this with the swiftness of a bullet fired from a gun." She had visions of Jesus, initially brief episodes, but later on they would last for days at a time. She saw angels and "a light far brighter than the sun." She saw one angel of such exquisite beauty that she was unable to adequately describe it. The angel "threw a dart" into her, which resulted in a state of supreme ecstasy.

Not only did Theresa experience extraordinary visions, but those visions spoke to her. She heard God say to her, "I do not want you to converse any longer with humans, but only with angels." During one period of extreme emotional anguish, she felt that the Devil was tormenting her. Then she heard a voice that said, "Do not fear, daughter, for it is I, and I will never abandon you. Do not fear." Theresa took the voice to be that of God.

In modern terms, Theresa sounds like someone suffering from a major mental illness, most likely schizophrenia, in which brain chemistry drives the person crazy, while psychological and social pressures throw the brain chemistry out of whack. Or she could be suffering from the euphoria of mania, which is caused both by a severe disturbance in brain chemistry as well as in psychological makeup. But this Theresa is Saint Theresa of Ávila, the great Spanish mystic of the sixteenth century.[1]

Saint Theresa was no schizophrenic. Rather, she learned how to live in two worlds, the world of the spirit and the world of ordinary people. Having developed an iron will, she commanded the respect of kings and popes, a feat impossible for a psychotic person. And unlike schizophrenics, who lose their ability to cope with the world, Theresa's ability continually grew. She founded an order of nuns and corresponded with officials, including San Juan de la Cruz, who became John of the Cross, and was a major organizing force of the Roman Catholic hierarchy. Once Theresa came to realize the spiritual truth of her voices and visions, her emotional suffering was transformed into joy and peace. Although her attacks of pain and physical weakness continued throughout her life, she learned how to live with them and to understand them in spiritual terms. For Theresa, happiness was the hallmark of spiritual progress.

At the age of 63, four years before she died, Saint Theresa called herself "an aged woman, good for little now, very old and weary. Yet my desires are still vigorous." Despite her physical frailty, she worked tirelessly until she died, trying to reform the Church. So strong were her will and her spiritual convictions that near the end of her life she pronounced, "If you faint on your way, if you die on the road, if the world is destroyed, all is well if you reach your goal." These are not the words of a person who has been defeated by mental illness. Rather, they are the triumphant words of a victorious soul, a person who can distinguish the voices of God and conscience from those that arise out of insanity and the whims of imagination.

If the signs, symptoms, and experiences of mysticism and enlightenment were confusing and upsetting to a saint, imagine how others feel when the inexplicable happens to them.

More and more people today are having spiritual, mystical experiences. Millions of us have experienced altered states of consciousness, have had visitations from deceased relatives, and have had strong premonitions that came true. People who have had these inexplicable experiences, these glimpses beyond time and space, always regard them as among the most meaningful and powerful experiences in their lives. Such experiences, to be sure, are not always blissful and pleasant; sometimes they are frightening. Spiritual experiences can bring on true spiritual emergencies that are not effectively treated with Valium, Thorazine, or Prozac. But invariably, people who have glimpsed a different reality begin to look at life differently. They gain a deep conviction that there is something greater than themselves, that there are ways of seeing that have nothing to do with the eyes, ways of hearing that have nothing to do with the ears, and ways of knowing that have nothing to do with the five senses or with "reason."

The average American already believes that modern science cannot explain many human experiences. Most of us already believe in a higher invisible order. In 1987 the National Opinion Research Center of the University of Chicago found that 67 percent of Americans have experienced extrasensory perception, 42 percent have had contact with the dead, and 29 percent have had visions. Gallup polls in the late 1980s showed that 43 percent have had an unusual spiritual experience; 46 percent of us are convinced there is life elsewhere in the universe; 15 percent have had a near-death experience—and 23 percent believe in reincarnation. According to a 1976 Gallup poll, 94 percent of us believe in God, 90 percent pray, and 88 percent believe that God loves us. One survey, reported in *Brain/Mind Bulletin,* revealed that 79 percent of psychiatrists accept the reality of psychic phenomena and that 33 percent have themselves had a life-changing religious experience.[2] A recent study reports that 60 percent of Americans believe in angels.

In fact, the average person has an unusual state of consciousness every day. We all experience at least a half dozen different states of consciousness every single day. Yet it seems that Americans believe in a "normal" state of consciousness, in one kind of consciousness only. Everything else is considered to be abnormal, whether it's nirvana or depression.

We need to pay attention to the other states of consciousness. Several books have already examined, at least partially, some of the altered states of consciousness and the "varieties of religious experience." *Are You Getting Enlightened or Losing Your Mind?* looks at varieties of *human experience.* Besides elaborating on the different kinds of experiences— "normal," "abnormal," and "supernormal"—this book will provide a Mental Fitness Program using imagery techniques from my practice. These mental fitness techniques channel your consciousness constructively to help you become more balanced psychologically and spiritually. It scares most of us just to consider that we may spend any part of our day in anything other than logical, linear, goal-oriented consciousness. My goal is to help you grow more comfortable with these different, sometimes disturbing states of mind, so that you may embrace each experience more completely, without fear and without judgment.

Before plunging headfirst into this book, a few words about my own background are in order. I write from the perspective of a medical doctor who has himself had numerous miraculous events in his own life, some of which I will share with you. I also will share a number of stories that patients, friends, and acquaintances have shared with me about their mystical experiences and about miraculous phenomena they have seen. As a psychiatrist, I have worked with literally thousands of severely mentally ill people, people I see in my office, people undergoing a few weeks of treatment in a psychiatric hospital, and people who are permanently psychotic and have spent years in a state mental hospital.

Based on my own experiences, I can say with confidence that the difference between a miracle and madness, between an angel and a psychotic vision, between clairvoyance and psychotic delusion, is vast. Yet it is essential that we learn to sort out the miracles from the madness. Not knowing whether one is having a nervous breakdown or getting enlightened is a terrible agony that can be lifted just by knowing the diagnosis.

If you're looking for double-blind controlled studies that prove the existence of miracles, you won't find them in this book. You'll never find a miracle in a test tube, and you'll never be able to count the number of angels dancing on the head of a pin. Someday scientists will be able to tell us exactly what the brain chemistry of an "altered state" like depression or schizophrenia is, but they'll never be able to put the *experience* of depression into a test tube. Likewise, scientists will one day, I believe, be able to identify the brain-wave patterns and blood chemistry parameters associated with samadhi, a mystical state of consciousness in which one experiences a sense of unity with God and all of creation, but they'll never be able to put samadhi into a test tube and measure the experience, any more than they can put God or the Infinite into a test tube or under an electron microscope. But there are still ways to find meaning in miracles.

As a psychiatrist, I have come to a new and better understanding of my job description. To treat depression and psychosis, I work with strong medications. But I also work with powerful mind-body tools, such as meditation and guided imagery, that have rapid and profound healing potential. And I work with what I believe to be the essence of our humanity—our striving for excellence, our yearning to be immersed in the moment, our ability to love, our quest to travel on our own personal mythological journeys, and our ability to rely on God as our primary healing ally.

As more and more people share with their physicians their glimpses into other realms of consciousness, the physicians may feel unsettled. But many of the greatest doctors and scientists of our time have been deeply spiritual. Here are a few of Albert Einstein's thoughts about God and the Spirit:

"That deeply emotional conviction of the presence of a superior reasoning power, which is revealed in the incomprehensible universe, forms my idea of God."

"The principal art of the teacher is to awaken the joy in creation and knowledge."

"The most beautiful and profound emotion we can experience is the sensation of the mystical. It is the sower of all true science."

The world's great religions have demonstrated that spiritual experiences, visions, angels, and a variety of higher states of consciousness are not only normal but also desirable and attainable through spiritual practice. I believe that the next quantum leap for psychiatry will be to integrate spirituality into clinical practice. Psychiatry needs to begin addressing a new order of questions, such as, How do we distinguish insanity from mystical ecstasy? How do we know if someone is hallucinating or seeing auras? Should we be treating auras at all? How do a person's attitudes about life after life or a higher dimension affect the way they live? As psychiatrists, how do our attitudes about these issues affect our ability to empathize with our patients? And how can any of us find out if we're getting enlightened or losing our minds? These are questions that psychiatrists are afraid to ask—but we need to ask them. And we urgently need to figure out how we can utilize the faith and beliefs of the average American—your faith—to help you heal your mind and body.

My role as a psychiatrist is neither to exorcise so-called "dark" or "evil" experiences nor to teach people paths to spiritual wisdom or enlightenment. But I and others in my profession—and lay people in all walks of life—need to listen respectfully to spiritual experiences and not discount them. We need to provide a safe place for people to talk about those experiences in a way that helps them come to grips with the significance that these experiences may have for their lives. An open, nonjudgmental attitude will help people accept the magical, mystical side of their personality and let it flourish. To modify slightly one of Einstein's quotes, I believe that the principal art of the *psychiatrist* is to awaken the joy in creation and knowledge and to help clarify what is a miracle and what is delusion.

## FINDING MEANING IN YOUR OWN MIRACLE

Of course, this book is not written just for psychiatrists. In fact, this book is primarily written for you, the average person. You are not a psychiatrist, and you don't need to see one. But you or someone in your family or a friend is likely to have had a spiritual experience. Maybe you're still in the closet about the experience, worried about how your loved ones would react if you told them about it. But if you and your loved ones understood that spiritual experience is normal, you all would feel freer to open up to one another in a deeper, more meaningful way, sharing your most profound experiences without fear of ridicule. I hope that by reading this book, you will come to embrace your spiritual experience, and that by the time you've finished it, you'll know more about such experiences as others have experienced them and will know how to make yours uniquely your own. I hope you will also learn what to call your experience. Being able to name it is a priceless treasure. Knowing that what you've had is a mystical experience, or a kundalini awakening, or a true vision of the departed, will comfort and reassure you, and you will feel united with others in a commonality of experience. You'll know you're not crazy.

Merely by listening to Pamela's frightening story of her mother's spirit, "the ghost at her window," for instance, I gave her permission to share and relive this experience. My acceptance was very healing for her. It told her she was not "crazy," and my nonjudgmental attitude calmed any fear she might have had. You too deserve the peace of mind that arises when you embrace your own spiritual experiences and can share them with your loved ones without fear of judgment.

I recently treated a man in a mental hospital who claims to be God. He claims to have millions of minds—that in fact all minds are his because he is God. Carl is a 40-year-old street person who has been diagnosed schizophrenic for many years. He mumbles, he hears voices, and he becomes frightened when I ask him direct questions about being God. Carl is so dysfunctional, I've had to apply for a conservatorship for him, which means a person will be appointed by the court to help him out, find him a board-and-care facility to live in, and help rehospitalize him if that is necessary. When I told Carl I was applying for a conservatorship, he got very upset and said, "How can you do that? All of my minds are perfect. How can you put God on a conservatorship?" I told him that was indeed a good question and that I would have to let the judge decide on it.

Other people who claim to have had miraculous or divine experiences *really are* having those experiences. That's part of what this book is about—helping you find out what your unusual experience was or is. This book is a diagnostic manual of mystical experiences. It will help you recognize when you're having a universally recognized experience that augurs spiritual development, and how to distinguish visual disturbances from spiritual visions, auditory distortions from oracles, and auras from migraine headaches.

Chances are, if you're reading this book, you're *not* going crazy. Yet you're living in a culture that—despite all its beliefs in God, religious practice, and higher purpose—does not accept the range of different experiences that some cultures do. For all our protestations of belief in God, for example, we are on, as Joseph Campbell put it, a "terminal moraine" of the fall of our traditional religious institutions. Many of us experience a spiritual void in our materialistic, competitive workaday lives. We need to make time to listen to what we already know—that love, faith, God, and spiritual experience are real and are the cornerstones of a meaningful life.

There is a huge gap between what the average person believes and the way the average psychiatrist practices. I have written *Are You Getting Enlightened or Losing Your Mind?* in order to provide a bridge between patient and psychiatrist—a bridge that allows spirituality to become a viable issue that either patient or doctor can bring up. It is my hope that we can destigmatize spirituality, altered states of consciousness, visionary experiences, extrasensory perceptions, paranormal phenomena, and other important experiences so that patients can discuss them without being labeled crazy by their psychiatrists. I hope this book will help you recognize your miracles and feel comfortable sharing them—even with your psychiatrist. (I also hope you don't use this book to "beat up" on your doctor or spouse for being "backward.")

In part, this book was written for the millions of misunderstood patients who were called crazy and put on Thorazine because they told their psychiatrist they were having visions. *An honest diagnosis is an incredibly healing tool in itself.* I cannot express to you the relief and hope that patients feel when they believe they are deeply understood: when I can clarify for them that they have a clinical depression that I need to treat with antidepressants—or that the vision of Mary they had is not part of their depression but is, in fact, a part of them that is turning them toward the light. I may not have to treat "Mother Mary"—I may have to inspire the patient to develop her relationship with Mary, at the same time that the Prozac is alleviating her depression.

It is my fervent hope that we can finally recognize the distinctions between mental illness and enlightenment. An ecstatic rapture may be either mania or samadhi. Sometimes it is drug-induced, a temporary high caused by amphetamines, cocaine, LSD, or ecstasy, which may produce a permanent "low." We need to learn how to sort out these different mental states, so that we're not treating samadhi or nirvana with Thorazine. I invite you to dive in and get comfortable with the different states of mind and body. I invite you to explore more deeply the many threads in the web of life—spiritual experience, enlightenment . . . and miracles.

What is a miracle? Like love, it is that which is not measurable. It occurs beyond our five senses. It is not limited by time or space. And yet a miracle is something we all have a sense about; a huge number of us have had direct experience with miracles. A miracle is a healing from an "untreatable" illness. It is extraordinary courage in the face of immense adversity. It is our subtle knowing of things that we're not "supposed" to know. It is a peaceful death.

Like dreams, spiritual experiences may not reveal their meanings without much probing and thought. As with any life experience, their full import is not instantly known, and sometimes may never be fully understood. We need to explore gently our spiritual experiences, our synchronicities, our miracles, and hold them lovingly up to the light of inquiry. And yes, that inquiry may produce uncertainty. Not all prophetic dreams come true the next day. Sometimes years may pass before one realizes that a dream was truly a prophecy and not the whim of the unconscious mind. Holding an experience with openness, humility, and a toleration of uncertainty will allow its deeper mysteries to be revealed to us.

Life is filled with experiences that have no name, with ecstasies that are not insanity, with love that is incomprehensible, with knowings of the unknowable—and with miracles. It is within this context that I work with people, hoping to coach them, to inspire them, to give them faith and hope to keep them going. My goal is to help them gain access to all their strengths—mental, physical, and spiritual—and to help them dream their grandest dreams, seek their higher *vision,* and go beyond the limited thinking that says "We will always need enemies. That's our nature."

Our real enemies are internal, and they are the most difficult foes of all. We must move beyond the kind of thinking that puts the enemy on the outside. This is the very thinking that makes change so difficult. Our recognition of our real enemies, by contrast, puts the power of change in our own hands. The heroes of history may seem to have been invincible people with few personal struggles, as if they had nothing to do but transform society. But even the great Mahatma Gandhi struggled with "demons," reporting candidly that his strong spiritual beliefs gave him his strength to drive the British out of India. Even as he lay dying from a fatal gunshot wound, he recited the name of the form of God he worshiped.

By his example, Gandhi teaches that nonviolent resistance can conquer the "enemy" with greater strength than can firepower. Without a personal life that was consistent with his public message, he would never have had all the strength and power he wielded. Likewise, as a physician, my personal self-work has lent me the strength to take seriously the famous Hippocratic oath. With that oath physicians promise to do what Gandhi taught, namely, "Do no harm." Decades later, that first and most fundamental promise remains more important for me than ever before—perhaps because of the importance I give to struggling with my own "demons."

In the spirit of doing no harm, I have taken great care to assure that, to the best of my knowledge, the strange, wondrous, and perhaps scary stories found in the pages of this book are 100 percent true. They have been carefully researched. Nothing has been sensationalized, dramatized, sanitized, or altered. Only the names of my patients have been changed.

So you see, I wrote this book with several hopes and goals in mind. First, I wanted to describe the vast array of human experiences—normal, abnormal, and supernormal—so that the reader could identify any experience he may have had, know what to call it, and know what, if anything, to do about it.

My second goal is to build a bridge that allows doctors and patients to better communicate with each other about spiritual experience. This book adds to the body-mind-spirit equation what I believe to be a missing element, namely—energy. In a new holistic medicine, I believe, the approach might be to evaluate a patient based on body, mind, spirit, and energy.

Third and most important, I want to provide powerful spiritual tools for mental fitness, tools that can transform your life, including a three-step system of Psycho-Spiritual Assessment, which is part of a total Mental Fitness Program. Finally, I wrote this book to give validity to the profound experiences that our society does not yet feel comfortable discussing. Even though you most likely already know you're not crazy, it is very easy to feel exposed, insecure, and misunderstood if you've had an experience that even comes close to those you'll find in these pages. After reading this book, you should be able to diagnose your experience, your vision, your hunch, or your intuition, and know what to call it.

When dealing with mental illness, there is no substitute for psychiatric training or for decades of experience in diagnosing and treating patients. But there also is no reason why lay people cannot have a more empowering understanding of their life experiences. For the vast majority of readers, merely finding out what to call the experience will be liberating. Knowledge by itself is a powerful tool. For too long the medical profession has maintained a mystique of secrecy, elitism, and technological knowledge, as if nonphysicians were incapable of understanding their own health. The mystique of psychiatry has prevented its most fundamental concepts from being incorporated into the everyday thinking processes of the average person, and so it has also prevented the merging of the spiritual outlook with the psychiatric outlook.

Every week in churches and in temples around the world, a clergy person stands in front of a congregation expounding upon principles that they hope their listeners will absorb. Now it is time for psychiatry to do the same. This book attempts to lift the mystique of psychiatry and provide an insider's view of mental illness. Information should be shared, not hoarded. Information is meant to lead to transformation.

I hope this book will help you recognize and embrace your miracles rather than chase them back into the recesses of your mind. I hope it inspires you yet also assists you in practical ways in your daily life. I hope it helps you recognize your miracles, strengthen your faith, and find deeper (and higher) meaning in your life. I hope it helps you come closer to your own sense of spirituality and God, tap your own healing power, and become comfortable with mystical or spiritual experience. I hope it helps you bring sacred awareness more fully into each moment of your life.

# PART I

*Opening the Mind*

*to Spirit*

# 1

# OPENING

# TO THE

# POSSIBILITIES

During the 1960s much experimentation was going on with hallucinogenic drugs. Some researchers wanted to see how LSD would affect Indian yogis. Would they hallucinate and lose touch with reality like everyone else?

When the yogis took LSD, an astonishing thing happened. Nothing. Nothing at all happened. But how could that be? Yogis have the same brains as everyone else, the same central nervous system. How could they not be profoundly affected? Perhaps spiritual discipline produces more than lower metabolic rates and deep relaxation—more than physical or bodily effects. Can the mind of the yogi be so completely transcended that mind-altering drugs, such as LSD, have no effect because they no longer have a mind upon which those drugs can act?

The mind, to be sure, hallucinates under the influence of LSD. But is it possible to go beyond mind, to uncover our "true nature"? Is there a "true nature"? Eastern religion teaches that there is—that the mind is not reality, that the mind helps *obstruct* reality. But the mind can also be used to lead us to the heights, to reach God. The mind can even be used to go beyond itself. That is the ultimate paradox. Yes, we can actually use our minds to slow down our minds, even to stop our minds. When the mind finally stops, we are no longer just loving, truthful, or peaceful; we have *become* love, truth, and peace. Our small minds disappear, and we become completely one with love, truth, and peace.

My theory about the yogis and LSD is that their minds had been so tamed, so disciplined, that the LSD had nothing to work on. That implies that the mind is more than just a philosophical construct that helps us communicate. It has real biological parameters. Thus, the mind *is* the biological level at which certain drugs such as LSD work. But these drugs have no effect on that part of us that is divine, that is beyond time, space, and matter, and that is also beyond the reach of medicine or chemicals.

## A POWERFUL MYSTICAL EXPERIENCE

By the time I was in my psychiatric residency, in 1976, I was meditating quite a bit every evening after coming home from the hospital. One night I got out of bed and inadvertently fell asleep on the living room couch. I dreamed that somebody was asking me about forensic psychiatry, the branch of psychiatry that deals with legal issues. In the dream I said, "Yes, I believe in forensic psychiatry." Then I took a step back and said, "No, I don't. I don't believe psychiatrists should play God."

I still don't totally understand why, but that dream preceded the most powerful spiritual experience of my life. I was suddenly hit with a gigantic blast of light. Immediately it threw me into a state that was neither wakefulness nor sleep, a state that transcended all states of mind I'd ever known. The light blasted through me as if it were being shot out of a fire hose about three feet wide. The energy moved from my feet up through my head.

The force of the energy was thousands of times greater than any force I had ever experienced. If the worst anger I ever had was like being pulled around by a strong Saint Bernard dog, the force of the light was like being pulled by a hundred wild horses.

All of this was quite instantaneous, and as I mentioned, it started while I was fast asleep. For a tiny fraction of a second, I was able to think and make a decision. I didn't say to myself, "I'm going crazy." I recognized that the energy was something called "kundalini energy" or "serpent fire," the immense dormant energy, the core energy of our existence, that lies at the base of the spine and in the solar plexus. I recognized it in that instant. Then I had to decide whether to fight it or surrender to it. For me, the decision was quick and easy to make. If I didn't surrender, I felt as if this energy would destroy me. So I said to myself, "Okay, here we go."

I have never enjoyed roller-coaster rides. I like being more in control than that. And I wasn't initially thrilled to be hit by this intense energy.

But I surrendered—and still within the same fraction of a second. The light, the awesome energy, moved upward and literally dissolved my mind. I could hear the light blasting through. It was loud. I could feel the substance of my mind dissolving. It was scary for a moment. I was rapidly moving into that state of being that allows yogis to be unresponsive to mind-altering drugs. I moved to where there is no mind to alter.

Up and up I went above this earthly existence. "Up and up" may not even be the correct way of describing where I went. In fact, the experience was completely ineffable, completely beyond any description in words. My being, my consciousness, expanded further and further, higher and higher—until I discovered that I was "next to" Michelangelo's statue of David. I don't know if I was in Italy, or if David and I met at some other time and place beyond time and space.

It was a divine experience. I studied the magnificent face of David, glistening white. I was with him for many minutes of "real time." Slowly the face faded, but I remained in this altered state for hours. It was a state of complete bliss. I could see that the normal way I lived, that almost all of us live, is totally unnecessary. I lived in the world of the mind all the time—the ups and downs, the highs and lows, the joys, sorrows, and depressions. I always thought that was life. But up there in the stratosphere, I could see that all of that was absolutely and completely untrue. Being in the stratosphere felt more *real* than anything I'd ever experienced in life.

Several hours passed before the experience faded and I slowly came back to normal awareness. My mind assumed its old form, with most of its old rough edges. But I was forever changed. I had had a beautiful glimpse of another way of looking at life. Finally, I woke up my then-wife. It was a bit strange trying to explain to her what had happened. She didn't panic, nor was she thrilled for me. Her reaction was more like "That's nice, dear. Now go back to sleep."

That morning I had a meeting to attend, at an address on Vision Drive. After the meeting I drove from San Diego to Los Angeles. I could sense that everything living in the world, human and nonhuman, animal and plant, was filled with the same energy I had recognized hidden in me. I could sense that every blade of grass had true "atomic energy" within it and that the entire world contained an infinite amount of this energy. Yet to all appearances that day, my energy was as normal as ever. Nobody could have guessed what I had just been through.

I came to believe that many people go completely insane when they are hit by the kind of energy I experienced. I already had an idea that it had something to do with spiritual enlightenment. If I hadn't known that, I would have fought it, struggled against it, and lost. You can lose your mind in a good way or in a bad way. Joe Montana, when he is "in the zone," loses his mind in a good way, as does Pepe Romero when he feels that God is playing through him during a concert. A patient in the back ward of a state mental hospital has lost his mind in a bad, destructive way. Losing the mind in a good way implies that you have a mind to surrender. The mental patient has not voluntarily surrendered his mind. He has not transcended the mind, but his personality has been destroyed along with his mind.

Did the experience make me a totally different person? I don't think so. But it did give me a glimpse of a reality that seemed much more real than normal awareness. Life is a journey, and that intense experience was a very bright lamppost on mine. It is as clear and bright in my memory now as it was in 1976.

A few years ago, in 1991, I had another interesting experience. All my most vivid spiritual experiences have come in the middle of the night, as if God has to sneak up on me when my mind is quiet, to reveal new levels of truth and experience. The experience I had in 1991 also began with a sudden burst of intense energy, although the energy was not cranked nearly as high as it had been fifteen years before. After the intense surge, I felt myself entering a state of bliss and peacefulness. It had the quality of being one with God, with the quality of total effortlessness. I understood that I didn't have to do anything—just *be* and *exist* in the bliss, in the moment.

This intense energy surge is called kundalini by many spiritual explorers. It is often depicted as a fiery surge up the spine, moving up through the body in a rush toward enlightenment or insight. Although it is most commonly called kundalini, a term from Eastern religion, the energy is a universal human experience. In fact, one of the earliest spiritual references to a burning, fiery energy is in the story of Moses and the burning bush, which "burned and was not consumed." Perhaps there was no burning bush at all. Maybe Moses was having a kundalini experience, in which the enormous power of kundalini was burning inside him but he was "not consumed."

Consider what might have happened if Moses, the great, revered leader of thousands of Jews, had returned from Mount Sinai and said, "I have just had the most incredible kundalini experience." Rather than looking upon him as a great spiritual leader, his people might have looked upon him as a lunatic. So he found a way of telling the story that would make sense to them. That's what Jesus did too. He taught in stories, in parables.

Legitimate, profound spiritual experiences may sound as ridiculous, when we speak of them to others. At that point in human spiritual history, it was more believable to the dejected, fleeing tribe that Moses had heard the voice of God from a miraculous source. Moses was able to reframe his experience in a way that was understandable and empowering to the Jews. Many "normal" people who have such experiences don't have the ability to convey them in such a skillful way. We may call them crazy, when in fact they've had profound experiences that they cannot describe in ways that make sense to us.

I am not promoting this interpretation of the Moses story in any way. Maybe it's correct, and maybe it's not. But maybe it has changed your view of the Bible. Maybe it has shifted your thinking slightly away from the worldly image of a "burning bush" and toward the mystical idea that a powerful lightning force shooting up the spine of Moses gave him an experience of samadhi. Consider this idea for a moment, and see how it influences your concept of Moses and the Bible, and your attitude toward unusual experiences generally.

Most of us have religious beliefs that are sealed in cement, locked into a dogma. We act as if we really *know* Moses, or Jesus, or the Bible. Likewise, when we are told of the spiritual experiences of others, we peg them as if we really know what they are. But each and every person's experience may be vast, which is why it is so essential that we expand our view. Even the "average" person doing laundry or the dishes can have an experience like Moses.

We all have life-force energy within us, and we all have access to higher states of consciousness. The Chinese call this energy *chi,* the Hindus *prana.* It is *yesod* in the Kabbalah, *baraka* to the Sufis, *orenda* to the Iroquois, and *megbe* to the Ituri. We can all come to understand and manage our energy better. A woman with terminal cancer who lives far beyond her expected life span in order to see her daughter's wedding day is one example of a conscious control over life-force energy. In the experience I had, my life-force energy was dramatically focused and released in a powerful new direction.

The range of experiences in life is infinite, as is the range of mystical and spiritual experiences. I do not want to imply that intense rushes of energy are anything to strive for. If I could strive for anything, it would be to be able to love more people, to be more forgiving, and to be of more service. I am not trying to have a special kind of experience. But my awareness of this spiritual energy makes it possible for me to help my patients move along on their own personal journeys.

Before I tell you how I bring my understanding of spiritual energy into my practice of spiritual psychiatry, let me tell you a bit more about myself, so you have a better idea of your guide through the strange territories we're going to enter.

## PSYCHIC BEGINNINGS

Spirituality was not part of my psychiatric training. My transformation from normal doctor to spiritual psychiatrist was gradual and was helped along by personal precognitive and extrasensory experiences, several extraordinary teachers, a severe bout with chronic fatigue syndrome (CFS), and lessons my patients taught me.

I entered the fast track to medicine at the age of four and later charged through high school and college, not enjoying life much. The only exception was sports. I was a real supporter of my high school's great basketball and track teams, and I was a big fan of the University of Colorado football team, the Buffaloes, for whom I spent many days shivering in the hope of seeing a long bomb caught or the halfback running eighty-five yards for a touchdown.

I was raised a Jewish atheist. At synagogue I was one of two atheists, and I argued my case vehemently. I had no respect whatsoever for the spiritual practices going on there. My friend David and I used to sneak out of synagogue before the Saturday morning service, go to the local drugstore, and read *Playboy*. Sometimes we'd return during the service and hide somewhere in the back, where it was dark, and play cards. We were smart, very careful, and never got caught. I was not interested in God.

Looking back at the rebellious Jewish boy at Temple Emanuel, it's amazing to realize how important God has since become to me. It's been a strange and slow process of opening up to spirituality. I started to come out of my shell of disbelief during college, when my intuitive perceptions and psychic experiences showed me there was something greater than myself. I began to sense ways of communicating that went beyond space and time. By the time I had become a young psychiatrist, these intuitive or psychic events were simply part of "the way the world was." They were not terribly unusual—they were the garden-variety experiences that well over half of all Americans have. I still didn't believe in God or a Higher Power, but I was coming to believe that the mind is not limited to the complex physical organ called the brain.

Medical school was a nightmare for me, as it is for many doctors. I forced myself to remember more facts than any poor brain should ever have to. I became affixed to my comfortable blue chair, day and night, only to rise at the end of the school quarter to walk in the park for a day before the whole misery started again. Medical school was like living in and under a dark black cloud—in a level of emotional coldness I had never experienced.

My class had a six percent mortality rate. That is, six of the hundred medical students I started with were dead by the time the rest of us finished, from suicides, freak accidents, cancers, and drownings. As far as I was concerned, medical school was not a very healthy place. In fact, it was a place where the human spirit was systematically trampled and destroyed. That any doctor produced by this system still has any love, humanity, and ability to touch the heart of a patient is a miracle.

After two years of medical school, I quit. I couldn't take it anymore and turned professional photographer. But after six months I realized that it wasn't the life for me, and I reapplied to med school. Getting in the first time had been a piece of cake. Getting back in now was a nightmare. I had started psychoanalysis in my second year so I could begin uncovering and chasing away some of my unhappiness and disillusionment. When I reapplied, the medical school dean told me that "psychoanalysis was not compatible with being a medical student"! I didn't know what to do, but I wouldn't quit analysis just to please the dean. My mother came through with a brilliant suggestion. "They want to hear that medicine is the only thing in your life that matters, that you're only in analysis to make you a better doctor. Tell them that you will quit analysis in an instant if it begins to interfere with your training." I repeated her words almost verbatim and was readmitted to school the next day. But the medical school had given me the message that understanding myself, exploring my feelings, coping with my inner demons was not important.

Still, medical school didn't keep me from being a little bit psychic. Even as a small child, I had had extrasensory perceptions. While riding in the family car, I would often hear the next song to be played on the radio—a few seconds before it was actually played. I just assumed that some kind of technical error with the radio or the radio station produced this phenomenon. I had no mental framework that allowed me even to guess that I was experiencing something extrasensorily.

My most intense childhood extrasensory perception took place when

I was three or four, during a family car trip from Denver to Mesa Verde and the Grand Canyon. I knew things that no four-year-old had any business knowing. I knew the names of the composers of music we heard on the radio. "This piece is by Tchaikovsky . . . this one's by Corelli." At one point my father was discussing lung physiology, and he mentioned the phrase *vital capacity*. My mother said, "What's that?" I said to her, "He just explained it." My father replied, "No, I did not explain it." I then explained that the term referred to the amount of air one has in the lungs, one's breathing capacity.

On and on it went during that two-week period. We were walking through the Painted Desert when I picked up an odd-shaped stone and proudly said to my father, "Look, Dad. This is a fossil clam." He looked at it, tossed the stone as far as he could, and said, "No, it's just a rock." Later that day we went to a museum at the edge of the Painted Desert—and saw a collection of fossil clams that had been found nearby. My father, distraught, went back to the place where I had found it. He searched and searched, with no luck. Later he bought me one to replace it.

One day after I had become a psychiatrist, I woke up in a state of absolute panic. I knew deep down in my soul that that day was going to be tragic. I went to work at the Veterans Administration hospital and shared my fear with one of the nurses. I wanted to "go on record." It was the day President Reagan was shot. I don't report this as some amazing or earth-shattering event. It's the kind of event in which the vast majority of Americans believe. I was finally catching up!

In my twenties I looked back at my early childhood experiences and realized that something had been unusual about them. Like millions of other people, I had seen and heard things without using my eyes or ears. These odd and inexplicable experiences piqued my curiosity—they helped me look at the world a little differently and redefine reality. I don't consider these childhood experiences important in the overall context of my life—and certainly thousands or millions of people have developed their abilities far more than I have. I mention them merely to explain how and why I began to look at life and ultimately psychiatry in a new light.

## A SPIRITUAL TEACHER REMAKES A PSYCHIATRIST

In San Diego, where I now live, I performed my psychiatry residency. I had been working at the La Jolla VA hospital for only two weeks when one of the nurses with whom I was working handed me a photograph of an Indian holy man. She simply said, "I know you need to know about this man.

His name is Sai Baba." A week later my chief resident in psychiatry told me about a psychiatrist in San Diego, a Dr. Samuel Sandweiss, who incorporated spirituality into his practice and who was also a follower of Sai Baba. Shortly after that, the ward chief also told me about Sai Baba—and Sandweiss!

During my first year of psychiatric training, I was certainly developing an interest in spirituality, but I had neither the time nor the energy to look into it. I had my hands full learning how to diagnose and treat severe mental illness; how to tell if someone threatening suicide was really going to kill himself or herself; how to treat extremely violent patients; and how to talk with schizophrenic people who think they are John the Baptist and have been standing in the middle of the street letting everyone know it. Learning emergency psychiatry included learning what to do when a veteran walked into a VA hospital emergency room to talk to the psychiatrist—me—and opened his briefcase, which contained a loaded revolver.

It was truly fascinating work, challenging, difficult, scary—and fun. Yes, fun. Although medical school had not been fun, with my psychiatric residency I felt I had finally come home, that I was finally learning to be what I had wanted to be for so long. I felt at home working in the psychiatric ward of the VA hospital, even though it was sometimes dangerous, noisy, and frightening. But by the end of that first year, I was ready to jump into something entirely different—something that wasn't part of the regular psychiatric curriculum.

In the second year of my residency, without really knowing what I was getting into, I called up Dr. Sandweiss and asked him to supervise me, to teach me about psychiatry and spirituality. My budding interest in spirituality was really quite cerebral. I knew that there was something more to life, something beyond what we can see and touch, but I didn't have any real experience other than my moments of intuition. My meetings with Dr. Sandweiss changed all that. We spoke about God as a living presence that applied to everyday life, as a divine presence that was part of every person, that was with us and around us. We talked about miracles, the power of love and faith, and the role of spirituality in psychiatry. We talked about consciousness and kundalini. And we talked about Sai Baba.[1]

Three years later I was in India meeting with Sathya Sai Baba, who has become a great teacher and resource for me. Through his teachings I came to know how important it is to help my patients on all levels—mentally, physically, and spiritually. Through his teachings I came to know the importance of love and service to others.

Sai Baba has slowly taught me how to bring spiritual principles into everyday life. He has taught me to try to see everything and everyone as a spark of divinity, and that the highest good, the greatest peace, is to be attained through serving our fellow living creatures on this wonderful, singular planet. The practical principles I learned from him have helped bring me happiness, and the feeling was contagious. Experiencing a deeper sense of peace and love has spread to the people around me.

Although I have a teacher in India, I rarely guide people in his direction. Sai Baba has said in his writings, "Who are you to publicize me? I have no need of publicity." I try to put his teachings into action without invoking the teacher. One of his teachings is pertinent here: "There is only one language, the language of the heart; there is only one religion, the religion of love; there is only one race, the race of humanity; there is only one God, and He is omnipresent." I am concerned with trying to live the message: to be loving; to treat all races, all religions, and all people with love, respect, and equality; to open my heart so I can respond to the suffering of others; to try to limit my ego and personal needs and allow my higher qualities to shine through; to value service and personal sacrifice; to face my inner demons, hold on to the vision, be persistent, and reach the goal; to respect awe, mystery, and uncertainty; to learn to experience the moment more fully.

The core of the spiritual teaching I have learned is to help people deepen the convictions and faith in which they already believe. With my Muslim patients, I speak about Allah; with Christians, I am very happy to talk about Jesus. One of my patients brings in his Bible, picks out a passage or two, reads it, and then tries to apply the principle to his life in a practical way. Believing in Jesus is quite a stretch for someone raised as an atheistic Jew, yet through the guidance of my spiritual teacher, I have come to love Jesus—and not only Jesus but the teachings and teachers of all religions.

## ILLNESS: A DOCTOR LEARNS COMPASSION THE HARD WAY

The third major twist of fate that shaped my thinking and my practice was my struggle with chronic fatigue syndrome (CFS).

In October 1984 I got pneumonia. I'd never had it before, and it really knocked me out. I went to the doctor, who listened to my lungs, took my temperature, and made the diagnosis. I took antibiotics for ten days, and the pneumonia cleared up. But after the pneumonia departed, I was not the same old me. I was exhausted. I could hardly get out of bed. By the time I made breakfast, showered, and reached my car, I was already wiped out.

Those of you with CFS or any other serious chronic illness will instantly relate to my story. To the rest of you, I ask you to remember what it's like to have a severe case of the flu—then imagine that it never goes away. That's CFS. By the way, exhaustion and feeling tired are entirely different. When you have severe exhaustion, you often can't sleep. You're too exhausted to sleep. I used to pray to feel plain old *tired*.

It's impossible to convey the agony of that year. Being a psychiatrist is not easy when you're drained to the bone. By Friday each week, I was so exhausted that I could hardly move. Sometimes I would be on the verge of convulsions. Every muscle in my body would contract randomly, as if the brain's normal modulation of such functions were completely gone. I would see halos of light around things and around lights. I couldn't even walk straight. Having CFS was like living in quicksand. No matter where I turned, no matter where I looked for help, I sank.

During 1985 I avoided any socializing whatsoever. I couldn't predict, a day in advance, if I would be able to function the next day. On a rare occasion I'd go out for dinner. One time a friend said to me, "You know, there's no life left in your eyes. They really look dead." I didn't need her to tell me that. I knew it. I felt it. I lived it. The exhaustion had taken a toll on my body and my mind. I couldn't think straight—couldn't concentrate. My memory was a fraction of what it had been. My IQ dropped by 30 or 40 points. I felt that I was losing it, physically and mentally.

I won't bore you with the details of my recovery over the past ten years. My journeys to medical doctors, homeopaths, nutritionists, Chinese acupuncturists, Indian Ayurvedic doctors, and Mexican faith healers would fill a book in their own right. But in the end my bout with CFS deepened my faith, shaped the way I incorporate spirituality into my life and my work, and helped me to help others sort out their miracles from their madness.

CFS gave me a crash course in being a patient. In this respect it has taught me more than any university could have. I have much greater compassion and empathy, as a result, for people with chronic illness. As a human being, I have changed enormously, losing my old moodiness. It leveled out my moods completely. I am much happier and more alive than before. CFS has helped me open my heart. It's helped me love and accept myself more, and to love and accept others.

CFS also taught me about surrender. When animals get sick, they have excellent instincts about how to recover. A bat with a broken wing will stay put and not try to fly until its wing is mended, even for weeks. But humans tend to go right on pushing and pushing, abusing ourselves in the face of illness. Finally I learned about surrender. Finally I could just lie there, sometimes in real agony, and say, "Dear Lord, I don't know what I'm supposed to be learning from this, but help me surrender to whatever it is. Help me realize that everything is a gift from you—whether it brings me joy or pain. Help me stop resisting. Help me stop fighting this thing the way I do." Now this idea—stop fighting—may sound pretty weird and cowardly. But it doesn't mean giving up hope. It means learning to feel what you feel, not trying to push it out of your consciousness. It means allowing feelings, thoughts, and pains to enter your consciousness, arising and dissolving. Sometimes this is the best way to handle unfamiliar or uncomfortable spiritual experiences too.

Surrendering means *allowing oneself to fully experience one's current condition*. Before we can change, we must learn to experience where we are right now. Sometimes we need to stop struggling and be like that bat with the broken wing. We need to let it mend in its own time. The process of surrendering teaches us patience. Illness—like enlightenment, mystical callings, and strange visions—can be terrifying, upsetting, and painful. But it also can be a real gift, if we open our hearts to the full experience, pain and all.

Some readers may consider my bout with illness a spiritual failure. If I have such faith and belief, why couldn't I heal myself completely? But it is a clinical and technical error for any healer or therapist to tell a patient, "You're sick because you're not praying hard enough," or because "You're not doing your imagery techniques correctly," or, "You're not sticking to your diet a hundred percent." That attitude, blaming the patient for spiritual failure, constitutes medical malpractice, in my opinion.

Spirituality is a source of faith, hope, and comfort. My illness helped me reach out to God and say, "Help me make it through another day." Spirituality allowed me to see meaning, purpose, and lessons in illness. And it gave me the strength to keep trying to recover.

Spirituality helped me feel as if my divine friend were always by my side, holding my hand, picking me up when I fell, inspiring me to smile while I was in the grip of the lion's jaws. Throughout my illness I have never felt alone. Perhaps most importantly, I have learned that healing is not just what happens to the body. It's also what happens to the heart.

Thus, both my life and my professional outlook were transformed. From extrasensory perceptions, from extraordinary teachers, and from

CFS, I learned that love, faith, hope, spirituality, God, joy, surrender, forgiveness, compassion, and self-acceptance are essential tools of a healer. All of these experiences—the pain of CFS, the psychic experiences—were part of my preparation to become a better healer.

With awe and gratitude for my own experience, I encourage you to keep going, to keep searching, to keep hoping, never to give up unless you choose to give up. Dig deep inside yourself, and look for reserves of strength and courage that you never dreamed you had. They are there, waiting to be tapped.

Don't ever let anybody take away your hope or tell you that nothing more can be done. To some extent, you *must* be your own doctor. If you expect your doctor to have perfect answers, you are not taking enough responsibility for your illness. Do your own research. Go to the library. Search the medical literature. Doctors are overwhelmed with ever-increasing piles of paperwork, ever-more-complicated bureaucracies, HMOs, and PPOs, rising overhead costs, and the ever-present threat of lawsuits. They can't always keep up with fast-breaking developments in medical research.

I have no intention of trying to pit you against your doctor. Rather, you must work *with* your doctor. Help your doctor. Educate him or her. Educate yourself, and try to have some compassion for why your doctor may lack compassion. Remember, he or she is human. Don't expect perfection. And that is one of the great lessons I learned from CFS: how to cope with chronic illness, how to go beyond the notion that everything can be instantly fixed. Look for the lessons in your own suffering. Look for the hope that is there, and embrace your spirituality.

# 2

# TWENTY-FIVE SPIRITUAL
# QUESTIONS PSYCHIATRISTS
# ARE AFRAID TO ASK

Comedienne Lily Tomlin has asked, "Why is it we're said to be praying when we talk to God—but we're called schizophrenic when He talks back to us?" Many of my seemingly ordinary patients, when I ask them about their spiritual experiences, give me extraordinary responses. A 60-year-old man who was hospitalized for treatment of alcoholism cried as he told me his story: "When I was thirteen, I was riding my bike one day when something amazing happened. I came around a corner, and suddenly right in front of me was the Father and the Son. I've never mentioned this to anybody in my whole life—not my wife, not my minister." I asked him, "By 'the Father and the Son,' do you mean God the Father and Jesus?" He said, "Yes, that's who I saw. I know it sounds really crazy, and that's why I never told anybody—ever." He cried tears of joy. What a relief he felt, after forty-seven years, to finally be able to share his most extraordinary experience! And sharing his experience accelerated his recovery from alcoholism.

Had he really seen the Father and the Son? I didn't feel qualified to judge. It was his experience, and I respected that. He felt heard and understood by me. I don't believe that God comes only once every few thousand years, parts the Red Sea or heals the blind—and leaves the rest of us out. God is for ordinary people—and He is here, all the time. As a psychiatrist, I evaluate every patient to arrive at a traditional psychiatric diagnosis, and I did so for my alcoholic patient who had met Jesus as well.

I found no evidence whatsoever that, at the time of his vision, he was psychotic, delirious, or physically or mentally ill. If I had, it would have been a lot more difficult for me to diagnose the vision accurately. Regardless, the vision had a spiritual message for my patient, and he needed to explore it, not suppress it or try to forget it.

It is important for you to have a conscious understanding of your own spiritual beliefs. Your basic view of the world as benevolent or threatening and of your own place in it, is key to self-understanding. Yet spirituality is a complex concept, with many definitions. Even though the word is widely used, an adequate definition is difficult to find. It is much easier to define *spiritual quest, spiritual qualities,* or *spiritual practices.* For some people, spirituality is simply the pursuit of a moral life. For others, it is believing in angels; for still others, it is their relationship with God. I have found no dictionary definition worth sharing, so I will provide the broadest, most inclusive, and most understandable definition that I can.

Spirituality is the heart of religion, much as the soul is the spiritual heart of the human body. Spirituality is *sacred awareness,* the awareness of sacred ways of being, of our relationship to something sacred, something greater than ourselves. It is the awareness of sacred forms of action. It is our relationship to God or a Higher Power, or our belief in something larger than ourselves.

Sometimes people who are aware of the sacred don't act in a sacred or kind way. But the person who has ultimate sacred awareness knows that all of life is one. Everything, everyone is interconnected. As a result of that deep knowing, the person's actions automatically become pure and sacred. Partial awareness leads only to partial results, part-time spirituality, and part-time morality.

One of the most important aspects of sacred awareness is understanding the relationship between oneself and one's chosen form of God. To quote producer and composer Richard Del Maestro, "Spirituality is the relationship between the devotee and God. It is the relationship between himself and his higher Self. Just as in physics the observer becomes part of the equation, in spirituality too the observer becomes part of the equation. If the person is a Buddhist, and God is not the central theme in his spiritual life, then spirituality is about one's relationship to moral values and to society at large. On the other hand, if the person is a Christian, Muslim, Jew, or Hindu, spirituality is defined by the relationship with one's chosen form of God. The more you focus on God or on human values, the more spiritual you become."[1]

Spiritual practices—prayer, meditation, fasting, charity, and service—are all intended to foster spiritual qualities, such as love, sacrifice, detachment, honest speech, simple living, a sense of unity with all of life, and sacred awareness. So is a practice of spiritual psychiatry. A major goal of both spiritual practice and psychiatry is to attain peace of mind through the ups and downs of life, as well as joy and happiness. The thread that unites them is love. Love is the goal of spiritual practice. Love is also the way of reaching that goal, for love is both the way and the goal.

Spirituality, or sacred awareness, helps us address life's most profound questions: How do I fit into this universe? Who am I? Where did I come from? Is there a purpose for my life? What is it? Where do I go when I die? Can I do anything here to make my after-death experience (if there is one) better? Spirituality helps us understand why bad things happen to good people—and why good things happen to bad people—and what good and evil are. Spirituality is awareness of God or something greater than ourselves. (For the sake of custom, I refer to God as *He* rather than *He/She*. By *God,* I mean both the God and the Goddess, the male and the female, the yin and the yang, and the Absolute. I look at God as a force, a presence that is not separate from us, not far away, and the universe as the body of God or a manifestation of God.) Spirituality asks higher questions—questions that psychiatrists are afraid to ask.

Spiritual *qualities,* such as faith and belief in a purpose, give us the courage to persevere in a world that we really don't understand. They give us the hope that some Higher Power is taking care of business, because as human beings, most of us truly do not know what we are doing. Doctors tend to believe that truth can be measured, stored in bottles, and replicated in controlled, double-blind studies. But the truth that Western civilization clings to is temporary, for each technological advance displaces or modifies the old truth. Thus we cling to ever-changing explanations of reality. Spirituality deals with that which is unchanging and eternally true. It helps us seek unity rather than distinctions and to realize that the spark of life, and of God, is contained within each living creature.

Because the word *spirituality* is so difficult to define, I want to summarize my discussion here before I go on. Spirituality, I have said, is sacred awareness. Spiritual practices are intended to help us develop spiritual qualities so that we may lead a more sacred or spiritual life. Our sacred awareness expands with conscious practice. Sacred action arises out of sacred awareness and out of spiritual practice.

Many years ago I heard psychologist Ram Dass talk about interpersonal relationships. We categorize other people as "potentials" (that is, as potential lovers, friends, or business opportunities—people who can potentially fill a need for us), "not-potentials," "competitors," or "irrel-evants." We tend to categorize everyone we meet in this way, which means that there are a lot of people to whom we pay no attention whatsoever because we don't "need" them. Spirituality—sacred awareness—helps us see that the most lasting thing, the only lasting thing about any of us is the soul—that spark of divinity that has been present in all of us from birth. Even though our bodies, minds, and personalities undergo tremendous transformations during the course of our lives, the soul remains un-changed, for that part of us is directly connected to God.

In the West we tend to believe that God is distant, above us, up in heaven. We pray by looking *up* to God. In the East the belief is that God is everywhere—outside us, inside us, and around us. He is the very center of our own being. Eastern religious traditions ask us to look within for God. Many Christian mystics throughout the ages have also looked for God within. Thomas Merton, the well-known Trappist monk and teacher, sought out the truth of spiritual mysteries through the practices of soli-tude, meditation, prayer, and silence. In fact, Christian mysticism like his is somewhat like Eastern mysticism. If one believes that God is present everywhere and in everyone, including within oneself, it becomes natural to look for God within—by visualizing God, by repeating or chanting your personal name for God, and by visualizing that form of God within your-self and within others. Whether one looks for God through Eastern or Western teaching is not important. But spiritual qualities—such as love, truth, peace, nonviolence, faith, hope, moral conduct, truthful speech, and devotion, which arise from spiritual practice—are important.

Most of us are comfortable with the external trappings of religion. But as we try to understand God and life's deeper meaning, we can end up exploring strange, esoteric practices, such as trances, channeling, heal-ing with crystals, psychic phenomena, stigmata, faith healing, working with pyramids, and speaking in tongues.

Spirituality is not only awareness of God or the Absolute; it's also awareness of human values. His Holiness the Dalai Lama, the leader of Tibetan Buddhism, never talks about God, only about human values and human character. Spirituality makes you aware that your actions count—every one of them. Rationalists, too, believe their actions count, but spir-itually motivated action is different from rationally motivated action. Reason may tell us that good actions are those in our own best interest. Spiritually motivated actions arise out of a desire for a pure heart. Action creates character—and character guides action. Our actions help form our character, and through our character we can all add something positive to the world. Positive actions build character. Negative actions destroy character.

I have no absolute answers about God or spirituality. I am writing merely from my own life experiences, from my personal spiritual experience, and from the writings of the world's great spiritual teachers. I hope that bringing together ideas and experience will help you see that there are no absolute answers; rather, there are many routes to spiritual awareness, many paths to spiritual practice, and many ways to arrive at an understanding of God.

A spiritual psychiatrist's job is to help patients identify their spirituality, their source of hope and faith, then help them use that source to heal themselves physically and mentally. The psychiatrist's job is not to judge an individual's beliefs as good or bad, correct or incorrect. Each person needs to find the light that leads him or her out of the tunnel— whatever form that light takes.

Though I firmly believe in God, I cannot begin to say how or why He sheds His grace. I believe He does, and that His grace can override *anything*—any illness, any problem. I believe that His grace is a power that I simply cannot ignore. As a doctor, I want to help my patients find everything that will alleviate their suffering. In my practice faith has proven to be an essential part of healing, as well as a way to cope with pain and suffering.

A theologian may say there is a correct way to approach God, but for a psychiatrist who is trying to bring hope and inspiration to patients, there is no room for notions of correct and incorrect. Each religion has a different name for God, and some religions have many Gods. For some religions, everything is God. Pantheism has existed in many forms, from the ancient Greeks up to the present. For Native Americans, all of nature is an embodiment of God—the trees, the sky, the rivers, the animals, the thunder, the rain. Native Americans from Cree to Cherokee believe that even hunting is a sacred activity, and they offer a prayer to the animal to be killed, one that acknowledges the spirit of the animal.

In many ways the Hindu philosophy is similar to most Native American religions. It feels God to be everywhere, in everything. Although God in this transcendent, all-pervading aspect is called Brahma, there are thousands of other Gods and Goddesses—of rain, prosperity, wealth, health, and so on. This pantheism can be very confusing for a Westerner, to whom it may seem that the Indians are worshiping stones and trees. But they are actually worshiping the divine principle that manifests itself in the stone and the tree.

Buddhism does not rely on a notion of God. Rather, it teaches mindfulness and nonattachment, living in the *now*. Spirituality, for the Buddhist, is sacred awareness of each moment, sacred awareness that all suffering on earth must be alleviated, for if one person suffers, all people suffer.

Psychiatry, practiced in the light of spirituality, is about God, faith, and hope. It is also about right action. It's not about what feels good at the moment, or about how to milk the most from the system. It's about love. It's about the therapeutic role of service. It's about how one can lead the most meaningful, happiest life—whether one is rich or poor, sick or healthy. It's about learning to share, to love, to care—to take a real interest in the people and the world around you. It's about learning "giveness" and forgiveness.

Spiritual practice teaches a kind of love that responds to other people's pain and reaches out to them. It teaches us to rejoice at others' good fortune—whether we ourselves have been beneficiaries of good fortune or not. Teaching this love is also the aim of spiritual psychiatry. Any practice of awareness and kindness is, in effect, spiritual psychiatry.

The essential message of the sacred Hindu texts, the Vedas, has been summed up as: "Speak the truth, and act righteously, or with moral conduct." Telling the truth is essential to both psychological and spiritual growth. Besides, it's far easier to tell the truth than it is to lie and then have to cover one's tracks. But how often do we try to get away with a "little" lie? How many of us cheat on our husband or wife? Cheating reflects a lack of the sacred awareness of the power of truth. It is almost impossible to make spiritual progress if one is lying. My job is to help people feel safe enough to look at their own pain, then to dive into that pain, embrace it, swim through it, and get to the other side. But when people lie, they short-circuit the process. The lie hides the pain, making it impossible to get to the other side.

In my struggle to define spirituality, I have read numerous books and spoken with experts. But I have also asked one of my patients, Rosanne, for her definition of spirituality. "Spirituality," she told me, "is letting go of everything you thought was true, so that the Truth may embrace you. It is the practice of becoming unhitched from illusions and fleeting distractions, and awakening to eternal Truth, breathing through life, enlivened and supported by boundless love. Spirituality is arriving at the realization that salvation, satori, mercy, samadhi, enlightenment, and the omnipotent and benevolent beingness that suffuse this moment, this universe, and beyond, lie nowhere outside of but within all animate and seemingly inanimate manifestations. And spirituality is a rising up of empathy, compassion, selflessness, equanimity, and unconditional love, and acquiring a stance of being here, now and always. Spirituality is bringing daily life into concert with the cosmos." Rosanne shares the view of Buddhist nun and writer Pema Chodron, in *The Wisdom of No Escape:* "Spirituality is coming into profound knowing by releasing what you 'think' you know."[2] Rosanne's spirituality is shaped by her Buddhist practice, her love for and practice of Navajo teachings, and her Indian spiritual teacher. I find her definition as compelling as any I've run across. The thread that runs through her definition is awareness.

Spirituality—sacred awareness—includes *sacred vision*, the desire or ability to see with one's inner eye, with one's intuition. It means having faith in that which cannot be physically seen or measured. That's one reason modern medicine and science don't have much respect for spirituality, and why psychiatrists are afraid to ask these questions—and why it's hard to get an honest diagnosis that addresses the body, mind, and spirit. Science cannot say anything about love—or God. Yet so much of the world believes in God or a Higher Power. And as for love, who in the world denies its existence? Yet love is entirely invisible. Oh, sure, certain physiological signs, measurable phenomena, go along with love. And even watching a film of Mother Teresa ministering to sick people with her extraordinary love can enhance the immune function. But these physical signs are not love. They're by-products of love.

Looking back over my professional training, it absolutely astounds me that love was never seriously mentioned by my professors or in the textbooks. How to cultivate love was never discussed. Yes, they said a psychiatrist must take a good history of the patient's work and sex lives—but not a spiritual history. In fact, taking a spiritual history could get you labeled "weird" in a hurry, which makes psychiatrists a little timid about asking some very important questions.

Modern psychiatry has become very Cartesian in its outlook, having now developed a body of technical knowledge. Some psychiatrists are even calling their field a "hard science." But many of them are focusing so exclusively on the brain that they're starting to ignore feelings! One psychiatrist friend recently attended a conference on psychopharmacology. The word *feeling* never came up once during the entire conference. Psychiatry wears the mask of science at a great price.

As a psychiatrist, I try to be open to all the possibilities, open to psychiatry as both art and science. In psychiatry you tend to get the information for which you are looking or for which you have formulated questions. If you have to find out about a patient's work history or sex life, for example, you'll find out. If you're a Jungian, your patients will have Jungian dreams. If you're a Freudian, your patients will have Freudian dreams. Likewise, taking a spiritual history will elicit spiritual information.

The usefulness of integrating God, spirituality, and psychiatry has led me to stop beating around the burning bush. I confront issues about God as directly as I confront any other issue in my patients. Here are some of the questions that I may ask when taking a spiritual history:

## TWENTY-FIVE SPIRITUAL QUESTIONS PSYCHIATRISTS ARE AFRAID TO ASK

1. In what religion were you raised?

2. What religion are you now?

3. What do you believe in? Is there a God?

4. What is God's "job description"?

5. Is God an important part of your life?

6. Is He nearby or out on a distant star?

7. Do you feel there is a purpose to your life?

8. Is there life after death? What is it?

9. Do you pray? If so, how often?

10. Do you meditate? If so, how often?

11. What do you call God?

12. Have you had any experiences that you couldn't explain? Have you ever known things that you simply had no way of knowing?

13. Do you go to church, synagogue, or some other organized place of worship? If so, how often?

14. Is God a man or a woman? Or both? Neither?

15. Are there saints or other holy figures who have special meaning to you?

16. Does God listen to you?

17. Are you and God on good terms?

18. Does He scare you? How do you feel about God?

19. Do you deserve God's love?

20. Is God critical, watching every move you make, looking for mistakes?

21. Have you ever had a mystical or spiritual experience?

22. If so, has that experience changed your life? How?

23. Do you believe there is a heaven or a hell? If so, where do you believe you'll be going?

24. Do you have any particular spiritual practices?

25. If you met God, what would you ask for?

These questions are both spiritual and religious in nature, for religion is the structure within which spirituality may flow. Religion is the rites, rituals, and beliefs, the external or expressed form that spirituality takes. Spirituality depends on one's direct and immediate experience of God or Spirit, and rites and rituals can facilitate that experience. Unfortunately, for some people, the rites and rituals of their first religion have lost their power. Their spiritual challenge is to rediscover the tremendous depth, power, love, beauty, awe, and divinity that these rituals can convey, or to find a new spiritual direction. Currently, I am treating a Catholic woman who told me that she once experienced a blazing light piercing the glass of the church and passing through the Eucharist. For her, religion and spirituality came together in a beautiful visual way.

Most readers of this book don't need to visit a psychiatrist to have their vision or miracle diagnosed accurately. But you do need to know what to call your vision or nonordinary experience. We'll get to that shortly. Meanwhile, I invite you to explore your spirituality, your sacred awareness, so that your life and the lives of those you love may be richer.

# A DAY IN THE LIFE

# OF A SPIRITUAL

# PSYCHIATRIST

By calling myself a "spiritual psychiatrist," I would not want to be misread as claiming to be more spiritual than other psychiatrists. In the professional world, I do not actually call myself a spiritual, holistic, or New Age psychiatrist at all. The general labels *doctor* and *psychiatrist* are noble and lasting ones and need no embellishing. For the purpose of inquiring into human experience, however, thinking of me as a spiritual psychiatrist may be useful to you.

For some people, experiencing nature helps them connect with the sacred. For others, surfing the California waves brings a sense of peace and spirituality. For still others, it is contemplating Jesus, Allah, Mazda (the deity, not the car), or the Buddha; or reading the Torah, the Bible, the Koran, or the Bhagavad Gita. Some find the sacred in jogging, swimming, gardening, or fly-fishing. One way is no better than another. All paths lead to the mountaintop and to God, and He answers to a thousand different names.

In order to make healing sacred, the healer turns his or her mind from the material world and directs it inward, to a place of peace, love, and truth. Of course, we all live in the material world, and there's no getting out of it alive! Yet one needn't live in a cave in order to be spiritual; one needn't live in poverty or renounce physical pleasure and convenience. The key to spiritual living in the world is practicing *detachment*. One may be a billionaire yet be detached from wealth; a billionaire may be humble, loving, and honest. It's not what we do and what we own, but how we live and how we are. Bringing the sacred into one's life changes everything.

And bringing sacred awareness to the everyday practice of psychiatry means changing the therapist! A psychiatrist cannot practice spiritual psychiatry if he is not already practicing what he preaches. It is not necessary that the psychiatrist's spiritual efforts be successful all of the time. Even when I am not succeeding in my own spiritual efforts, I am aware of my failure. My awareness of how difficult spiritual practices can be allows me to work with my patients compassionately. I do not expect them to change their lives overnight. And when a patient drifts away from the therapy I prescribe, I can respond nonjudgmentally—it is easy to get caught up in the dramas of our lives, whether that drama is about finances, romance, career, family, or health.

Who the psychiatrist is is as important as the specific techniques utilized in helping people. With the attitudes of love, peace, and reverence, prescribing medication becomes as sacred as prescribing meditation. Prozac or Thorazine can be administered in a holy way (and imagine the difference it would make). On the flip side, meditation and prayer can be prescribed in an unloving way, which would defeat the purpose of using these techniques.

When patients are given treatments that will help them grow, embrace their suffering, and live more meaningful lives, they are being treated in a holy way. If, on the other hand, the psychiatrist conveys the message, "You are creating your illness, and you can use these tools to create a new reality with complete health," he is not practicing in a sacred way. Rather, he is using techniques associated with spirituality to the detriment of his patient, beating him up psychologically, and making him feel guilty for being sick.

It may be easier for you to see how spiritual psychiatry works if I walk you through a day in my own life. I try to follow the teachings of Sathya Sai Baba by practicing his message every waking moment, whether I am cooking a meal, driving the car, writing a book, or seeing patients. Baba teaches that "the goal of spirituality, and of life, is to always remember God and to live a noble life." I do not fully succeed in my daily spiritual practices, but at least I try to walk the talk.

When I arise each day, I say this prayer: "Oh Lord, I am born again from the womb of sleep, and I am determined to carry out the tasks of this day as an offering to you. May all my thoughts, words, and deeds be ever sacred and pure. Let me harm no one. Let no one harm me."

After I drag my body from the bed, I often imagine God in the house with me. I will not share with you my chosen form of God, since that is not important for you to know. It is only important for you to know who *your* chosen form of God is. It is as if I "carve God" out of thin air, until I can "see" His form. I try to keep him with me all through the day.

Much as the Native American prays to Nature and thanks the Great Spirit present in everything, I pray before I eat breakfast. Then, while showering, I chant the Gayatri mantra, a prayer that God will illuminate my intellect. As I'm soaping up, I say a prayer of surrender: "Think through me. Feel through me. Act through me. Love through me. Speak through me. Heal through me. Thy will be done. Help me remember your name. Help me see you everywhere. Help me see you in everyone." A few minutes of yoga follow.

And then I'm off and running to work. Before I see a patient, I try to remember to dedicate the session to God. As I run up the three flights of stairs at Mercy Hospital on my way to the Behavioral Health Unit, I imagine God climbing the stairs beside me. I am truly filled with happiness as I mentally say to him, "Okay, God, let's go and help this person." Strangely, I find it easy to feel His presence and have an inner dialogue with Him in that craziest of places, the mental hospital.

Often I *practice the presence* (as this technique is called) as I sit with patients in my office. I imagine that God is sitting in one of the chairs, helping and guiding the session. Sometimes when I get stuck, I silently ask, "God, what does this person need right now?" Immediately I get a thought, feeling, or image that guides the session like an arrow flying toward a bull's-eye.

Another important technique I practice is the repetition of a mantra. I chant *"Om Sai Ram,"* which translates as "Divine Mother and Father." The ideal of my spiritual practice is to repeat it constantly, but that is not what I actually succeed at.

Now, if you were a patient of mine, you wouldn't know that I had prepared myself in this way. Let's say I have an imaginary new patient named Mrs. Diamond. She has some problems that are common in the Western world. Here is what her experience—or *your* experience—in my office might be like.

"Hi, Mrs. Diamond. I'm Dr. Gersten. It's very nice to meet you. Please come this way." I show her to my office. As she enters, I ask her to sit in the chair on the left. But before she can sit, she takes a good look around my office. Plants fill the office and grow to the ceiling, some of them with beautiful white flowers. Kermit the Frog is on my desk because I work with children and he helps me connect with them.

As we get down to business, I ask Mrs. Diamond why she has come to see me and what her problems are. I want to know about her whole life: her mental life, her social life, her marriage, her kids, her work, her stresses, her finances. I want to know about any physical problems she has, and I probe deeply into any subtle metabolic difficulties, such as those associated with chronic fatigue syndrome, candidiasis, or adrenal sufficiency, which are often overlooked by psychiatrists as well as internists. I may or may not ask about her childhood. I ask about her creative outlets, her special talents. I ask about her religious upbringing as well as her current spiritual beliefs. After this first session, I will have some idea of her life as a whole, not just the reasons she came in to see me. I need to learn how her symptoms fit into the fabric of her life.

Mrs. Diamond is stressed out, she tells me. She's having trouble making ends meet. She's a wreck by the end of her workday, and the tension is spilling over into her marriage. She gets frustrated and angry with her husband over trivial matters—and she's not sleeping very well. She could go on living like this indefinitely, but she knows something just isn't right. My most important goal is to "connect" with Mrs. Diamond. If I don't, I have failed her.

## THOUGHT WATCH
### Mental Fitness Technique

During the first session, I teach Mrs. Diamond the importance of getting perspective on how her mind works: "I now want to do a thirty-second exercise," I tell her. "Close your eyes, and simply observe your thoughts. Remember what comes into your mind. Don't try to change or alter your thoughts. Just watch them. I'll tell you when to start."

Why don't you try this exercise now? Set a timer for thirty seconds. Close your eyes, and observe your thoughts.

"Okay, go." After thirty seconds have passed, I tell her to open her eyes.

I say to Mrs. Diamond, "Okay, let's review your thoughts." As she tells me about them, I write them down on my notepad. You can write yours down at this point, too, according to the following format:

Write down every thought, image, feeling, or sensation that floated through your head during those thirty seconds. If you had the same thought five times, write it down five times.

After you've written down each thought, go back to the top of the list, and after each thought, place a check mark in one of the three right-hand columns, indicating if that particular thought was negative (−), positive (+), or neutral (±). Add up the number of positive, negative, and neutral thoughts you had.

(+)  (−)  (±)

1. _____  \_\_  \_\_  \_\_

2. _____  \_\_  \_\_  \_\_

3. _____  \_\_  \_\_  \_\_

4. _____  \_\_  \_\_  \_\_

5. _____  \_\_  \_\_  \_\_

6. _____  \_\_  \_\_  \_\_

7. _____  \_\_  \_\_  \_\_

8. _____  \_\_  \_\_  \_\_

9. _____  \_\_  \_\_  \_\_

10. _____  \_\_  \_\_  \_\_

11. _____  \_\_  \_\_  \_\_

12. _____  \_\_  \_\_  \_\_

13. _____  \_\_  \_\_  \_\_

14. _____  \_\_  \_\_  \_\_

15. _____  \_\_  \_\_  \_\_

16. _____  \_\_  \_\_  \_\_

17. _____  \_\_  \_\_  \_\_

(+)   (−) (±)

18. _____ __ __ __

19. _____ __ __ __

20. _____ __ __ __


**Total Positive Thoughts** _____

**Total Negative Thoughts** _____

**Total Neutral Thoughts** _____

**Total Thoughts** _____


The next step is to figure out how many thoughts you have in a single day. Let's say you had five thoughts in that thirty seconds. That's ten thoughts per minute, or six hundred per hour. When you're working, your mind is probably fully engaged in the work, but when you're not working, your mind, like every mind, flies. How many hours per day are left over after sleeping and working? For example, if you sleep eight hours and work another eight, you have eight hours left. Multiply six hundred thoughts per hour times eight hours, and you have 4,800 random thoughts each day.

Now make your own calculations.

How many hours per day are you neither working nor sleeping? This figure is the number of hours per day your mind is free to wander. _____

A. Total thoughts in 30 seconds × 2 = number of thoughts per minute _____

B. Multiply A by 60 minutes = number of thoughts per hour _____

C. Multiply B by the number of hours per day your mind is free to wander = total number of random thoughts per day _____

If any other thoughts enter your mind, simply allow them to pass through like clouds passing through the sky. Don't try to push away "bad" thoughts or hold on to "good" ones. If your mind drifts, slowly bring it back to the mantra. People often get upset with themselves when their minds drift. Please remember that mental drift actually is part of meditation. You drift, and then you refocus. Drift, then gently refocus.

Practice your mantra two or three times a day, for five minutes each time. Practice when you wake up, at noon, and before you go to sleep. Stick with one mantra for at least a week. If it doesn't feel right, change to a new one. Eventually, you will have to settle on one mantra—otherwise, no progress will be made.

If you do this Mantra Meditation exercise for one month, you will notice a difference. You'll feel calmer, less hurried, less worried, and better centered. After practicing for one year, your personality will solidify at a new level of wholeness. And after you've practiced for ten years, you'll hardly recognize the person you once were. The essence of you will always be there, but your rough edges will be smoothed out.

Mantra Meditation has three important purposes. One is to slow down the always-buzzing mind. We've already seen how the mind is a two-cylinder engine that runs on attraction and repulsion. But another analogy is that the mind is like a fan that's furiously buzzing around all day. Every time you say your mantra—*every* time—it's like turning off the switch to that fan, so that it turns a little more slowly. So if you practice your mantra for five minutes two or three times a day, which is what I recommend, your mental fan will begin to turn more slowly, and you'll begin to feel less stressed out. But you don't have to limit saying your mantra to two or three times a day. When you're driving and come to a red light, recite your mantra until the light turns green. Do it with your eyes open. But when the light turns green, please focus your attention back on the road. Recite your mantra when you're walking from your car into the supermarket. Maybe you'll do it while you're sitting on the can! These are all opportunities to slow down the mind.

The second purpose of the mantra is to give your mind something positive to do. The mind needs to do work. If we don't give it work, it will simply run itself, lurching this way and that. In ten days you will have had 60,000 random thoughts; in a hundred days you will have had 600,000. That is an incredible thing to think about. (There's *another* thought!) You don't want your mind running you around. You have to be your mind's master—or else you will be its slave. You will have this need whether you're depressed and living in poverty—or you're a billionaire. The mind does the same thing to everyone. So give it something positive to do. There's nothing more positive for your mind to do than to remember the name of God.

And the third purpose of the mantra? The mantra is your mental home base. It's the place in your mind that you can come home to over and over again. Even if you've been frazzled and haven't chanted your mantra in five hours, you can come back home to it. The vast majority of people simply have no mental home base. Your mantra can be your anchor, if you practice Mantra Meditation.

It's the simplest, most effective technique in the world—and it's free. But although it's simple, Mantra Meditation isn't as easy as it may seem. Your mind has years of momentum built up, years of spinning of that mental fan, that flywheel. You're going to have to throw that mental switch over and over again. I've been practicing my mantra since 1979. In the beginning, I sometimes forgot to say my mantra for days at a time. My mind was just running so fast and so far. But now I can always return home to my mantra within seconds, no matter what's going on in my life. It's almost effortless. It's been absolutely transforming for me and has helped me become a lot more peaceful.

You—and Mrs. Diamond—might be worried that your mantra will make you so peaceful that you won't get anything done. But the amazing thing is that the quieter our minds become, the better we are at what we do. We don't get lazy. We don't become worse at what we do. We become better. We clear out the mental clutter that interferes with our purpose and happiness.

Here's something else I do to help get rid of the clutter: I carry a three-by-five card with me, on which I write down all the things I have to do—people to call, things to buy. Once I write it down on the card, I don't have to worry about remembering it or clutter up my mind with it.

As I teach my clients about Mantra Meditation, I periodically "check in" with God. Sai Baba teaches that work is worship. We needn't retire to a cave and meditate in order to progress on a spiritual path. By regarding my work as worship and remembering to dedicate every session to God, the work of psychotherapy is transformed. I continue to remember God throughout the session. Sometimes He's in sharp focus, and sometimes He's in soft focus. I believe that divinity is present within everyone, that all of creation is not only made by God but is permeated by God. In my work in clinical psychiatry, I try to see God in the patient I am working with.

Sometimes, I must confess, God is hard to see. Sometimes when I'm looking at someone, I will mentally say, "You-hoo. Hello, God? Are you in there? I know you're in there!" To most psychiatrists, all of this surely must appear as sheer madness, but to me, it is part of an integrated approach to life.

A traditional psychiatrist might be saying to himself, "Mrs. Diamond suffers from a fixation at the Oedipal stage of development. Her depression reflects repressed rage, which is a reaction formation. She secretly hates her mother for stealing away her father, but she is not aware of her hatred. Her current problems with her husband, who works too late, are triggering early feelings of abandonment and reactivating her Oedipus complex." Mrs. Diamond doesn't know what her psychiatrist is thinking, be he the traditional one or myself. But I think that the therapist who regards psychotherapy as a sacred process and keeps God in mind throughout uplifts the patient—instead of confusing her or, worse, making her feel pathological or defective. A spiritual therapy process can help take the patient to a new level of consciousness. Perhaps Mrs. Diamond has never felt herself to be loved. A psychiatrist who is quietly considering God to live inside her and treating her with respect and compassion will certainly help her heal.

After my first five or six years as a psychiatrist, I discovered that my medical theorizing about my patients' problems was actually getting in the way of treating them. Both my patients and myself were stuck at the level of the mind. Therapy is most effective when we are engaged on levels of consciousness much higher than the mind. Through the years, as my own mind became quieter as a result of spiritual practice, that quietness began to carry over into my clinical work. Finally, I reached the point where I just stopped the whole process I had been trained to follow. I threw out all the theories. I was left with an experience in which I was there with the patient, with nothing between us. In place of those theories, I now have a much quieter mind, a mind that is seeking the divinity in my patients.

I don't come right out and say to my patients, "You are God. I can see divinity within you. You are a divine light. No need to be depressed or anxious anymore. Just let that God that is in you, that you really are, come right out." No! On the outside I maintain a professional, doctorly manner. Although I do not narrate my inner workings to my patients, however, those inner workings *are* the therapy. Therapy is not just the talking, the listening, the guided imagery, the Mantra Meditation, the exploration of spiritual experience, the use of nutritional supplements, the use of antidepressant medication, the variety of strategies and suggestions. Therapy is *the moment*. The therapist is not merely a dispenser of drugs. He is a dispenser of the moment. The therapist creates the atmosphere in which healing will or will not take place. Therapy is *what* he does and *who* he is. Eventually, the patient becomes his or her own therapist or inner authority, just as you—the average reader—becomes his or her own therapist. In many ways, I am merely a consultant to my patients, as I am your consultant, providing information that may or may not lead to transformation, information that you may or may not choose to integrate into your life.

Mrs. Diamond almost certainly has had her spirits lifted by her first session. She understands a bit more about how her mind works and how it gets her into trouble. She takes home a mantra that can help her today, tomorrow, and I hope for the rest of her life. As our first session ends, I give her an overview of her problem.

"Here's what I think is going on. You have a number of life stresses that are leaving you depressed, anxious, and worn out. I believe I can help you feel less moody and anxious quickly. I wouldn't worry about the marriage right now. Once you're more relaxed, you'll probably experience many positive changes in your life. Your marital problems may simply go away. If not, we'll deal with them in the future. The mantra should begin helping you soon.

"Most people I see with this degree of stress have a variety of metabolic imbalances caused by the stress. We'll go into this in more detail next time. But let me say briefly now that nothing in our life exists in a vacuum. Your moods are not confined to your brain or mind. There are four major systems within us that are very interdependent: the brain and nervous system, the immune system, the endocrine system—consisting primarily of the adrenals, pancreas, and thyroid glands—and the digestive system. When you're stressed out over a long period of time, your immune system suffers. You get sick more often. The adrenal glands get drained by constant stress, and when that happens, the pancreas and thyroid get out of balance. Basically, the endocrine system helps maintain our energy level. And stress begins to impair digestion. I don't see this as a serious problem for you, but in this society of high stress, high pollution, pesticides, foods laced with hormones, and land that has been leached of its nutrients, most of us simply are not running at our metabolic best."

In general, I recommend that my patients enhance their physical health by avoiding junk food, eating a wholesome balanced diet, and taking a variety of nutritional supplements, depending on the individual's particular needs. In this high-stress society, I generally recommend high doses of vitamin C, spirulina (a high-protein food, made from plankton, that is an immune system booster), an antioxidant such as vitamin A, selenium, pycnogenol, coenzyme Q-10, and a multivitamin. I also recommend specific amino acids, depending on the particular problem (tyrosine or L-tryptophan for depression; taurine for nervous system instability and anxiety; alanine and serine for problems with blood sugar; lysine for a stressed immune system and frequent viral infections). I'll also advise them to take pyridoxal-5-phosphate (a form of vitamin $B_6$) if they're taking any amino acids, because $B_6$ is needed in order for amino acids to work.

I may or may not tell Mrs. Diamond if I am considering medications for her, but I will have assessed that need. Mrs. Diamond has been hit with a heavy dose of information. Most of all, I want to see her walk out of my office with a sense of hope. I want her to feel that she can talk about anything with me, from sex to samadhi.

## GUIDED IMAGERY

I specialize in the use of guided imagery techniques, and I usually begin using them in the second session. Suppose Mrs. Diamond and I are working on her relationship with her husband. Rather than simply talking about him, I'll ask her to close her eyes and imagine that he's right in the room, so that she can tell him things mentally that she may not have thought of saying at all. It's far more powerful than simply talking about him.

How does the imagery process work? The mind is like a garden. When you use your mantra, you're weeding the garden. After you've done some weeding, imagery work is like planting seeds into that fertile ground. If you haven't weeded the garden, then flowers *and* weeds will be growing once we start imagery work.

Here's a brief imagery exercise for helping you deal with the little stresses in your life that rob you of energy:

## MAGIC BOX
### *Mental Fitness Technique*

*Imagine you have a magic box beside you. Now get in touch with any worry, fear, or problem that is bothering you.*

*Allow the problem to flow out into your hands. Notice what the problem feels like in your hands. How big is your problem? What color is it?*

*Toss your worry or problem into the magic box, and leave it there. Your magic box can hold an infinite number of worries, fears, and problems.*

If imagery is new to you, this exercise may seem foolish. But please suspend your judgment, about this and all other techniques in this book, until you have tried them. Imagining tossing your worries into a magic box actually can help relieve stress. In fact, this simple imagery technique will go a long way toward reducing stress.

Now that you know how to de-stress, you can "carry" your imaginary magic box with you wherever you go. Put it in your office, and another one at home.

When you combine breath techniques with imagery work, you can relax at an even deeper level.

## REGULATING ENERGY WITH BREATH
### *Mental Fitness Technique*

The ancient Hindu texts, the Vedas, describe a complex system of breath control called *pranayama*. Breathing can either raise or lower your energy, depending on how you choose to breathe.

If you want to lower your energy and become calmer, practice this method of breathing:

1. Inhale to the count of four.
2. Hold your breath to the count of four.
3. Exhale to the count of eight.

If, on the other hand, you want to bring your energy up, the method you'll want to use is the opposite:

1. Inhale to the count of two.
2. Hold your breath to the count of two.
3. Exhale to the count of one.

If you're always exhausted, this energizing breath is for you. If, on the other hand, you have too much energy or are anxious and stressed out, practice the first technique. A general rule is to practice for one minute four times a day.

These techniques affect not only your energy level but your consciousness and alertness. If you are extremely energized, you may become overactivated, and as a result, your focus will begin to narrow. You'll see less. You'll be fully aware only of what's right in front of you. We can illustrate this by taking an example from football. If you're a defensive tackle, all you have to do is knock down the guy in front of you and then tackle whoever is carrying the football. So you need high energy and a narrow focus of attention. If, on the other hand, you're the quarterback, you need to have a much wider focus of attention. You don't want to be as pumped up as the defensive tackle. You want to slip "into the zone," like Joe Montana, and see everybody on the field—all your receivers and everyone defending against your receivers. In a high-pressure game, like the Super Bowl, a quarterback usually needs to practice the first kind of breath technique, the relaxing kind.

The same principle holds true for any event in which you're participating. If you're about to give a speech in front of a thousand people, you'll want to bring your energy down so you're centered and relaxed. But you don't want to be too calm, for a certain amount of tension is necessary for you to connect deeply with your audience.

Whatever situation you're in, you can consciously use your breath to optimize your performance and make yourself feel better.

Now, back to Mrs. Diamond. She'll have a good idea, after that first session, about the direction our therapy will take. Psychotherapy, as I practice it, is actually fun and inspiring, and she may already feel that it is. She certainly does have a lot of questions to mull over, though, for I've given her enough information and ideas to think about for months. And she has received something that she doesn't consciously know about yet. By describing the way the mind works and how it gets us into trouble, I've conveyed to her a subtle but powerful message: We *have* a mind, but we *are not* our minds. Meditating on a mantra allows one to witness the mind— the thoughts that pass in and out, like clouds passing through the sky. But *who* is it who is doing the watching? It is the eternal witness within us, the part that has witnessed the drama of our lives since childhood, yet that stays the same despite the ever-changing landscapes of our lives.

Automatically, by meditating with her mantra, Mrs. Diamond will begin to get in touch with that part of her that is eternal, the witness. As she becomes more aware of her witness, her mind will lose some of its self-limiting control over her. She (the "real she") will become the master of her mind and not its slave.

My approach to therapy is radically different from traditional ones because conventional psychiatry does not recognize anything above or beyond the mind. It gets stuck in the mind and stays there, mucking around sometimes for years. But when therapy is launched from a spiritual foundation, the trajectory is quite different. And the spiritual context continues, even as my patient is walking out the door.

Traditional psychiatry deals with our dark side, our shadow, our unconscious, and it does not lead toward the light side, the bright side. It is essential to deal with both sides. The dark side, the painful experiences, the anger, the shame—all of these must be brought to the surface, expressed, and released. But released *from* what and *to* what? Spiritual psychiatry releases the person to something that has God and spirituality in its psychiatric equation. That "balanced equation" allows the patient to identify with their strengths, not dwell on their weaknesses. It helps them develop those strengths, to become better than better, and to find their unique place on this planet. It can help them see the light, to see their inner divinity, their love, their courage—their positive side.

The patient need not already have a spiritual practice in order for spiritual psychiatry to benefit them. My patients are Jane and John Doe—they're your next-door neighbors. They are you. They are doctors, nurses, lawyers, musicians, beauticians, private investigators, businessmen, salesmen, and psychics. They come from all walks of life, all religions. They're very rich, and they're unemployed. Amazingly, spiritual psychiatry seems to have a universal appeal. It resonates with almost everyone, because the human mind works the same way no matter who you are, no matter your sex, race, creed, color, or religion. Everyone has a mind, and almost everyone believes in God. Therefore, almost everyone is very happy to experience this spiritual approach.

As my day winds down, I'm a little worn out as I drive north on the interstate. During the half hour I'm stuck at the merge, the site of daily traffic jams, I chant my mantra, or listen to NPR (National Public Radio), the country-western station, the classical station, some classic rock. Always looking for a song that I like, no matter what style.

Before I go to sleep at night, I read from spiritual books for about a half hour. And then I begin a long prayer, starting with the Gayatri mantra (the prayer to illuminate my intellect), followed by *Loka Samastha Sukino Bhavantu*—"may all the beings in all the worlds be happy." I continue with, "Dear Lord, the tasks of this day, whose burden I placed upon you this morning, are now over. It was you who made me think, feel, and act as I did. Now I offer all my thoughts, words, and needs to you. Please receive me. I am coming home to you."

These prayers are rather fixed and routine, but then I go on "talking to God" for a while: "Dear God, I pray that you fill me with your love and grace. I pray for liberation. I pray that you will work through me as a healer. I pray for [family, friends, the world]."

God and I talk for a while. Rather, I talk. He listens. And then I recite my main mantra over and over again: *Om Sai Ram . . . Om Sai Ram . . . Om Sai Ram . . . zzzzzz.*

# 4

# THE HEALING POWER
# OF HUMAN VALUES

In all arenas of life, human values are fundamental to success. Values
form the core of character and the foundation of spiritual development. The Indian yogi and scholar Patanjali outlined an "eightfold
path" to enlightenment, in which the first step is the development of
human values. The second step has to do with our obligations to society,
which gave birth to us and continues to provide for us.

Patanjali's third step is *asana,* the physical postures that we commonly think of as yoga. The fourth step is *pranayama,* or regulation and
control of the breath. Step five is *pratyahara,* or sense control. Through
pratyahara, we learn detachment, how to be in the world, and how to have
objects but not be "owned" by them. Step six is concentration, which pre-
pares us for meditation. Despite the common view that meditation is the
beginning of spiritual development, it is the seventh step in Patanjali's view.
Samadhi, or nirvana, is the final step, the state in which all is one. Here
all mental agitation ends. In samadhi, we are more than peaceful. We are
peace, and we are love.

The true healing of mind, body, and spirit requires attention to our
values. You can be cured of an illness through high-tech surgery or antibiotics, but you won't find out why you became vulnerable to the illness
in the first place unless you attend to the life and spiritual issues at its
source. In psychiatry, fostering human values is the first step toward self-
understanding and insight. Understanding a patient's values helps a psy-

chiatrist diagnose and treat. The goal of psychiatric treatment, however, is not samadhi. It is healing—healing of one's suffering, healing from illness, even healing into a good death.[1]

Sathya Sai Baba understands the importance of human values for mental health—as well as for politics, business, and education—and has created an entire educational system, from kindergarten through graduate school, based on the premise that the fostering of human values and character is the main goal of education. Not only is the Sathya Sai Education in Human Values (Sathya Sai EHV) system prevalent in his native India, it is being taught all over the world. According to this educational system, the five core human values are truth, right action (moral conduct), peace, love, and nonviolence. Each human value evolves out of the one prior to it. For example, truth is the first human value. When one knows the truth, one can proceed with right action. When one has taken right action, one develops peace of mind. Where there is peace, love soon follows. Finally, nonviolence evolves out of love.[2]

All other values are subvalues of these five core human values. For example, compassion is a subvalue of love. Sai Baba asks, "Are you practicing brotherliness, tolerance, equanimity, charity, compassion? These are the armors that guard the mind from the arrows of sorrow and pain."

Sai Baba's teachings are essential to my practice of psychiatry, and I am convinced that tolerance and compassion really are medicines for the mind. Spiritual psychiatry is not just about gathering *information* or incorporating the latest data on mind-body medicine and the latest thoughts on spirituality. It's about *transformation* and *goodness of the heart*. In order for transformation to occur, psychiatry becomes "sacred," creating a space in which trust, healing, and even miracles can take place, where truth and love can be experienced and shared. In almost all doctor-patient relationships, compassion and trust are the essential healing ingredients.

The exceptions include the approximately 40 percent of psychotic people who don't believe they have a problem. For a paranoid schizophrenic in the middle of a psychotic episode, determining the treatment may not be so easy. The patient will require powerful antipsychotic medication, but since he doesn't think there's anything wrong with him, he will probably resist taking the very medicine he needs. In these cases the psychiatrist must treat even though no trust has been established. I would order Haldol or Navane and, along with the nursing staff in the hospital, gently try to persuade the patient to take it. (Paranoid schizophrenia can be difficult to treat even when the patient is cooperative, but the law makes involuntary treatment with medication almost impossible.) If I can get the patient to take the medicine, however, he'll start to recover—and then may begin to trust me. In such rare situations trust may come after treatment, not before.

For each patient, doctors must look at body, mind, and spirit—and diagnose and treat each aspect. The patient needs to become aware of mind, body, and spirit too. (There is actually more to us than body, mind, and spirit. In the East six aspects of man have been explored for thousands of years: the physical body; prana, or life-force; the mind; the intellect; the "layer of bliss"; and the soul. In Eastern medicine, chi, or life-force energy, is not the same as spirit. Spirit, or soul, is eternal, unchanging, limitless, not bound by time or space. The physical body is the most dense form of energy, followed by life-force energy, mind, intellect, the "layer of bliss," and finally spirit. We'll limit our discussion to the body, mind, and spirit for now.)

Among psychiatrists, the word *morality* is used as infrequently as *God* and *love*. But spiritual psychiatry looks not only for signs of mental illness and psychological stress but for *deficiencies in human values*. After determining which human values are deficient and need to be fostered, I incorporate them into my treatment plan. You may consider which values are strengths of yours and which you would develop more fully, first by visualizing symbols for them and then by prioritizing the ones you most need to work on.

## VISUALIZING SYMBOLS OF HUMAN VALUES
### Mental Fitness Technique

Because human values are so important—they are, in fact, the core of character—you'll want to do everything you possibly can to foster truth, right action, peace, love, and nonviolence in yourself.

Find an image or symbol to represent each of the five human values. Do not simply ask your unconscious to provide you with an image or symbol. Instead, ask God, or a Higher Power, to show you the right image. In this sense, imagery becomes prayer.

Ask God for images of the human values. Take a minute with each one, and then write down and draw the image for each value in a notebook:

1. **Truth**
2. **Right Action**
3. **Peace**
4. **Love**
5. **Nonviolence**

It is extremely important to understand that mental illness and moral illness are not the same thing. I have worked with very sick schizophrenics who were quite moral—and I have worked with people who were normal psychologically, but severely impaired morally. I have also worked with people who were both mentally and morally ill.

It is not only patients who suffer from these problems—psychiatrists themselves have been known to have moral deficiencies. A psychiatrist I know who practices in San Diego is an example of someone who is mentally healthy but morally impaired. A nurse in the hospital, a married woman, confided in me that Dr. T. had walked up to her, slid his hand inside the elastic belt of her pants, and pulled the fabric a few inches away from her waistline, so that he could stare down at her underwear. Dr. T. shows no signs of mental illness to me, but his action was clearly immoral. Another San Diego psychiatrist, Dr. A., has been in prison for several years for hiring a hit-man to murder a former lover. One may argue that only a mentally ill person would plan such an evil deed. But regardless of the degree of his mental instability, Dr. A.'s moral illness is far more serious. I attempted to have him removed from his residency program before he was licensed, but sadly my pleas fell on deaf ears. He was given a year of probation and a slap on the wrist, then completed his training.

Some people suffer from both mental and moral illnesses. Ben, a 35-year-old, had requested psychiatric hospitalization because he was depressed and was hearing voices. I treated Ben for three weeks in the hospital, and as I was preparing to discharge him, he asked me to read a note he had written. Grinning slyly, he explained, "You asked me to write down some goals. So here they are." I concealed my horror as I silently read Ben's twenty goals: "I plan to buy a semiautomatic rifle and kill as many people as I can." "I plan to blow up the police station." "I plan to carry a large hunting knife with me at all times and randomly attack people."

"What do you think, doc?" Ben asked, without a trace of guilt, shame, or fear.

"Ben," I replied, "what is the worst physical harm you've actually done to another human being, or to an animal?"

"Oh, one time, about ten years ago, I set a bum on fire. It was pretty funny to watch."

Upon pursuing the details, I learned that Ben had discovered a homeless person, smelling of alcohol, who was sleeping beside a building. Ben doused him with lighter fluid and then set his big toe on fire, as if it were the wick of a candle.

"Did he die?"

"Yeah. I killed him," Ben responded.

I told Ben that he had given me some serious things to think about and that I'd have to talk to him further at another time. I went into the doctors' lounge and notified the homicide division of the San Diego Police Department. A detective met with Ben in the hospital, then investigated, telephoning the city where Ben said the murder had occurred.

I waited for a week without hearing back from the police department. When I called them, they told me that the city had no murder or death on file that corresponded to Ben's story. I informed the police that Ben no longer needed psychiatric treatment, but that he had a severe case of moral illness. The police would now have to assume full responsibility for him. They said they'd get back to me. I kept Ben in the hospital for a few more days, then called the homicide division again. They told me they were dropping the investigation and that Ben was free to leave the hospital.

Ben's case is a clear example of mental illness (borderline personality with psychotic features) combined with moral illness. He was primarily lacking the human values of nonviolence, love, peace, and right action. It is my opinion that the police department may have also exhibited a degree of moral illness. I remain convinced that the murder did take place, and if the victim had been wealthy, powerful, or famous, the case would have been investigated and Ben would have been transferred to the county jail. Perhaps an unknown homeless person was the victim—someone who mattered to nobody else in the world.

Rosanne, the patient whose definition of spirituality you read in Chapter 2, suffers enormously, both mentally and physically. Her history of abuse is more like a history of torture. Yet her honesty, her sincerity, her compassion, and her urge to help others are immense. She and I have worked with her suffering as part of her spiritual path, and a major part of her recovery has been to find a highly structured spiritual community. After she had a half-dozen overdoses in one year, followed by even more psychiatric hospitalizations, I told her, "We've reached the end of the line. We need to find a long-term facility for you—and that is either going to be a locked long-term mental hospital, or a spiritual community." Rosanne was terrified. Both of us researched spiritual communities, and in accordance with her Buddhist leanings, we found the ideal place for her. She has lived and worked for six months there, trying diligently to practice the teachings of the Buddha every day.

Rosanne is no saint, and few of us are. Except for saints, sages, and enlightened masters, everyone has to overcome moral deficiencies—deficiencies in honesty, or love, or truth, or nonviolence, or courage. Yet morality is essential to mental and spiritual wellness. Practicing nonviolence, loving speech, forgiveness, and forbearance will help you make progress with your emotional suffering. Adhering to these virtues is essential to our progress as human beings, whether we are progressing from mental illness to "normalcy," or from "normalcy" to supernormalcy, or to enlightenment.

Much of psychiatric healing is based on awareness and understanding. The greater the awareness, the deeper the healing. Awareness leads to appropriate action: Once you are aware, once you know what to do, you have to do it. If you can't or won't do it, you must become aware of the obstacles that are preventing you from taking right action, and eliminate them. In a sense, spiritual philosophy is simply an extension of traditional psychoanalytic thinking, which also values understanding highly.

A primary goal of physicians is to encourage patients to become aware of their own inner resources, to better understand what to call their experience, to know how they feel about it, and to discover what to do about it. Awareness must lead to action if real change is to occur.

In order to become more fully aware of values in our lives, we'll explore them in more depth.

## WORKING ON HUMAN VALUES FOR PERSONAL GROWTH
### *Mental Fitness Technique*

Let us move forward to prioritize the human values you most need to work on. It is invaluable to be aware not only of the five human values but of which ones you feel most confident about, and those that need the most work.

In the list that follows, rate each human value from 0 to 5. Five means that that value is fully developed in you. Zero means that it is not developed at all (which would be a rare condition).

RATING (0–5)

1. Truth           _____
2. Right Action    _____
3. Peace          _____
4. Love           _____
5. Nonviolence     _____

If you have a problem with your temper, rate item 5 between 0 and 3. If you find yourself lying a lot, or twisting or exaggerating the truth, rate item 1 from 0 to 3. You will quickly see where your human value deficiency lies. We all have these deficiencies, so don't worry about being the only person in the world who needs to work on them.

In order to consolidate your experience thus far with the human values, recall the symbols that you developed for them, and write the word for each symbol to the right of its value.

Use a pencil when you write in your ratings. Because we are constantly changing and having new life experiences, our relative strength and weakness in the values varies, and so will the value ratings. This page is just your starting point for identifying and prioritizing them. Add this exercise to your notebook. Check in with yourself and with your notebook on a regular basis to make sure that the value at the top of your priority list is still the one that needs the most work.

Keep in mind the values that you feel you need to develop the most. Throughout this book, you will find many techniques for self-improvement, and each technique will say whether it fosters truth, right action, peace, love, or nonviolence. Some techniques specifically target a particular value; others will help you develop all of them.

## PSYCHO-SPIRITUAL ASSESSMENT

Psycho-Spiritual Assessment (PSA) can be a powerful tool for transforming your life. It helps people understand their spiritual and life experiences in a commonsensical way so they can integrate them into their lives. For my part, Psycho-Spiritual Assessment helps me zero in on patients' core issues so that I can help them work through those issues and move on to their next challenges in life. Because of PSA, many of them have been able to meet their challenges courageously and feel empowered by the experience. Many of these patients had spent years in traditional psychotherapy without making much headway, but they were able to "see the light" when they realized that there was a light to be seen. When spiritual questions are included as a viable and important part of therapy, both psychiatrist and patient gain a larger perspective on the patient's life, which in turn leads to faster personal growth, transformation, and healing.

In a sense, the major goal of all forms of therapy is to convey the message "Everything is going to be all right." I deeply believe that for all of us, everything is going to be all right. The obstacles we face in life are challenges and opportunities for growth. They are not to be dismissed or avoided. Even death can be a healing experience, a time of releasing, letting go, and completing unfinished business.[3] To heal, in the sacred sense, means to convey hope at all times—even in so-called hopeless situations.

From the moment I first shake hands with a new patient, I am working to create hope. I am simultaneously diagnosing her to see what feels hopeless to her and treating her with a dose of hope. For many people, compassionate diagnosis inspires hope and alleviates fear. People want to know if they've really seen a ghost or if they're crazy. On dozens of occasions while writing this book, when I've shared the title, people have told me their stories to find out if I think they're crazy. It's a kind of abbreviated therapy. They tell me their ghost story or spiritual experience; I tell them what I think their experience is called, and they feel better.

I use this three-step Psycho-Spiritual Assessment to evaluate patients. If you believe you are capable of honestly evaluating your own belief systems, even of allowing them to change, then you may apply the PSA to your own life, without the assistance of a psychiatrist. The PSA is meant to give you diagnostic information, which you then use to take appropriate action.

It will also clarify for you what you want to work on in life. Before you begin self-transformation with the PSA, however, you should gain better control over your mind through Mantra Meditation. Once your mind is a little quieter, you will be in a better position to go deeper, to clarify what you want out of life.

## PSYCHO-SPIRITUAL ASSESSMENT
### *Mental Fitness Technique*

*Human values fostered by this technique:*
*Truth, Right Action, Peace, Love, Nonviolence*

1.  What is your main concern in your life right now? It could be a symptom, problem, experience, or goal. A *symptom* or *problem* is

something you want less of, such as: pain, depressed mood, insomnia. A *goal* is something you want more of, such as: money, friends, peace of mind, or work-related or athletic goal. An *experience* is neither. Examples of experiences are: angels, near-death experience, past-life memory. You will need to identify your main concern, find out how you feel about it, and discover what it means.

Be as specific as possible about identifying your main concern. For example, if you have cancer, your main concern may be the pain caused by the cancer.

_____

_____

_____

_____

2.  How do you feel emotionally about your main concern?

_____

_____

_____

_____

3.  How does your main concern affect your belief system or your sense of meaning in life?

_____

_____

_____

_____

Keep your main concern in mind throughout the remainder of this book. Because your main concern may change from week to week, use a notebook for the PSA, leaving pages on which to complete future assessments.

Let's run through one Psycho-Spiritual Assessment, using the symptom of pain as the main concern. Here are some possible answers to the three questions:

1. What is your main concern? "The symptom of pain."
2. How do you feel emotionally about your main concern? "I hate it!"
3. How does your main concern affect your belief system or your sense of meaning in life? "The pain makes me question if God exists."

Here's another PSA, in which the "experience" of angels is the main concern:

1. What is your main concern? "I saw an angel."
2. How do you feel emotionally about your main concern? "It made me feel ecstatic."
3. How does your main concern affect your belief system or your sense of meaning in life? "I believe I'm losing my mind. I don't believe in angels. They're not real. Even though it *felt* real, I'm sure it cannot *be* real."

Your main concern may very well be of no interest to anyone else. Moreover, whether it is a concern or not depends not on how others might view the event but how you react to it. Some events that others might think extraordinary may be routine to you. For example, if you've just seen your first angel, you will probably be startled, wondering what it is and what it means. If, on the other hand, you've seen so many angels that you've actually lost count, then seeing one more angel will concern you about as much as going to the mailbox.

All symptoms, problems, experiences, and goals that cause you concern are worthy of your attention. Don't dismiss an experience as insignificant if you care about it. If something has grabbed your attention, that something is your main concern, if only temporarily.

Now that we've completed the diagnostic phase, let's look at Psycho-

Spiritual Assessment in more depth, as a form of treatment. The three questions can help you either overcome a *problem* or attain a *goal*. Because the PSA is so widely applicable, it can help you achieve a variety of goals, from mundane problems at work or home to physical challenges.

Aaron, a 55-year-old, came to see me at his wife, Penny's, strong urging. Penny had asked Aaron to move out after twenty-five years of marriage, mainly because he drank too much. After he moved out, I saw Aaron weekly for several weeks, then met with them both together. When I asked Penny what she wanted from Aaron, she replied, "I just want him to stop drinking."

Aaron replied, "But I *have* stopped drinking. I haven't had a drink in three months. You can check it out. There's not a can of beer or a bottle of liquor in my apartment." Penny didn't believe Aaron, but I did.

"What else is bothering you, Penny?" I asked.

"I'm really sick of the whole situation. I work fifty or sixty hours a week. I come home and the house is a mess, and he expects me to do all the cooking. I've just had it."

"So tell me this, Penny," I asked. "Is this marriage a hundred percent over for you? Is there a fifty-fifty chance? What are we dealing with here?"

"Well, doctor, I'd say this marriage is ninety-nine percent over."

"Okay, at least now we know what we're dealing with. We have one percent to work with here. It's not much. Do you two want to work on that one percent or just call it quits? Frankly, it looks pretty bleak to me." Without hesitation, Aaron said he was ready to give saving the marriage a good try.

Penny took a little longer to answer, but then she sighed and said, "We might as well try. I don't see much hope at all, but . . . whatever."

We now had answered question one of the PSA. The main concern was a goal, and the goal was to save the marriage. Aaron and Penny then answered question two, how they felt about it, differently. Aaron was frightened that it wouldn't work out, while Penny felt confused. She had been preparing herself for divorce and now had to face an uncertain situation.

Here's how they answered question three about their belief systems. Aaron was overwhelmed with sorrow at the thought of completely losing Penny. He deeply loved her and felt that life would not have much meaning without her. Penny's beliefs were in greater conflict. She didn't believe the marriage could be saved, but at the same time, she was willing to try. Trying to save the marriage itself was a leap of faith. She too was scared. They were both grappling with the Human Value of Love.

Having assessed the situation as thoroughly as possible, it was time for me to take action. The diagnosis was clear. The treatment soon would be. "You guys really have a lot of problems. Let's start with something small and try to solve one problem at a time. Let's start with anything small, I don't care what. What small thing would either of you like to see the other change?"

Both of them felt stuck and didn't answer, so I said, "I have an idea. Penny says she's upset that you never cook. She hates coming home and feeling as if she has one more person to take care of, one more mouth to feed. Now she wants to be taken care of. Aaron, I suggest you begin cooking for her."

"But I really don't know how to cook," Aaron replied. I grilled Penny and Aaron about their favorite foods. They both liked fish.

"Okay, Aaron, how do you feel about starting to cook fish?"

"I have no idea how to do that, doc."

Patiently, I gave Aaron a cooking lesson. "Aaron, here's a piece of paper and a pen. Take some notes. I want you to go to your grocery store. Go to the fresh fish section. Do you like sea bass?"

They both agreed on sea bass. "Ask your grocer to pick out two terrific sea bass steaks—let's say a half-pound each. Then buy a lemon, some olive oil, salt, and garlic powder. You can buy fresh garlic, but let's keep things simple." I went into details about how to prepare the fish and told him to cook the sea bass for four minutes on each side. We then ended the session.

When they returned next week, I asked them how the cooking was going. Penny was very pleased with how the fish tasted and with the fact that Aaron had made the effort. Aaron was relieved. He hadn't been sure if he had had the skills to cook, and now he knew he did. Both were happy with the outcome.

This fish story actually was the turning point for their marriage. Immediately, hope and trust began to return. I continued to help them with specific, detailed tasks—with more "fish stories." Within a few months, Aaron had moved back in with Penny. The marriage was saved, and over the years since I last saw them, it has grown even stronger.

I still find this story amazing. Love was rekindled and a marriage restored simply because a man learned how to cook fish. It may not sound like spiritual psychiatry to you, but the "practical" thing to do, the "right" thing to do, is "spiritual." For some who complete the PSA, the practical thing to do is intensive meditation and guided imagery work to assist them in deepening their faith in God, and in removing obstacles to progress on their chosen spiritual path. In the case of Aaron and Penny, the practical thing to do was to save a sacred bond, a marriage, through a mundane activity.

Psycho-Spiritual Assessment may not always provide you with the ultimate answers or the relief you seek, but at the very least, it can help you organize your thoughts, feelings, and experiences so that you can begin to understand them and do something about them. Here's a simple exercise you can use when confronted by your main concern.

## MOOD WORDS
### Mental Fitness Technique

*Human values fostered by this technique: Confidence (a subvalue of Right Action), Truth, and Peace*

Suppose you are battling a serious physical problem, like cancer. As part of your mental fitness program, you may want to incorporate mood words like "conquer," "win," "overcome," "triumph." But don't just say these words in a repetitious way. Pour your heart into the words so that your own deep emotions empower them.

Suppose you're about to take an exam. First calm yourself by using your mantra. Then you may use mood words throughout the exam, but not mood words that make you feel pressured. You want to be able to glide through the exam without getting hung up on any particular point. So "glide" or "fly" may help you do better and feel better during the exam.

If you're giving a speech, lecture, or sermon, first become clear about your intentions. Are you trying to inspire your audience, educate them, or move them into a particular course of action? Let's say you want to inspire them, in which case, you can inspire yourself with mood words like "inspire," "breathe," "glorify," "unify."

Perhaps you work in some kind of production business in which you must meet deadlines. Every month you're under the gun, and there never seems to be enough time. Time is a big issue. As deadlines come and go, mood words can play a part in "expanding time" and helping you relax. You may feel the need to "speed things up," but that attitude almost invariably makes you run out of time, so try mood words like "slow down" or "expand." Yes, you can expand time, so by telling yourself to expand, you actually can expand psychological time.

I used mood words to assist one elderly woman who was recovering from a stroke. She had to learn how to walk again and was started with a walker while in the hospital. Because her feet no longer seemed to obey her wishes, mentally she was saying, "Damn these useless feet." I suggested she use the word "lift" every time she wanted to lift her feet. It made a big difference for her.

No matter what your situation, problem, goal, challenge, or experience, you can find a mood word that will help you.

By helping you identify your main concern, the PSA has already provided a valuable service, for you cannot arrive at your destination without knowing what that destination is. You have to start somewhere. Begin where you are this moment—and where you are this moment is your main concern.

Although seemingly simple, the PSA is intended to be all-inclusive. It is not intended solely for spiritual aspirants or theists. Atheists and agnostics benefit equally from using it. Everything in life can be seen as part of one's spiritual process. To the spiritual seeker, the real challenge is finding meaning in everyday things—in cutting a loaf of bread, doing the dishes, balancing the checkbook, investing wisely, planning vacations, and even learning to cook fish.

# 5

# YOUR MENTAL
# FITNESS PROGRAM

So that you can gain maximum benefit from the techniques in this book, this chapter has been designed to help you create your own personalized Mental Fitness Program, a strategy to help you strengthen your psychological and spiritual health. Your Mental Fitness Program is a progressive 12-week program, which you can tailor to your own particular needs. Whether you are suffering from anxiety, are trying to understand a strange or mystical experience, or want to clarify your values, this chapter will help you achieve your goals, overcome your problems, and integrate your inexplicable experiences in an accelerated fashion.

You may find some of these techniques "mundane," while others may appear to be more "spiritual." My goal is to help you become more whole, so that your body, mind, energy, and spirit may come into balance. Even if your main concerns at the time you begin this program are (seemingly) simple headaches that aspirins can cure, the 12-week program will help you understand these headaches better, maybe even discover their origin, and certainly understand your whole life better.

Each mental fitness technique is intended to foster one or more of the five core human values: truth, right action, peace, love, and nonviolence. In this way, a "mundane" technique, such as "stress-reduction," can become as "spiritual" as hours of meditation, for it too fosters the human value of peace.

All religions teach us how to be better people, to love more, to serve more, to give up greed, anger, envy, and jealousy; to embrace a spirit of unity and begin to perceive the world family as our very own family. And that is exactly what these techniques will help you achieve *if* you practice them. These techniques are not intended to induce you to have an out-of-body experience or to go into a state of samadhi, but if you've had one of these special and unusual happenings, these techniques will help you put those experiences into their proper perspective. Don't remain attached to the experiences, however. The experiences occur to foster deeper values, lasting values. The effect of the experience is valuable, not merely the experience itself.

As you read the following pages, have a notebook handy to write down your observations, experiences, insights, images, brainstorms, and solutions. First, organize your notebook or journal by writing the week number at the top of each page. As we proceed through the program, you will find specific instructions regarding which techniques to use and for what length of time. It will help you to write the instructions in your journal. You might also consider tape-recording the many imagery scripts on your own so that you have your own set of tailor-made audiocassettes.

Because of the multiple goals of this book, your Mental Fitness Program has been set up in a unique way, which allows you to read the entirety of the book at your own pace, as well as work on the Program at your own pace. Don't try to complete this 12-week program in one week! All of the guidelines for your Mental Fitness Program are contained within the pages of this one chapter. Begin slowly. After you've read about and begun your program for week 1, put aside this chapter and continue reading through the rest of the book. Then, one week from now, return to this chapter. Once a week for 11 more weeks, return to this chapter. Of course, you may not want to work on a Mental Fitness Program at all, or may not want to at this time. That is quite all right. If that is the case, simply proceed directly to the next chapter. But you should know that you actually already have begun the program by having learned the Thought Watch technique, the Mantra Meditation, and Psycho-Spiritual Assessment. These are actually the techniques you'll want to practice in week 1.

The techniques and guidelines that make up your Mental Fitness Program are presented throughout this book, but all of the techniques marked MFT for Mental Fitness Technique are listed in Appendix A at the back of the book.

Your Mental Fitness Program will progress in the following way:
After your mind is quiet, deeper changes can occur. You can learn

the next techniques "targeted" for specific symptoms, problems, goals, or experiences. You'll begin to embrace problems in a whole new light, deepen your spiritual practice, and more fully develop your capacity for love. Finally, you will reassess the entire program and be able to create your personalized "Long-Term Mental Fitness Program." You will discover that, while you will be focusing in on a particular problem, all of these techniques are aimed at fostering love.

Remember to try to approach each technique with an open mind, and practice each technique with the attitudes of love, reverence, and confidence. Therein lies the deepest transformation.

Here's what your Mental Fitness Program looks like:

Week  1:   Quieting the Mind

Week  2:   Psycho-Spiritual Assessment (PSA)

Week  3:   Main Concern: Focusing on What's Important

Week  4:   Breathwork

Week  5:   Communicating with Your Main Concern

Week  6:   Deepening Spiritual Practice

Week  7:   Profound Self-Acceptance

Week  8:   Exploring Resistance

Week  9:   The Power of Paradox

Week 10:   Developing Love

Week 11:   One-Minute Imagery Rituals

Week 12:   Long-Term Mental Fitness Plan

## WEEK 1:   QUIETING THE MIND

**Day 1     30 seconds**

*Thought Watch: Recognize the volume of your thoughts (MFT).*

**Days 1–7     5 minutes, 2 times a day (morning and evening)**

*Mantra Meditation: Channel your thoughts (MFT).*

Mantra meditation is central to your Mental Fitness Program, and you will want to practice it throughout the 12-week program. Please copy into your journal the names of the techniques and the number of times you will be practicing them.

## WEEK 2:   PSYCHO-SPIRITUAL ASSESSMENT (PSA)

*Continue practicing Mantra Meditation daily.*

### Day 1      10 minutes

*PSA: Become more aware of your current main concern in life (MFT).*

In week 3, you will be going deeper into the PSA. During this week, you are invited to begin exploring PSA. You will begin to zero in on your main concern in life, find out how you really feel about it, and discover how your main concern affects your belief systems and sense of meaning of your life.

### Days 2–7      5–10 minutes per day

*"Who Am I?" Meditation: Ponder life's deepest questions (MFT).*

If you are feeling stuck with the exercise above or are wondering how honest you are being with yourself, try the following exercise.

## FACING UP TO SELF-LIES
### *Mental Fitness Technique*

*Human value fostered by this technique: Truth*

You may think you know what you want, what your goal is, and what your talents are. Yet, many of us are unrealistic with ourselves. We exaggerate, either telling ourselves we're "worse" than we really are or that we're "better" at something than we really are. No matter what you want to succeed at, you've got to start with an accurate and honest self-assessment, brutally honest.

Almost all of us fail to tell ourselves the full truth about ourselves. We lie to ourselves. We pretend to be something we're not. We fool ourselves into thinking we're better at something than we actually are, or that we're worse than we really are. By facing our personal reality, free of lies and distortions, we become free. Every lie we tell ourselves requires mental effort to keep that lie in place. We have to keep telling the same lie.

For some people, it's not so much a question of lying to themselves, but rather a question of exaggerating or distorting the truth. This exercise is an opportunity for you to write down the lies you've been telling yourself or those things you've been distorting or exaggerating.

This technique may reveal some obvious self-lies, or you may have to think about it before you discover ways in which you may be hiding from the truth about yourself or your life situation.

Information can and should lead to transformation. By working with this technique, I am not encouraging you to beat up on yourself. Just tell yourself the truth. Write down your self-lies, exaggerations, and distortions in your notebook.

After you've written down your list, review each entry and ask yourself why you've been distorting that particular item. And then, if you really want to accelerate your personal growth and spiritual advancement, vow to stop lying to yourself about anything no matter how petty or small it might seem. This vow of truth will clarify some of the shadow parts of your personality, allowing you to shine some light on that area. Telling the truth is immensely powerful. Start by telling yourself the truth, the whole truth, and nothing but the truth. Once you have shared your soul with yourself, you can proceed toward your goal without being hindered by false notions. You'll know exactly how much higher you have to jump and how much longer you'll have to persevere in a particular endeavor. If you think you're going to be an overnight success as a rock-and-roll star, harsh reality will clash with your dream, and reality is likely to win.

## WEEK 3:   MAIN CONCERN: FOCUSING ON WHAT'S IMPORTANT

*Continue practicing Mantra Meditation daily.*

**Day 1     5–15 minutes (total time for steps 1–3)**

*PSA, Main Concern Monitor: Learn how to zero in on your life's most important concern (either a symptom/problem, goal, or experience) (MFT).*

In order to zero in on which is truly the most valuable concern for you to work on, you will first want to become aware of all the major concerns. After listing all of your concerns, prioritize them, and then finally select your number-one main concern, the pivotal issue around which you will center the following 9 weeks. This is a big commitment, so we place a lot of emphasis on choosing the main concern. You will also select your specific imagery technique for dealing with your main concern during this week.

### STEP 1 PRIORITIZING MAIN CONCERNS

   **A.** Make a list of your 10 top concerns.

   **B.** Number from 1–10 from most important (1) to least important (10).

   **C.** Cross out the ones you know are least important.

   **D.** Cross out all but 1–3.

   **E.** Of these 3, decide which is the least urgent, important, pressing and cross it out.

   **F.** Of the remaining 2, pick the most important one, and it becomes your main concern. If you cannot yet decide, proceed to step G.

   **G.** Using the scales imagery from Decision-Making (MFT), decide which of the remaining 2 concerns is your Main Concern.

### STEP 2 NAME YOUR MAIN CONCERN _____
   Write down your main concern in your journal.

STEP 3

Which of the five human values (truth, right action, peace, love, non-violence) best reflects the "value deficiency" caused by your main concern? For example, if you are suffering from either physical pain or emotional stress, "peace" is the human value you need to develop. Relationship problems, on the other hand, call on us to develop "love" or "nonviolence." Use Visualizing Symbols of Human Values (MFT) to create an image representing this one human value.

Once the symbol has been visualized, it will often become immediately apparent how you are to use that symbol. If its use is not readily apparent, close your eyes and ask God what to do with the symbol. Here are four ways in which you can work with the symbol: (1) You may simply picture the symbol whenever your main concern is bothering you, (2) you may imagine bringing the symbol inside your body and keeping it there, (3) you may imagine your main concern pouring out of you and into the symbol of the human value, or (4) you may communicate with this symbol, using the Communicating with Your Main Concern technique (MFT).

By visualizing a symbol of the human value related to your main concern, you will not only be working directly on your main concern, but will be bringing more of that particular human value into all aspects of your life.

**Days 2–7　　5–10 minutes a day**

*Practice visualizing your symbol of a human value.*

## WEEK 4:    BREATHWORK

*Continue practicing Mantra Meditation daily. Visualize your symbol of a human value for 2 minutes every day.*

**Day 1**

*Practice Deep Breathing.*

Working with the breath contains tremendous potential for effecting change. During this week, you will learn to calm your mind so profoundly that creative, unforeseen solutions to your main concerns will begin to surface spontaneously. These techniques can also release vast reserves of energy.

You will become more aware of how you breathe, and you may notice that on numerous occasions throughout the day that you actually stop breathing. This is a common problem in the West.

When westerners first arrived in Hawaii, the Native Hawaiians called them "haoli," which means "without breath." The Hawaiians were struck by the lack of deep breathing. The importance of breath can be understood by examining language. The phrase "to inspire" means "to inhale" and also "to be moved by the Gods." The word "inspiration" dramatically shows the connection between breath and spirit.

### DEEP BREATHING
#### *Mental Fitness Technique*

*Human value fostered by this technique: Peace*

For 15 seconds every hour observe whether you are taking deep breaths. If you are, you'll feel your waistline expand, or you'll simply notice that your diaphragm is rising and falling. Most of us take very shallow breaths, primarily using the muscles of our rib cage, rather than our diaphragms. When we're stressed out, our respiration becomes very shallow, sometimes even to the point of holding our breath. This is exactly the wrong thing to do, as it intensifies stress even more.

Try this experiment. Place your hands on your ribs and then take a deep breath. You should feel your ribs expand. Now place your hands on your abdomen and take another deep breath. You should feel your abdomen expand. When you are breathing properly, both your abdomen and rib cage will expand with each inhalation. Monitor your breath so that you breathe deeply from your abdomen.

### Days 2-7    2 minutes 3 times a day (morning, noon, evening)

Practice deep, slow breathing, making sure you are moving your diaphragm.

### Day 3    2 minutes 3 times a day

*Regulate the Energy with Breath (MFT).*

Practice the two techniques: one that increases energy, and the other which relaxes and lowers energy. By practicing these two techniques, you will easily identify which of the two is best suited to your needs in a given situation. In your journal, write down which of the breath techniques suits your needs.

### Days 4-7    2 minutes 3 times a day

After you've decided which of the two techniques is best suited to you, practice that one for the remainder of the week.

## WEEK 5:   COMMUNICATING WITH YOUR
## MAIN CONCERN

*Continue practicing Mantra Meditation and visualizing your symbol of a human value daily.*

### Days 1, 3, 5, 7      20 minutes

*Practice Communicating with Your Main Concern (MFT).*

Use symbols to achieve direct contact with your symptom or goal. Few of us hesitate to pick up the telephone and communicate with a friend or loved one, but how many of us consider that it is possible to communicate with a symptom, goal, or experience? This technique enables you to create a temporary separation between you and your symptom, goal, or experience. In other words, there is the person who has a problem, the problem itself, and that part of us called the "witness" that is eternal, unchanging, and "beyond" the problem. Once you recognize these three aspects, you can symbolically reach out and touch that which you want to affect. But rather than using the language of words, which you'd use when communicating with a friend on the phone, you'll be using the language of symbols.

This symbolic work is very deep and powerful and is a technique that has facilitated many "miracles" in the lives of my patients. This technique allows your unconscious, conscious, and higher conscious minds to communicate with each other, and also allows your mind to communicate directly with your body.

You will continue practicing this technique every other day for 20 minutes during weeks 6 and 7.

## WEEK 6:   DEEPENING SPIRITUAL PRACTICE

*Continue practicing Mantra Meditation and visualizing your symbol of a human value daily.*

*Practice Communicating with Your Main Concern every other day for 20 minutes.*

**Days 1–7     5 minutes before bedtime**

*Practice the Judgment Review (MFT).*

By week 6 of your Mental Fitness Program, you will have learned how to quiet your mind so that you can become calmer, allowing for deeper changes to occur within you. You've determined your main concern and have worked on it using human value imagery techniques, as well as a symbolic technique.

During week 6, you will shift your focus from the purely mundane and practical and will consciously explore and deepen your own spiritual beliefs and practices. By focusing on the spiritual, you will not be losing sight of all the work you've done thus far on your main concern, but your focus will also include spiritual techniques.

In order to develop a solid foundation in these spiritual techniques, we'll start with the  Judgment Review, a technique which will help you let go of blaming, judging and comparing, which all hinder spiritual progress.

## WEEK 7:   PROFOUND SELF-ACCEPTANCE

*Continue practicing Mantra Meditation and visualizing your symbol of a human value daily.*

*Practice Communicating with Your Main Concern every other day for 20 minutes. On the alternate days practice the Judgment Review for 5 minutes.*

**Days 1–7     15 minutes before bedtime**

*Profound Self-Acceptance and Embracing Overwhelming Pain and Fear (MFT).*

Profound Self-Acceptance is a combination of a meditation technique and an imagery technique, and is one of the most transformative of all techniques. During this week, you will not be trying to get rid of a symptom, nor trying to attain a goal. Rather, you will be consciously practicing the acceptance of "what is." Through this technique some of our deepest fears can actually be embraced. For example, this is the only technique which works for the overwhelming fear of a cancer recurrence. No matter what is gnawing away at you, no matter how "large" or "small" your main concern may appear, by practicing profound self-acceptance, healing begins to occur at a deeper level. The connection with God or Spirit becomes more profound, and one begins to see more clearly what is really important in life and what is not.

## WEEK 8:   EXPLORING RESISTANCE

*Continue practicing Mantra Meditation daily.*

*Begin Practicing the Presence (MFT) in order to deepen your spiritual awareness 5 minutes 3 times daily.*

**Days 1, 3, 5, 7      15 minutes each day, preferably before bed**

*Practice Overcoming Resistance.*

Analyze your progress with your Main Concern Solution to find out how you can increase results.

This week will be spent dealing with that which is hidden, our resistance, a force that can only be overcome once it is known. Therefore, you will uncover, meet, and face that hidden force buried below the surface that accompanies every experience, goal, or problem. Very few of us are 100 percent behind our own success, even if we think we are. However, after working with resistance, you will come close to a 100 percent commitment to attaining a goal, overcoming a symptom/problem, or integrating an experience.

### OVERCOMING RESISTANCE
#### Mental Fitness Technique

*Human values fostered by this technique: Truth, Right Action, Peace, Love, and Nonviolence*

You *know* you want to attain your goal. You *know* you want to be free from pain, suffering, symptoms, and problems. Yet, when I ask my patients (and you) if they are 100 percent ready and willing to work toward that goal (or away from that symptom), they usually pause and say, "Well, I pretty much want it. Even if they tell me they definitely want "it," I'll ask them how committed they are. "Are you 100 percent committed, 90 percent, 50 percent, 25 percent? I almost never hear "100 percent."

That part of you that is not 100 percent behind success with your main concern is your resistance. There is some part of you, maybe only one percent, that is sabotaging your best laid plans. Until you are aware of your resistance, it will be nearly impossible to actualize your dreams fully or to resolve your symptoms or problems.

*Get in touch with that part of yourself that is resisting, that is not fully committed to attaining your goal or overcoming a symptom—that 1, 5, 10, 25, 50 percent of yourself. Allow an image to emerge from your unconscious mind that represents that resistance.*

*Once you have seen, heard, touched that image of resistance, you will immediately have more information about how to proceed and about what obstacles you may be putting in your own way.*

For example, when I asked one patient of mine to get in touch with her resistance to romance, she immediately "saw" and "felt" her elbows being pulled back into the chair as if drawn by ropes. She then had to work with those ropes in her mind. One month later, she resumed dating for the first time in many years.

Once you have visualized your resistance, you can gain more information and deepen your transformation by proceeding in this way:

*Give the image of resistance a voice. Express your feelings toward the image of resistance. Ask what it needs and wants from you. Ask it why it wants what it wants. Ask it if it is protecting you from anything.*

## WEEK 9: THE POWER OF PARADOX

*Continue practicing Mantra Meditation and Practicing the Presence daily.*

**Days 1–7**

*Practice the Power of Paradox.*

Up until this point, your Mental Fitness Program has been helping you move forward in the direction you have chosen. Because the mind can be so difficult to control and direct, an allowance needs to be made for the very nature of the mind itself. If this is not done, subtle forms of resistance beyond anything we dealt with in week 8 can still sabotage your efforts. In other words, continuously working in one direction is not always the best approach, even though your mind thinks it is. Therefore, in the 9th week, we will work paradoxically, which will accelerate progress dramatically. We will go beyond "profound acceptance" and will move to "active resistance."

Let's start with the definition of paradox from the *Random House Dictionary*—"a statement or proposition seemingly self-contradictory or absurd, but in reality expressing a possible truth; an opinion or statement contrary to commonly accepted opinion."

While working paradoxically, we won't be "fighting" a symptom or problem or striving to attain a goal. We may, in fact, be "encouraging" the symptom or "discouraging" the goal. My experience is that change occurs most rapidly and most dramatically when paradoxical and straightforward interactions are interwoven with each other.

In Step 1, by ceasing to work on your problem, you will free your subconscious mind to begin its work, which until now, it has not had the available energy to begin. Here we are actually diverting energy in the same way a train is diverted from one set of tracks to another with a toggle switch. We are redirecting our minds, which have been charging in one direction all of our lives. It's time to switch tracks.

In Step 2, by putting off all change, by resisting change, by even refusing to change, you will fatigue your ability to resist change, and will begin to recondition the way your mind thinks change must occur.

## THE POWER OF PARADOX
### *Mental Fitness Technique*

*Human values fostered by this technique: Truth, Right Action, Peace, Love, and Nonviolence*

### STEP 1    STOP WORKING ON YOUR MAIN CONCERN.

Because paradox may seem foreign to many, I'll illustrate this technique with an example. Let's say that your main concern is that your sex life with your spouse has fallen apart, and that every day for the last year you've been asking yourself, "Will tonight be the night?"

During this paradoxical week, there is a clear answer to that question. "No, tonight will not be the night." Your main concern may have been bugging you for months or even years. This week is your sabbatical. You are not allowed to have sex this week. In other words, sex ceases to be a problem whatsoever, at least for seven days.

If you're depressed, stop trying not to be depressed. Just be depressed this week. You not only have my permission but I am asking you to do so. Of course, some discretion must be applied here. If your depression is so severe that you're on the verge of suicide, do not work paradoxically.

Similarly, if your main concern is a goal, stop trying so hard to attain it for one week. The goal won't disappear, even though you may fear it will. In other words, take the pressure off the need to attain a goal or remove a symptom.

### STEP 2    ACTIVELY RESIST CHANGE. CHANGE BY REFUSING TO CHANGE.

#### 5 minutes 3 times a day

Step 2 takes us further than you may ever have imagined you could go. You will want to make your symptom/problem "worse" this week. If you're always anxious, always terrified about when the next panic attack is coming, desire to be more anxious. Set aside three periods a day during which you will actually try to be more anxious (or depressed, etc.).

Step 2 is a major attitudinal shift. *Do not* use this step as an excuse to hurt yourself: in other words, *do not* stop your medication, vitamins, meditation, or anything else that you feel benefits you. Do not use this week as an excuse to resume smoking or overeating. We're striving for a constructive quantum shift in attitude this week.

Here are some further tips for how to work paradoxically. Let's continue with the example of anxiety and panic attacks. During this week, try to have more panic attacks, and when you do feel one coming on, rather than fighting it, find a nice, comfortable chair in which to be in a panic.

If you're not smiling or laughing yet, you haven't gotten the point. We haven't talked about this yet, but change does not have to be a long, arduous, painful process. Change can be fun . . . and funny. Paradox is a very funny step for two reasons: It sounds absurd, and it works. Something in you right now is probably registering the thought, "This is so strange it probably does work." I can tell you from years of experience that working paradoxically does work.

## WEEK 10:   DEVELOPING LOVE

*Continue practicing Mantra Meditation daily.*

*Practice the Presence in order to deepen your spiritual awareness (remember now to saturate the technique with love). 5 minutes daily.*

This entire week will be devoted to love. Everything we do can help us develop love. Love is the goal, and love is the means to that goal. By developing love, we achieve the real transformation of the heart. We go way beyond either removing pain or understanding a vision. Those are great achievements, but only if their attainment makes us better people, more lovable people. During week 10, you'll be focusing entirely on developing love. By practicing "removing obstacles to love" and by "encouraging the expansion of love," you will be better able to: (1) give love, (2) receive love, (3) feel love in the face of rejection and (4) love safely in "unsafe" places.

Over the last few weeks, you have been practicing techniques aimed at expanding your awareness, deepening your belief systems . . . even working paradoxically. In other words, you are now not only transforming a problem or symptom, you are in the process of healing your life, your beliefs, your connection with God, your connection with yourself, your sense of purpose and meaning in life.

Now that we are consciously focusing on love, we need to take a deeper, loving look at love, rather than simply "techniquing" our way through love. Here's a brief, very sweet story about love: Sai Baba approached some school-age boys who live near Baba's ashram and attend his school, which is based on the principle of "Education in Human Values." Baba asked the boys, "What is love?" The boys each provided a variety of answers. Baba listened, smiled, and then said, "Love is ice cream—very sweet."

## LOVE IS ICE CREAM
### *Mental Fitness Technique*

*Human value fostered by this technique: Love*

> *Think about ice cream. Close your eyes and picture your favorite kind of ice cream. Imagine yourself taking a bite and then experience the sweetness.*

Silly as this may sound, I want you to keep this image with you though the rest of the program. Practice each technique as if it were creamy ice cream, slipping off your tongue and down into your stomach. You can practice all the techniques in the world, be the "perfect" spiritual seeker, but if your spiritual practices are not saturated with love, they will have little benefit. Saturate these techniques with the sweetness of ice cream. In the rare case that you do not like ice cream, substitute your favorite dessert or fruit—perhaps a juicy plum.

### Days 1-3

*Remove obstacles to love.*

### Day 1     10 minutes

Identify ways in which you are greedy, selfish, judgmental, angry, jealous, envious. These are all obstructions to love. By identifying these obstacles, you can accomplish the first step in developing love. Write down these "obstacles to love" in your journal.

### Day 2     10 minutes

*Practice Ceiling on Desires.*

Excessive material desire decreases our "love capacity." By cutting down on our desires, we can continue to remove obstacles to love. Identify areas of excessive material desire by practicing the Ceiling on Desires imagery.

## CEILING ON DESIRES
### *Mental Fitness Technique*

*Human values fostered by this technique: Love and Peace*

Here is an imagery technique to help you let go of excessive attachments:

A. Allow an image to emerge representing ways in which you are wasting money.

B. Allow an image to emerge representing ways in which you are wasting food.

C. Allow an image to emerge representing ways in which you are wasting time.

D. Allow an image to emerge representing ways in which you are wasting energy.

By putting a ceiling on our desires, by identifying ways in which we waste money, food, time, and energy, more love begins to flow.

### Day 3

*Explore Resistance to Love.*

A. Identify ways in which you are greedy, selfish, judgmental, angry, jealous, envious. These are all obstructions to love. By identifying these obstacles, you can accomplish the first step in developing love.

B. Excessive material desire decreases our "love capacity." By cutting our desires, we can continue to remove obstacles to love. Identify our material desire.

C. Allow an image to emerge that represents resistance to love.

D. Practice the ABCs of Anger Control (MFT). The more your anger is under control, the more love will flow.

E. Practice forgiveness. Pray that you may forgive everyone whom you feel wronged you in any way. Your own resentment is a great obstacle to love.

## RESISTANCE TO LOVE
### *Mental Fitness Technique*

*Human value fostered by this technique: Love*

> *Allow an image to emerge which represents resistance to love. Ask your Higher Consciousness how to deal with this image of resistance to love.*

### Days 4-7     5 minutes 3 times a day

*Encourage the Expansion of Love.*

Take up selfless service. Serve each individual by using "Divine Vision" to look for the spark of the divine within everyone. In other words, don't just go through the motions of service. Rather, perform acts of service that are soaked with love. Remember that the more love you give, the more love you will have to give. Love, without attachment, does not run out.

*Live and love fully in the moment.*

Imagine that you only had one more week to live. During that week, you would want to convey your love, at the deepest level, to the people in your life whom you really care about. But you don't have to be on your deathbed to express this kind of love. Make believe you're going to die next week, and live today as if it were the last day of your life. If you were about to die, you would overcome all fears about expressing love at the deepest level. So don't wait until you're dying. Be bold and courageous and express your love openly—today. Write letters to those whom you deeply love and tell them why you love them so much. And tell people directly. Speak to them. Say those words that so many of us find so difficult. "I love you." Live this way for four days.

### Days 6, 7     5 minutes a day

*Practice random acts of loving kindness. Start with one more act of love, generosity, or service today than you are used to.*

## CONNECTING TO GOD'S LOVE
### *Mental Fitness Technique*

*Human value fostered by this technique: Love*

> Picture your chosen form of God in front of you. Imagine that a hollow tube connects your heart to God's heart. Imagine that divine love flows through that tube into you. Allow it to continue flowing until you are filled with love. Notice if love has a color as it flows into you. If there are any places within you that do not fill with divine love, focus your attention there and allow love to pour in.

## WEEK 11: ONE-MINUTE IMAGERY RITUALS

*Continue practicing Mantra Meditation (saturated with love) daily.*

**Day 1      5 minutes**

*Create One-Minute Imagery Rituals.*

Learn to create your own personal imagery ritual for powerful results. You will create your imagery ritual based on your main concern as well as the techniques which you've practiced during the previous 10 weeks.

Review your PSA and determine your current main concern. Then select the symbol of the human value that you've been practicing. This one visualization will become the "heart" of your imagery ritual.

Design your personalized imagery ritual using the following outline. The idea is that you will want to be able to focus on your symptom, problem, or experience in a very focused, quick manner. Because the imagery ritual lasts only one minute, you can easily build it into your life. Not only will the imagery ritual help you directly with your main concern, these mini-breaks will also provide a great relief from the high-stress, high-pressure lives under which many of us live. If you were told you needed to take an hour a day to "relax," the idea alone might make you more anxious. On the other hand, knowing that you can accomplish a great deal in one minute is a tremendous relief for most people.

### ONE-MINUTE IMAGERY RITUALS
#### *Mental Fitness Technique*

Pick the specific times when you will do this exercise—for example eight A.M., noon, four P.M., and eight P.M. Plan to begin on the hour.

**STEP 1   RELAXATION AND MENTAL CLEARING   15 SECONDS**
    Close your eyes. Take three deep breaths, and allow yourself to let go of tension with each breath. Imagine that a wave of relaxation spreads from your head to your toes with each breath.

    Silently recite your mantra along with each breath you take. Allow yourself to sink into the peaceful stillness of your own mind. By so doing, you center yourself and temporarily withdraw from life's distractions.

### STEP 2 REGULATE ENERGY WITH THE BREATH 15 SECONDS

Decide if you need to bring your energy up or down. If you're drained most of the time, practice the energizing breath:

**A.** Inhale to the count of two.

**B.** Hold your breath to the count of two.

**C.** Exhale to the count of one.

If, on the other hand, you're anxious or stressed out, use your breath to continue to deepen relaxation:

**A.** Inhale to the count of four.

**B.** Hold your breath to the count of four.

**C.** Exhale to the count of eight.

### STEP 3 SPECIFIC HUMAN VALUE IMAGERY 25 SECONDS

### STEP 4 COMING BACK 5 SECONDS

Take one more long, deep breath, and completely bring yourself back to normal consciousness.

### Days 2–7　　1 minute 4 times a day

*Practice Your One-Minute Imagery Ritual.*

If you practiced every technique in this book every day of your life, you wouldn't have time for anything else.

That's why I encourage my patients, and you, to create one-minute imagery rituals that you can practice three or four times a day. If your doctor told you to take a pill four times a day, you'd probably do it. And each time it would probably take about sixty seconds for you to remember to take the pill, get a cup of water, swallow the pill, and then dispose of the cup.

One-minute imagery rituals don't take much longer than taking a pill. But do not underestimate their transformative power.

## WEEK 12: LONG-TERM MENTAL FITNESS PLAN

Through the past weeks, you have learned how to determine your main concern, how to solve a problem, attain a goal, or integrate an experience by using a combination of techniques.

Your main concern will forever be changing, for life is not static. These tools provide the flexibility necessary to handle life's ups and downs and the fact that life simply cannot be predicted.

With these thoughts in mind, review what you've discovered so far and craft a program you can use indefinitely.

**Day 1**

*Review Program and Current Beliefs.*

STEP 1 JOURNAL REVIEW   15 MINUTES
Review your notes and drawings that you've made thus far. Write down the techniques and guidelines which were most helpful. Those techniques which were most helpful you may want to continue using.

STEP 2 TWENTY-FIVE SPIRITUAL QUESTIONS   10 MINUTES
Review the twenty-five spiritual questions and write down your new answers in your journal.

STEP 3 "WHO AM I?" MEDITATION   10 MINUTES
Review these questions upon which you already meditated during week 2. Notice if your beliefs have shifted.

**Day 2**

*Assess Your Progress.*

STEP 1 EVALUATING YOUR MENTAL FITNESS PROGRAM   10 MINUTES
Determine if this program felt like too much work for you, too little work, or if it was just right. This is critical information for you. If you found that the program was too difficult, you'll want to scale back. If, on the other hand, you feel you could have worked a lot harder, you can design a much more intensive program for the future.

### STEP 2 FILLING IN THE MISSING PIECES   15 MINUTES

No 12-week program can provide 100 percent of the people what they need and want 100 percent of the time. Ask yourself what piece of information is missing in your Mental Fitness Program. What problem remains unsolved? Write those down, and then review the technique list at the back of the book to see if you may have missed or overlooked a technique that could be beneficial.

If you cannot find the "missing piece" in this book, begin your own research into that particular problem, goal, or experience.

### Day 3

*Character Building, Integrating Core Human Values*

Before embarking on your Long-Term Mental Fitness Program, we need to address a major, underlying theme of this book, namely the importance of the five core human values: truth, right action, peace, love, and nonviolence. Every technique you've practiced thus far has helped develop one or more of these qualities in you.

Although you may have begun this program with the idea of getting rid of a symptom/problem, or at least coming to terms with it, I'd like you to conclude this program (and begin the rest of your life) by consciously building character. In other words, we need to put our main concerns into perspective and realize that they are changing all the time. When we foster the core human values, they do not wither with time. Character is what is eternal.

### STEP 1 PRIORITIZE HUMAN VALUES   10 MINUTES

Through this technique, you will determine which of the five core human values you need to work on the most.

### STEP 2 VISUALIZE SYMBOLS OF HUMAN VALUES   10 MINUTES

By allowing your own imagination to provide symbols that represent each of the five core human values, you will have a valuable tool to draw on whenever you feel deficient in truth, right action, peace, love, or nonviolence. Review the symbols you've already visualized.

### Days 4–7   10 minutes a day

*Learn how to set yourself up for long-term personal growth with this program-planning technique.*

Your journey has just begun. The best way to continue growing is to recommit to your personal growth and transformation. Continue using the techniques you've learned in your Mental Fitness Program, but you'll now want to design a system that has staying power, is fun, creative, powerful, and flexible. Don't become another victim of "personal growth burn-out." Don't struggle so hard to do this program so well, so perfectly, that the life is drained out of it, and out of you. Because you now are aware of which techniques worked and which did not, and whether the program was too much for you or too little, we can begin building a program for the rest of your life. I will outline two kinds of programs: (1) a maintenance program, and (2) a transformational program. A final reminder: Do not judge one program or one approach as better or worse than the other. Just decide what is right for you.

After reading the "Maintenance Program" and the "Transformational Program," take time over the next five days to develop your long-term program. Write down a variety of programs. Brainstorm. Now that you've been practicing imagery, you can use your imagination to help you tailor your own program. Close your eyes. Ask yourself what your personalized program should look like. Allow an image to emerge, which will help guide you in organizing your long-term program. Don't forget to use the Decision-Making scales imagery (MFT), if you're having difficulty deciding whether you want to incorporate a technique into your life or leave it out.

## MAINTENANCE PROGRAM

A. Mantra Meditation 5 minutes twice a day

B. One-Minute Imagery Ritual twice a day

C. Select the one human value which you need to develop the most. In Appendix A, you will find several lists of the techniques in this book. Look for "MFT by Human Values." Look for the particular human value you need to develop and then select any of the techniques that foster that human value. Incorporate that technique into your Long-Term Mental Fitness Program.

D. Review the PSA every six months, in order to reassess your main concern, and thereby construct a new program.

## TRANSFORMATIONAL PROGRAM

**A.** Mantra Meditation 20 minutes twice a day.

**B.** Practice Mantra Meditation during every waking moment when your mind is not engaged in work.

**C.** Select the one human value that you need to develop the most. In Appendix A, you will find several lists of the techniques in this book. Look for "MFT by Human Values." Look for the particular human value you need to develop and then select any of the techniques that foster that human value. Incorporate that technique into your Long-Term Mental Fitness Program.

**D.** One-Minute Imagery Ritual four times a day.

**E.** Review the PSA every month, in order to reassess your main concern, and thereby construct a new program.

**F.** Symbolic Imagery. Communicate with your current main concern (symptom/problem, goal, or experience) 20 minutes every other day.

**G.** Evaluate Resistance once a month by practicing the resistance imagery for 20 minutes.

**H.** Build prayer into every moment of life so that life becomes a prayer. Dedicate each day, word, thought, and action to God.

**I.** Actively look for opportunities to serve. Pray for opportunities to serve.

**J.** Consciously reevaluate your life every 3 months to see if you are happier, more loving, more peaceful. Determine if you are solving your problems and attaining your goals.

## FINAL THOUGHTS

*Meditate for 10 minutes a day on the following two attitudes:*

### BE HAPPY

Above all else, be happy. Enjoy your personal Mental Fitness Program. If you're not enjoying it, modify it. Don't make yourself fit into this program. Make it fit you. Let yourself glide into the zone. Don't force yourself into the zone. It can't be done. If the techniques become "dry," remember to take them along with a "double-decker ice cream cone."

## LET LIFE BE YOUR TEACHER

Life provides each of us all the opportunities we need in order for us to grow, in order for us to reach complete liberation. If we believe that life is random and cruel, we will miss the lessons that come our way. If, on the other hand, we believe that the Universe is intelligent, and that meaning and purpose underlie everything, then every day of our life will be a lesson, an opportunity for growth, an opportunity for our egos to be brought down in size, an opportunity for our hearts to expand into love.

As you move beyond week 12 into the rest of your life, put things in their proper perspective. Realize that your main concern, which changes from week to week and from month to month, is a relative truth. We need to deal with our goals and problems without losing sight of Absolute Truth. I hope that your Life-Long Mental Fitness Program directs you toward Absolute Truth. With this in mind, you will realize that no matter how dramatic one's main concern may be, it still is a passing thing. Keep looking for that which is eternal and lasting, even though you must work on that which is impermanent and changing.

# 6

# BELIEF MEDICINE

Most of us believe in God. Half of us have been visited by the spirits of the dead. Most of us believe in angels, and many of us have had close encounters with them. Even though millions of Americans have had these experiences, we still consider these phenomena to be stunning and unusual. The rest of the world, for its part, has similar experiences, and most people take them in stride as part of everyday life. Of course, there are cultural differences: Among the Hopi and certain Japanese villagers, the dead always visit—the lack of such visitation is considered abnormal.

Healing through faith, magic, potions, spells, spirits, hexes, divination, "irrational" belief systems, and nonscientific thought is prevalent throughout the nonindustrial world. Some of these healing systems may appear as strange to Americans as our own spiritual practices appear to them. Still, an understanding of the difference between mental derangement and miraculous occurrences can help us sort out our attitudes toward spiritual experience in our own culture.

One theme pervades the indigenous world: Everything, whether animate or inanimate, contains spirit. All of life is interconnected, and we can communicate with it. So even rocks and trees have some type of consciousness—and people can listen to the rocks.

Another belief commonly held by indigenous peoples is that thought has the power to heal or harm. The Balinese have a curious courtship ritual. A man pursuing a woman in marriage will send her a bouquet of flowers. If he is determined that she will answer in the affirmative, he places a pea-sized package in the bouquet. That package is made by wrapping a boar's tooth with a banana peel, then wrapping that with boar's hair. If the woman discovers this addition to her flower bouquet, she believes she must marry him or else she will fall ill immediately and die. Up until the mid-1960s, this practice was prevalent in Bali. Many women married because of this practice, and many women died because they refused to marry.

For thousands of years in India, spiritual experiences, paranormal phenomena, and the power of thought have been accepted as so commonplace that many Indians are distrustful of ochre-robed gurus with *siddhi* powers.

Not only do Indians give considerable weight to the power of the mind, but hundreds of millions of people accept the power of the gods. It is believed that deities cause rain, fire, and every other natural event. Droughts and natural disasters are believed to be Nature's response to man's evil deeds. In Hawaii, Nature is worshipped and feared in the same way. Great care is given to propitiate Pélé, the Goddess of volcanoes, for her wrath can bring death. Every year post offices in Hawaii receive a vast number of packages mailed from all over the world. They contain pieces of lava. Tourists who had brought a little bit of Pélé home with them later became frightened by stories of Pélé's powers and returned the lava to its natural home.

In every culture, including our own, belief systems form the foundation of the diagnosis and treatment of illness. People all over the world have visions and talk to spirits. For them, spiritual beliefs and practices are central to the diagnosis and treatment of illness as well.

## SHAMANISM AND SORCERY

Every culture has its shamans and sorcerers. India is well known for its yogis and gurus. Yogis have the same powers as shamans, but they do not use them in the same way. The shaman acquires power with a specific intention of healing, while the yogi acquires power as a kind of side effect of spiritual practice. The yogi is interested in spiritual liberation as well as the uplift of his fellow humankind. But unlike the shaman, the yogi rarely displays his powers, for such a display is considered a sign of ego and an obstacle to spiritual progress.

Shamans and sorcerers practice their craft in every inhabited continent. They work not only in the villages of Africa and Asia but in cities across America. In my own hometown, there are several shamans of whom I am aware and very likely others of whom I am not aware. On the eighteen Native American reservations in San Diego County there are shamans. San Diego itself has Chinese healers, Thai healers, *curanderas,* and kahunas.

Anthony is a psychiatric nurse with whom I work. You would not know, from listening to his beautiful English diction, that he comes from the Ibo tribe in Nigeria. Nigeria consists of three main tribes—the Ibo, the Yoruba, and the Hausa. Anthony's Ibo name, Chukwura, means "God is great." As for the Ibos' beliefs and practices, according to Anthony, "five to ten percent of our people talk to the spirits and the spirits talk back. These are the traditional healers, and that's all they do—they talk to the spirits and heal people. Many of them throw stones, bones, or feathers in order to make their diagnosis. My village has between five and ten thousand people—and there's one major shaman in each village. There are no psychiatric hospitals in the villages. The crazy people are treated by the shaman, who usually considers insanity to be caused by possession."

With "rational" psychiatry, we spend billions of dollars on brain research, and we treat psychotic people with powerful mind-altering drugs—and of course, we keep looking for those genetic markers. The drugs are great. They work. But the collapse of traditional societies, like the Ibos', has everything to do with why the schizophrenic no longer fits in and no longer functions. In Anthony's tribe the schizophrenic is not an outcast. He is considered sick, but he is not discarded. Schizophrenia is not just a disorder of dopamine metabolism in the brain. It's a disorder of society itself.

Hermana Sarita is an urban healer in San Diego, a shaman world-renowned for her healing abilities. For more than twenty years, Sarita was very ill with asthma and got little relief from years visiting traditional doctors. Because her own father was a medical doctor, it was certainly logical that she be treated allopathically. But at age 45, as a last resort, she visited a *curandera,* a Mexican folk healer or a shaman. The psychic surgery she received permanently cured her. During the healing, she intently observed two "medical assistants" who were working beside the shaman. When the healing was over, Sarita asked who the two helpers were. The shaman responded, "Oh, you can see them? They are my spirit guides."

Restored to full health, Sarita decided to learn the art of healing and devote her life to healing others. She practices a blend of Mexican folk healing and Native American practices. Through the years I have very discreetly referred three or four patients to her, one of whom she cured of a fatal, inoperable brain tumor.

To a Western-trained psychiatrist, Sarita sounds insane. When she heals, she goes into an altered state, where she feels the presence of Bate de Agala (Eagle's Leg), a spirit guide who assists her—and when she is doing her healing work, she feels and sees "angels of light" pouring out of her fingers into the patient. She claims to be able to see into people as if she had X-ray eyes. She talks to the spirits, and the spirits talk to her. Bright lights swirl around her while she is in a trance.

Sarita is the daughter of a physician and has two sons who are medical doctors—surgeons. In her family, the ancient and the modern come together and are embraced fully and completely. There is no either-or, no debates about which form of healing is better. The only question they ask is, Which type of healing is needed in a given situation?

Sarita is unusual only in the extent of her healing gifts and in her generosity. She charges fifty dollars for the entirety of treatment, whether it takes one session or one year. Herbs cost extra. She has an extensive outreach program, routine follow-up care, and a devoted group of patients who visit from all over the world. But Sarita's beliefs are not unusual. They are part of healing in Mexico and in the rest of Latin America. Like the Ibo shamans of Nigeria, the *curanderas* believe that spirit is present everywhere, and that we can communicate not only with the spirits but with all of creation. Both believe in the interconnected web of life.[1]

In order to acquire their special healing powers—and the ability to predict the future—shamans like Sarita undergo a variety of spiritual practices, which may include meditation, prayer, fasting, dancing, yogic postures, chanting, drumming, and the use of natural hallucinogens such as peyote. By contrast, sorcerers use these same techniques to acquire power, but they use them for malevolent purposes or in difficult cases of tribal justice.

In Panama and in many other Latin American countries, sorcery is commonplace. Usually the person who is about to have a spell cast on him is notified ahead of time—not so that he can repent but so that he might live in fear. In one of their most highly developed types of sorcery, the kahunas of Hawaii cast a spell without the targeted villager being aware of this "attack." A group of kahunas will meet in order to decide how to cope with a problem villager and, on some occasions, will decide to kill him through spells and "black prayer." Illness and death proceed the same way in each case, with the villager developing a progressive paralysis which eventually leads to death. The symptoms and course of the illness are identical to a poorly understood Western illness called Guillain-Barré syndrome.

It is widely believed that sorcerers have intense willpower and supernatural powers and can use these powers to inflict harm on those who are spiritually unprotected. It is also accepted that people who come under such psychic attacks fall prey to accidents, fires, theft, illness, or death. Whether an afflicted individual is living out a self-fulfilling prophecy or is actually being attacked psychically cannot be scientifically determined. But these beliefs are widespread throughout the world.


## EASTERN HEALING SYSTEMS

More than a billion people live in China, and almost a billion in India. That's 40 percent of the world population. Throughout the millennia the people of China and India have shared the same basic healing philosophy of all preindustrial people. Central to their healing systems is the idea of chi, prana, or life-force.

Acupuncture is based on working with chi. Although Western medicine has begun to accept the efficacy of acupuncture for a variety of conditions, most Western doctors are not aware of the philosophy that underlies it. The Chinese understanding of mental illness is particularly interesting. According to some practitioners, mental illness is caused by problems of the liver, because the liver is "the house of the mind." Rather than labeling mental illness with a name like *schizophrenia* or *manic-depressive illness,* the doctor of Oriental medicine looks for "an excess of fire in the liver," "ascending fire," "liver chi stagnation," "liver yin deficiency," or "liver yang deficiency."[2] The liver is believed to be closely linked to the expression of anger.

Chinese medicine also believes that the kidney and spleen are linked to mental health. The kidney is associated with fear, memory, and forgetfulness. According to Chinese medicine, "If someone with a mental problem complains of an episode of absent-mindedness, they probably have a liver-kidney problem." Worry is caused by problems with the spleen, so an emotional problem characterized by an "excess of worry" would be diagnosed as a liver-spleen problem. Many mental-emotional problems are treated by "reducing liver heat," then balancing spleen or kidney yin and yang energies.

Because Chinese medicine involves an understanding of body, mind, and spirit, reports of visions of spirits or other paranormal phenomena do not surprise the Chinese doctor. He knows that an angelic vision requires no treatment at all. If the patient desires deeper spiritual understanding or further spiritual experiences, the Chinese doctor may encourage them by using specific acupuncture points to urge the flow of chi through the chakras, up toward the head, and out the "third eye." If, on the other hand, a patient is troubled by "spirit possession," the Chinese doctor will treat by focusing on the patient's chi, helping him build up his own defenses, and his own mind, body, and energy, so that the spirit can be overcome.

Even more ancient than Chinese medicine is Ayurveda, the ancient holistic medical system of India, which was first written about in one of the Hindu sacred texts, the *Atharva Veda* and which has gained acceptance in the United States through the writings of Deepak Chopra, M.D.[3]

Like Chinese medicine, Ayurveda is based on an understanding of chi, or prana, as the life-force is called in India, as well as an understanding of three body types, or *doshas:* kapha (water), vata (air), and pitta (fire). The Ayurvedic physician decides whether his patient has too much water, air, or fire and then prescribes herbs and a diet that will balance the three doshas. For more than five thousand years, Ayurvedic physicians have been practicing and perfecting their medical science. Western doctors who want to know if Ayurveda really works will have to examine the source of Ayurveda. Ayurveda is believed to have originated in "cosmic consciousness," handed down from God to the ancient Indian *rishis,* who in turn, transmitted their knowledge and wisdom, by word of mouth, to their students.[4]

Belief in something beyond the mind and body pervades Asia and affects many other aspects of life besides medical and psychological diagnosis. In Burma, people who spend years meditating have visions of creatures that live in another dimension of consciousness. These pale creatures with large dark eyes fit the common description of aliens. According to the spiritual adepts who see these creatures, they are not aliens but live right here next to us, although they generally cannot be seen without "spiritual sight."

In looking at the beliefs and customs of other cultures, we may initially be struck by the differences between "us" and "them." But beyond the obvious differences, we discover commonalities. Body, mind, and spirit matter to people in every culture, from every religion, and from every age in history. In addition, core healing principles are universal, common to

Western medicine, Oriental medicine, Ayurvedic medicine—and even faith healing.

## UNIVERSAL HEALING PRINCIPLES

While the spiritual healing systems of different cultures may seem different from Western approaches, they actually share the key components of every healing system in the world, which are: *hope,* inspired by the healer; *trust* in the healer, his diagnostic methods, and his treatment modalities; and a shared *belief* in the causes and cures of illness.

Even if, in physical terms, penicillin is the most effective treatment for pneumococcal pneumonia, the treatment will work even more effectively if both doctor and patient share the same belief in it. Shared belief inspires hope, deepens trust, and allows our built-in healing systems to kick in. Part of how penicillin works is through our deep belief in the awesome power of antibiotics against bacteria.

Dr. Frank Lawlis spent years treating Native Americans in the Southwest, which taught him some powerful lessons about the power of belief systems. He noticed that the chronic-pain patients came into the clinic only three or four times a year to refill their Demerol prescriptions, instead of every few weeks, as the typical American would. Dr. Lawlis was amazed to learn that the Indians were not ingesting the Demerol tablets! They were placing them around the house to ward off the "pain spirits." This treatment was very effective, but it would wear off after a few months.[5]

Belief systems have everything to do with the onset of illness, the treatment course, the recovery rate, and every other aspect of health and healing. When I was a resident in psychiatry, I met Chang, an 18-year-old Chinese man with clear-cut paranoid schizophrenia. Chang knew he was sick. When I asked him why he thought he had developed the mental illness, he replied, "When my grandmother was buried, my back was to the sun and my shadow was cast across her grave. That is very very bad luck." This deep belief, widespread among the villagers in the southern provinces of China, may have been the straw that broke the biochemical back of Chang's brain, bringing on the full-blown schizophrenic psychosis. Although I treated Chang with antipsychotic medications, this story gave me a broader view of how his illness fit into his life and worldview.

One's cultural belief system can trigger illness, or at least contribute greatly to its onset. Cultural beliefs can also determine the course of the illness. Remember that the schizophrenics in the Ibo village in Nigeria do not appear crazy—they fit in. However, schizophrenics decompensate when they move from the village to a large city. Culture can trigger illness or prevent it!

In every culture on earth, health and illness are intimately woven into the fabric of life. We, in the West, believe that we can separate illness from the individual, from society, from culture. We try to separate the mind from the body and relegate the spirit to the clerics. But a complete diagnosis must take into account body, mind, spirit, and energy, as well as cultural beliefs, rites, and rituals. In a sense, all healing is faith healing, even our own.

American medicine men won't cop to being superstitious, but they really are. In Great Britain and throughout most of Europe, half of all medical doctors either prescribe homeopathic medicines or refer patients to homeopaths. A homeopathic remedy is created by taking a substance—say, the mineral phosphorus—and diluting it to the point that only a single molecule of phosphorus is in the solution. This solution becomes the remedy for an illness whose cause is associated with phosphorus. Well-controlled scientific studies performed around the world over the past ten years have demonstrated that homeopathy works, at least sometimes.[6] Yet American doctors argue that "homeopathy can't work because there's nothing in the medicine." Homeopathy is like chemical acupuncture. The molecule of phosphorus, or whatever the remedy is made from, charges the solution. Homeopathy works on the energetic body, or chi.

The belief that spirit has no place in healing is common in Western medicine, but it is important to realize that this is just a belief. The fact is that the absence of spirit in medicine is a major cause of our disenchantment with medicine, with our discomfort with some doctors, and with our shaken faith in the current health care system.

## FOLK MEDICINE OF THE AMERICAN TRIBE

Perhaps the strangest tribe I have had the privilege to study personally is the Americans. Anthropologist Horace Miner was one of the first to study and write about the Americans as if they were an indigenous tribe from a foreign land. In order to make his point about the "strange" habits of the Americans, he referred to this tribe as the Nacirema (*American* spelled backward).[7]

"The Nacirema," Miner wrote, "are a North American group living in the territory between the Canadian Cree, the Yaqui and Tarahumare of Mexico, and the Carib and Arawak of the Antilles. Little is known of their origin, although tradition states that they came from the East. . . .

"Each family has a shrine. The focal point of the shrine is a box or chest which is built into the wall. In this chest are kept the many charms and magical potions without which no native believes he could live. These preparations are secured from a variety of specialized practitioners. The most powerful of these are the medicine men, whose assistance must be rewarded with substantial gifts. However, the medicine men do not provide the curative potions for their clients, but decide what the ingredients should be and then write them down in an ancient and secret language. This writing is understood only by the medicine men and by the herbalists who, for another gift, provide the required charm."

In the American health care system the medicine man is not actually the highest authority on healing. After he has poked, prodded, and stuck needles into the tribesman, he must go to the herbalist, then confer with a ceremonial leader. This leader knows absolutely nothing about healing, but from him the medicine man must get approval for the healing, in a paper ritual dance, in order not to violate tribal taboo. The natives give gifts several times a year to these ceremonial leaders, who then transfer these gifts in part to the medicine men.

The poorest of the American tribespeople are not required to give to the same ceremonial leaders, but a special leader allots gifts to the medicine men working with them. Both types of ceremonial leaders exert incredible control over the medicine men, telling them what herbs and potions they can dispense and how long it should take them to cure a particular patient. If the medicine man does not comply completely with the ceremonial leader, especially the leader involved with the poor, the medicine man will receive no gift at all.

Much like the healers of Bali, who pierce their arms with arrows, the American medicine man must undergo a long, grueling apprenticeship, with brutal rites and rituals, under other medicine men. During his initiation the apprentice is shamed and humiliated repeatedly for many years. Part of the training is not unlike the Vision Quest of the Cherokee, who go into the desert or forest alone for days and days until they have a vision. Usually they do not eat or sleep until they have their vision. That vision gives guidance about what they are to do in life and what their totem animal is. The Vision Quest of the American medicine man, however, goes on for years, with extended periods of sleeplessness only briefly interrupted with sleep. The medicine-man-in-training lives in a state of almost complete mental and physical exhaustion. Some medicine men have told me directly that this method of training is ancestral: "It's the way it's always been done."

Horace Miner writes about the healing temple or latipso ("hospital"): "The latipso ceremonies are so harsh that it is phenomenal that a fair proportion of the really sick natives who enter the temple ever recover. . . . No matter how ill the supplicant or how grave the emergency, the guardians of many temples will not admit a client if he cannot give a rich gift to the custodian . . .

"From time to time the medicine men come to their clients and jab magically-treated needles into their flesh. The fact that these ceremonies may not cure, and may even kill the neophyte, in no way decreases the people's faith in the medicine men."

So powerful is the belief in the healing temple that tribal members will even go there in order to die, even though they know they have an incurable illness, for which care by an untrained family member would provide a more soothing ending to their life.

The American medicine man practices a powerful form of voodoo that can either cure or kill. It is among the most powerful in the world. I met a woman whose husband had been the victim of voodoo death by the medicine men. This poor lady's husband, who was in his seventies, went to visit the medicine man and was told he had a fatal disease that would kill him in thirty days. This man had been active up until the day he visited the medicine man. He returned from the visit, lay down on his bed for the next thirty days, and died on schedule.

The power to heal by the medicine man is also immense. The mere sight of a medicine man can inspire healing on the spot. So great is this awe and power that a client often recovers before he has taken the herbs and potions.

The healing and spiritual practices of our own and other cultures are strange and bizarre only when seen out of context of their cultural belief system.

## JUDGMENT REVIEW
### *Mental Fitness Technique*

*Human value fostered by this technique: Nonviolence in Thought*

One reason I've gone into such detail about the healing practices of other cultures is to help you understand that our judgments of other practices are just that—judgments—and not facts.

Not only do we judge anything and anyone we don't understand, but many of us are judging ourselves and others all day long. "That person is stupid. What a dumb thing he just said." "It's her fault. She's always messing things up for everyone else." "That guy is so fat." "Wow, is she skinny." "African-Americans are dumb." "White people can never understand." "The Mexicans are ruining our economy." "The Japanese are ruining our economy." "Ibo healing practices are insane."

Judging serves only one purpose: It temporarily removes us from our own pain. But it also harms each of us profoundly, stunting our psychological and spiritual development, keeping us isolated, separated, and walled off to love. Here is a simple way to become aware of your judgments and then begin to let go of them. Practice this just before going to sleep at night:

> *Imagine that you are with a Divine Being, a Higher Consciousness, a being who embodies love, compassion, wisdom, and strength. Scan this being from head to toe (or top to bottom, if this presence is a glowing light without form). Let yourself relax into being in His presence.*
>
> *Now begin to get in touch with the judgments you've experienced today. Review in your mind each and every person, place, or event that you judged. Remember each incident as completely as possible, recalling the thoughts, feelings, sensations, and images. Then imagine that each judgment flows out of you, into your hands, as if it were liquid. Offer each judgment to God, knowing that He is not standing in judgment of you. I'm sure He will gladly take the burden from you.*
>
> *Now review the past week, and go through the same process. Allow each judgment to flow out of you and be received by your Higher Consciousness. Finally, review your entire life. Look for the really big judgments—and then let go of them.*

Remember not to judge yourself over your judgments. Rather, try to adopt a meditative, witnessing attitude, in which you allow yourself to see how your mind has been working. Release the judgments one at a time. Practice this technique for a year, and you'll probably come close to stopping the flow of judgments completely. When that happens, your heart will begin to expand and open up. Love will begin to flow so that you can both give and receive it.

Of course, it's important not to judge yourself for being judgmental. If you judge yourself for being judgmental, release that judgment to your Higher Consciousness.

The process of growth is something like the process of peeling away the layers of an onion, one after another. Once you begin to peel away the judgment layer, a deeper layer can be seen. My patient Joe, a middle-level manager, wanted my help with his judgmental attitude. He was aware that the more judgmental he became at work, the more people backed off. In the process, his work relationships became more and more strained.

After Joe spent a session working on his judgments, he said to me, "I know why I do that. I need the distance, the separation, the space that judgments provide. This reminds me of my mother. She's sixty-five and still doing, doing, doing for others. She can never say no. And I'm like that. I can't say no. Being judgmental allows me to keep my distance from people and is kind of a way of indirectly saying no. I'm afraid if I'm more available to people, they'll want more of me, more of my time and energy. I'll be sucked dry."

I asked Joe to practice Judgment Review each night. This technique helped him peel away that layer of the onion so that he could examine the deeper issues in his life.

The Vedas proclaim that love cannot coexist in the heart of man along with greed, anger, jealousy, and envy. By practicing Judgment Review, you can begin to remove these obstacles to love.

Now that you're more clear about your judgments, let's look at some serious facts about the effects of spirituality and religion on health. If you find yourself judging the next set of facts, try to suspend judgment. Analyze the data carefully. If you can't stop judging, take another minute to practice Judgment Review.

## MIXED MESSAGES ABOUT HEALING

It is often asserted during medical school and psychiatry residencies that religious commitment is harmful to health. Yet scientific studies have proven that the opposite is true—that religious commitment is beneficial to both mental and physical health. Seventy-two percent of Americans agree with the statement, "My religious faith is the most important influence in my life."[8]

It is not surprising, then, that so many Americans feel uncomfortable with their doctors. Although most believe that religious faith is the single most important influence in their lives, medicine has largely ignored that fact. Instead, it has clung to Freud's dicta that "religiosity is in many aspects equivalent to irrational thinking and emotional disturbance" and "religious beliefs are illusions." In a letter to Reverend Oskar Pfister, Freud confided, "I am a completely godless Jew."[9]

Not one of Freud's major clinical cases, which formed the foundation for his theories, involved believing Christians or Jews. Not only did Freud dislike religion, he did not like to listen to music because he didn't want to be powerfully moved by something that he couldn't understand rationally. In his attempt to remain "rational," Freud did a disservice to psychiatry.

Modern medicine has come a long way since Freud, but the long-term effects of his pseudo-scientific rationalism have yet to be overcome. A recent review of four major psychiatry journals revealed that religion was evaluated in less than three percent of all quantitative studies.[10] When religion was evaluated, by far the most common variable studied was religious denomination—a variable that solid science has proven to be worthless in terms of health. What is vital to health is religious commitment—a variable examined in fewer than one percent of all psychiatric studies.

Since psychiatry and medicine have given so little study to religious commitment, one may well wonder about the scientific basis for the disregard of religion and the persistent view of religious experience as a health risk. Actually, there is no basis, other than a gut-level, irrational reflex. Scientific medicine is, in fact, out of step with the beliefs of the average American.

Scientific studies are now verifying that the beliefs of the average American have a positive effect on health. A review of all quantitative psychiatric articles over a twelve-year period found that 72 percent of the religious commitment variables were beneficial to mental health. Psychiatrist David Larson, M.D., has been studying the specific components of religious commitment—ceremony, prayer, social support, relationship with God, meaning and purpose—and has found that commitment is the most important religious variable.[11] Commitment is a powerful predictor of health and recovery. Among these "commitment variables," relationship with God, ceremony, and social support have been proven to be an overwhelmingly positive influence on health. According to Dr. Larson, "Religious commitment, when measured appropriately, is associated with mental health benefit at least 80 percent of the time." The effect even of regular church attendance is tremendous. One large study found that people who did not attend church were four times more likely to kill themselves than were people who attended church frequently.[12] Another study showed that church attendance predicted suicide rates more effectively than did any other factor, including unemployment.[13]

No matter what the illness, religious commitment has been shown to have a protective influence. Drug and alcohol abuse is a particularly interesting subject to examine in terms of religion. Drug abuse is related to an absence of religious commitment and, in particular, to a decline in faith during the teen years. Eighty-nine percent of alcoholics had lost interest in religion during their teen years, compared with 20 percent of a control group.[14] No wonder Alcoholics Anonymous and other twelve-step programs have been so successful in treating addictions. A crisis in faith may, in fact, be one of the main causes of addiction. So a program like AA, which requires acknowledgment of a Higher Power, is the appropriate "cure."

Religion is also good for marriage. Not only do religiously committed couples report a higher rate of marital satisfaction, they also report more satisfying sex lives, which is perhaps a surprising finding, since many people—especially psychiatrists—consider religion to be a repressive force. Women who state they are very religious report greater satisfaction and happiness with marital sex than do either moderately religious or nonreligious women.[15]

Religious commitment, as measured by church attendance, not only decreases stress and improves quality of life, it may also extend life. One study found that for men, the risk of dying from atherosclerotic heart disease was much less among those who attended church at least weekly.[16] A two-year study of the elderly in New Haven, Connecticut, showed that the less religious had a mortality rate twice that of the more religious.[17]

Other studies have shown that religious commitment reduces delinquency, psychological stress, and depression. Even hypertension is significantly alleviated by religious commitment. These studies have all been carefully designed and conducted. For example, the study on hypertension controlled for a variety of other factors.[18] Good mental and physical health could have just been a by-product of specific religious practices. It could have been that the religiously committed smoked less, drank less, ate better, and exercised regularly. In fact, they do, but even with those factors controlled for, the results remain significant. The findings also hold true for people who are not practicing a healthy lifestyle. Among smokers, those who consider religion to be very important were seven times less likely to have an elevated diastolic blood pressure than were those who did not value religion so highly.

The bottom line is that religious attendance, along with a host of other religious commitment factors, should be a major consideration in evaluating health. Lack of religious commitment is a reliable risk factor for illness and death and should be evaluated by physicians along with smoking, cholesterol levels, and exercise.

Religious belief has been studied for fifty years in America, with a consistent finding: 95 percent of the population believes in God. There is a huge gap between the average American's religious beliefs, the positive effects of religion, and how medicine practices. This discrepancy is part of the American belief system. We're ignoring the facts—but we can't afford to do so anymore.

Physicians can apply Psycho-Spiritual Assessment to any health problem, any experience, any life challenge. It is not enough for a doctor to say to a patient, "You have bone cancer—and I recommend a course of chemotherapy immediately." Physicians must find out what the cancer means to their patients, and why they think they have cancer. Once we know what our patients believe, we can work as a team, making shared decisions based upon shared, or at least respected, beliefs.

We must begin to close the gap, so that what the patient believes is similar to what the doctor believes and how he or she practices medicine. One of the most exciting findings of the new religious studies is that it is easy to teach doctors how to incorporate religion into their work. In one particular study, psychiatrists were taught how to take a religious history and how to treat depression with a cognitive approach that included religious content. Patients did better with this approach, but the doctors who considered themselves atheists had an even greater success rate using this "religious" technique than did believing doctors.[19]

What you believe should be similar to what your doctor believes. How can your doctor help you at the deepest level, if he thinks you're hiding behind your religiosity, or if he thinks your visions are the results of imagination or a nervous breakdown? If you've had a vision, you want someone to whom you confide it, to help you keep your head together and reinforce the importance of the event. You want someone who can reassure you that your vision is special and not abnormal.

# 7

# GETTING CONSCIOUS

# ABOUT CONSCIOUSNESS

Quarterback great Joe Montana (now retired) "steps back into the pocket. He's not the fastest quarterback, and he's not the strongest—but he is arguably the best ever. Montana looks downfield, calmly to the left, then to the right. He acts like he has all the time in the world to throw the ball—even with several three-hundred-pound linemen charging him. Montana throws deep, just as he's smashed to the ground—and Jerry Rice grabs the ball in the end zone, to clinch a third Super Bowl victory for the Forty-Niners."

The sportscast is imaginary, but Montana was the best, and that's partly because he often played football in an altered state of consciousness. Athletes call it "the zone." When Montana was in the zone, he saw all the receivers and defenders and felt as if he had all the time in the world. His mind was very steady and calm, not filled with thoughts, doubts, questions, or desires. When he was in the zone, he felt as if the games were being played through him. He had a sense of almost divine perfection, as if nothing could go wrong. And when he was in the zone, not much did go wrong. He "saw everybody on the field." And he "knew" that the football *would* arrive exactly where it was supposed to.

The zone is one of many altered states of consciousness. Consciousness is difficult to define, but it is easier to describe in terms of its qualities, which are time, space, level of alertness, and awareness. Most of us live in the consciousness of four dimensions: three dimensions in space, and a fourth in time. Those four dimensions are the parameters of so-called "normal" consciousness. Some of the top physicists in the world have speculated that there are as many as ten dimensions. Like the words *God, spirituality,* and *love, consciousness* is a word that medicine has chosen to ignore as much as possible.

Time is one of the most extraordinary aspects of consciousness. When we're bored, time seems to move slowly, but when we're really enjoying ourselves, time seems to move all too quickly. Under certain dramatic circumstances, our perception of time is radically altered. For three years race-car driver Dennis Adams raced in the NASCAR circuit and was in a few dramatic wrecks. He noticed that as an accident unfolded, time slowed down, and it slowed down more and more as his consciousness of the imminence of the accident increased. As time slowed down, Adams's thoughts and actions dramatically sped up, as if he had a lot of time to prepare himself.

Pepe Romero, the world-renowned classical guitarist, can consciously alter time to suit his own needs. If he needs to play sixteen notes in one second, he simply expands the second—rather than trying to play faster. For many musicians that blazing speed can be a real stress, but for Pepe it's quite simple. He has as much time as he needs. He simply makes the time and changes it as he needs to. In certain altered states of consciousness—states of merging, being at one with all—time ceases to exist at all. That is difficult for people who have not had altered states to comprehend, although most people have had some kind of experience of this slowing, whether it's after receiving some bad news, while "crashing" from hypoglycemia, or after driving on an interstate highway for ten hours. When time stops, one simply is. One experiences a sense of unity with life, God, and Nature and feels free from the laws of time.

Space is the second major quality of consciousness. Several years ago, as I was driving my car out of the driveway, my gorgeous and sweet 12-year-old cat, Daisy, ran under the front right wheel and was struck. I dashed out of the car and saw her covered with blood and having massive convulsions. I did a quick medical check, to see if I should take her to a veterinarian. But her heart was in ventricular fibrillation, and I knew she would die quickly. I held her, stroked her, and talked to her. She died, and the grief that I felt was so huge, it had no boundaries. I had never experienced such pure pain. Pure, raw pain. Such pain that the boundaries of my own mind melted away. Time stood still, and space took on new proportions. There was no past, no present, or no future, and my mind was not bound by space. There was no shame or blame or mental activity. I *was* pain. I realized that grief is an altered state of consciousness.

Imagine what a distorted view a psychiatrist would have if he didn't understand consciousness. Here's a hypothetical case. Suppose a patient—we'll call him M.J.—tells his shrink that he can jump so high and so far that it looks as if he is walking on air. M.J. tells his psychiatrist, "It's as if gravity doesn't affect me, like I can defy the laws of space. I've even seen videotapes of myself in the air, and I can't even believe it's me. Sounds crazy, huh, doc?" The doctor might reply, "Yes, this certainly sounds like a terrific fantasy, a deep narcissistic dream, a childlike magical wish that reality could be other than it is. This wish must be hiding a deep-seated depression." I do not mean to imply for a second that M.J. should see a psychiatrist. But if he did, the psychiatrist would have to acknowledge that when Michael Jordan is in the zone, he is in such an altered state of consciousness that he actually thinks he can fly. And of course, he can! Basketball great Larry Bird has said, "Michael Jordan is God incarnated as a basketball player." Jordan's feats of magic are an example not only of extraordinary physical skills but of extraordinary mental skills. He can handle states of consciousness as well as he can handle a basketball, and his genius lies in his skill in both.

Consciousness also involves various levels of alertness. One may be sharp and focused, or intensely aware, or dull, or in a coma. All these are levels of conscious awareness. How you process sensory input depends upon your level of alertness. Are you receptive or active? Are you aware through one sense, such as vision, or are you experiencing a multimedia show, through sight, sound, touch, smell, taste, and movement all at once?

Awareness is the most significant component of consciousness—and it is also the most elusive. By awareness, I mean one's sense of being, of existence, of "I-ness." And as we'll see later, your sense of awareness depends on which level of your being you are focused on: body-awareness, mind-awareness, or soul-awareness. Let's take a moment to find out more about your sense of "I-ness" and where you are focusing your awareness.

## "WHO AM I?" MEDITATION
### *Mental Fitness Technique*

*Human values fostered by this technique: Truth, Right Action, Peace, Love, Nonviolence*

If what you believe is not in sync with your thoughts, words, and deeds, you will have a *human value deficiency*. If your thoughts, words, and deeds are one and are in complete harmony with your beliefs, all the five human values will flourish. Few people in the world today have thoughts, words, and deeds that are one and the same, but they do exist, and they serve as great inspirations for the rest of us.

A spiritual quest requires personal effort and deep inquiry. In order to know where you're going, you'll need to know where you are right now. Where you are is *who and what you believe you are.* So let's take a minute to review some of life's most fundamental questions.

Before addressing each question, close your eyes, take a few deep breaths, and relax. Allow your mind to let go of all thoughts, worries, and concerns for just a minute. Then ask yourself the first question: "Who am I?" Meditate on that question, and allow answers to present themselves from your unconscious, conscious, and higher conscious minds. Your answer may come in the form of images, thoughts, sensations, or words. (One way to approach this first question is to ask, "Who am I not? What am I not?") Maintain the same kind of nonjudgmental, meditative, reflective attitude toward each question. Witness the answers that present themselves, and don't immediately dismiss the first answer that arises. Write down your answers in the space provided.

1.   Who am I? (not just my name!) _____

_____

_____

_____


2.   Where did I come from before I was born? _____

_____

_____

_____


3.   What is the meaning of life, if any? _____

_____

_____

_____

4.   What is the mission in my life, if any? _____

_____

_____

_____

5.   Where will I go when I die? _____

_____

_____

_____

While you were meditating on "who I am" or "who I believe I am," you experienced an altered state of consciousness, no matter how small that shift in consciousness may have been. If you deeply entered into the question "Who am I?" it may take you a moment or so to return to "normal" consciousness. Now—you're back!

Have you ever walked into a room at home or at work and suddenly completely forgotten what you were looking for—or why you went into that room? We all do that. That's an altered state. Most of us don't know how to handle altered states, and most of us don't like this one. Several years ago I decided to turn the tables on this state. Rather than struggle mentally to remember why I had gone into a certain room, I surrendered to this lost feeling and allowed myself to go into a meditation for a minute or two. I've done the same thing when I've opened the refrigerator and had no idea what I had been looking for—I proceeded to go into this "lost" meditation for a minute or two.

Consciousness is not a fixed quality that is the same all around the world. It differs from culture to culture. Culture shock is really "consciousness shock." When people go to a foreign country, they often feel stunned or shocked. One reason is the change in scenery, the differences in language, architecture, dress, vehicles, and so on. But another reason for culture shock is that the other culture exists at a different level of consciousness. Many people have written about India as a "hypnotic state," and I have certainly experienced that. The Indian people speak a different language and wear different clothing. They have a different rhythm and spirit. When you enter a country of nearly a billion people who are in a certain cultural consciousness, your own individual consciousness gets a jolt.

Women and men have different states of consciousness, too. In fact, Jeanne Achterberg, author of *Woman as Healer,* says, "Men and women may not communicate much of anything at all to each other since we live in such different states of consciousness and being."[1]

Different groups also have a group state of consciousness. A football team, a choir, and an orchestra all consist of people who must think and act with one mind. Anyone who's watched competitive sports has witnessed the rise and demise of team momentum. The group-consciousness "force" goes this way and that. It's either with a team or it's not. Suddenly the other team coalesces into a tight unit, and that one-mind force becomes unstoppable. One mind is also essential for an orchestra to play a beautiful symphony without a single instrument standing out inappropriately.

In contrast, mob consciousness—another kind of group mind—often has no conscious direction or goal. In a mob, the individual relinquishes his own personal awareness and conscience and surrenders to the mass. In the late 1960s at the University of Colorado, a group of students were trying to take over the administration building, and thousands of people were being swept this way and that. From my standpoint, observing at the periphery of the mob, the energy was frightening, like a tornado that could rip through town and go in any direction. The mob was an unpredictable, angry group that was surrendered into one-mind.

Social consciousness, still another kind of group mind, changes over time. Sometimes we are raising our social consciousness, and sometimes we surrender to it as it is. Our society's views of women's roles, African-American identity, national purpose and pride, and human evolution, for instance, have changed dramatically over the past half-century.

All the various components of consciousness—time, space, sex, societal orientation, level of alertness, and awareness—are determined by whether our mind is focused on past, present, or future. If we are focused on the future, our consciousness is narrow. Whereas when we are immersed in the moment, as when we are in the zone, our consciousness seems to expand. When we're fully in the moment, time seems more flexible, and we feel as if we have more room within which to work, even though the physical playing field is the same size.

In the West, we have a notion of "normal" consciousness: individualistic, goal-directed, linear, sequential, outer-oriented, task-oriented, and objective. We like it that way. We like to think that we have one state of consciousness, or maybe two—awake and asleep. This "normal" consciousness is actually a kind of binary outlook: good-bad, black-white, hot-cold, fat-skinny, Democrat-Republican, and so on. In "normal" awareness we judge, separate, and classify. We dissect experience. We hold fast to what we consider good, and we push away (or hate) the opposite. It's a kind of American male consciousness. This kind of "normal" thinking polarizes the world. Yet psychiatrist R.D. Laing, in his book *The Politics of Experience,* states, "Normal men have killed perhaps 100,000,000 of their fellow normal men in the last 50 years."[2] Laing wrote that in 1967. If he's even remotely correct, then approximately two percent of the present world population has been murdered during this century. We call it war and consider it more or less normal. But war is not the creation of schizophrenics or other psychotic people. It's a product or a result of our *normal* consciousness!

Most of us live at the level of our body, mind, and personality. We identify ourselves, for example, as a "forty-year-old American male high achiever." But the person who is experiencing mystical union with the divine or with Nature is no longer identifying with his or her physical body or even personality. His or her awareness has risen to the level of soul, whose boundaries are limitless.

According to Eastern thought, consciousness can be fixed at any of the levels of human being: the physical body, the energy body, the mind, the intellect, the layer of bliss, and the soul. The more we identify with the outer levels, the more "normal" our consciousness seems to be. The more we identify ourselves as spiritual beings, or beings full of spirit, the more our consciousness expands, until time and space no longer hold any significance.

In the final analysis, our state of consciousness is determined by our level of spirituality, or sacred awareness. The great ones—the saints, sages, and mahatmas—are the true masters of consciousness. Masters of time, they live in a state of consciousness in which "normal" time does not even exist. They live in "God's" time, unbound by ideas of past, present, and future. They're like Michael Jordan when he's in the zone—except that they can enter higher states without a basketball in their hands and can stay there as long as they choose.

## THE LANGUAGE OF CONSCIOUSNESS

Eskimos have more than fifty words for snow; Americans have more than thirty words for money but fewer than ten words for consciousness. There are more than four hundred words in Sanskrit for consciousness. Just for those beginning with the letter A, there are fifty-six Sanskrit words for consciousness.[3]

Obviously, if you want to know a lot about snow, ask an Eskimo, for Eskimos live in "snow consciousness." If you want to know about money, ask an American, for they live in "money consciousness." And if you want to know about consciousness, study Sanskrit, for Indians live in "consciousness," having made it their business for thousands of years to study the inner landscape.

The few English words we do have to describe the different states of mind and consciousness, especially those related to mysticism, have negative connotations, such as *unreal, bizarre, ominous, spooky, weird*! Because Western culture considers "normal" consciousness to be the state in which we *should* live most of the time, it considers altered states of consciousness to be abnormal.

Why should Eastern and Western thought be so different? Why should it be that Eastern religions have mapped out the territory of altered states of consciousness? One hypothesis involves language itself. Western language is linear. We read one letter, one syllable, one word. We read one word after another, until a thought, a sentence, is complete. Eastern languages (like Sanskrit, Chinese, and Japanese) are written in symbols, not in a sequential, linear structure. It is the very nature of symbols, of images, to lead us deeper into meaning and experience beyond language.

Put another way, the West uses left-brain language: logical, linear, object-oriented, goal-oriented, analytical terms that help us separate one thing from another. Through our left brain we see differences. The right brain, however, does not obey the laws of time and space. The right brain synthesizes and finds similarities rather than differences. This brief summary of brain function is an oversimplification, but it highlights some of the general differences between the right and left hemispheres of the brain.

Today we are learning to fuse the incredible left-brain problem-solving capacity of the West with the synthetic, right-brain, mystical experience of the East. Neither function is "better" than the other. All endeavors, inspiration combined with perspiration, intuition combined with intellect, bring greater understanding and skill than either component taken alone. Both intuition and intellect are needed to understand and experience different states of consciousness.

The Sanskrit language describes a range of consciousness that all of us go through to some extent every day. Throughout the day, we move through the obvious ones: from full alertness to dreaming, to deep sleep, to waking up—to falling back asleep. We also go through phases of being sharp or dull, alert or out of focus. We shift our sensory awareness from inner- to outer-directed. We take a little break to relax and close our eyes. The physical changes in our bodies affect our consciousness, so that a dip in your blood sugar will make you foggy, while caffeine will jack you back up. We have television consciousness, in which, after a long day at the office, we "zone out." We're not sharply focused, yet not tired enough to go to sleep. We're on consciousness's version of autopilot.

Giving birth is still another altered state of consciousness, one that I won't pretend for a second to have experienced. There's even bowel movement consciousness! Aren't you in an altered state sitting on the toilet?

Making love definitely produces an altered state of consciousness, one in which many people feel their individual boundaries drop and themselves merge with the other. The guys in the gym or at the bar won't talk about it that way, but it's not just the orgasm that's the charge. It's love and the union of consciousness.

In many Western societies we have a "holiday" consciousness. There are times of year when we're allowed to feel happy all the time. It's a feeling in the air. But we're not supposed to feel great all the time. We're not even allowed to. And we wouldn't even know how to.

Mental illness involves a split, shattered, or contracted consciousness. Consciousness can narrow to a fine point, as in hypnosis; shatter, as in schizophrenia; or contract, as in depression and anxiety. But consciousness can also expand, taking us to realms beyond space and time, beyond the physical body. Yogis, shamans, and other spiritual seekers are intentionally striving to expand their consciousness, to attain a state of perpetual joy and love.

By examining both kinds of consciousness, we'll begin to see just how different mental illness is from mystical and other altered states. But we must also avoid the pitfall of glorifying these higher states. A Buddhist monk in training enthusiastically ran to his roshi, or teacher, to tell him that he had just experienced nirvana, or unity consciousness. The roshi replied, "Don't worry. It will pass." We need to remain balanced about all our experiences, not attaching too much or too little significance to any of them, appreciating that we will eventually see them in their proper perspective, despite of the tendency of medicine and psychiatry to dismiss or denigrate them.

## KUNDALINI: A GREAT MASQUERADER

Medicine has always had to face illnesses that are difficult to diagnosis and that masquerade as other illnesses. Syphilis is a disease that has fooled many doctors. AIDS was the same. Chronic fatigue syndrome is still a great masquerader—it can look like depression, arthritis, lupus, AIDS, or cancer. But kundalini energy puts on one of the greatest masquerade acts of all time. Kundalini, a sudden release of intense energy throughout the body, may look like mental illness—like mania, depression, or anxiety. It may look like physical illness—like gout, arthritis, muscle spasm, or "an acute abdomen," a true medical emergency. It may sound like encephalitis, a brain infection. But kundalini is none of these. It is a prolonged altered state of consciousness, and the various physical symptoms it produces demonstrate its powerful body-mind-spirit connection.

Kundalini exists within all of us. Certain spiritual practices that stir it up should generally be avoided—especially kriya yoga, which should be practiced only under the guidance of a master teacher. Yet what feels like a crisis is an opportunity for extraordinary mental and spiritual growth.

Like other states of consciousness, kundalini is viewed differently in different cultures. In 1967, Gopi Krishna, an influential teacher of Eastern philosophy, wrote the classic *Kundalini: The Evolutionary Energy in Man*. His experiences with kundalini energy began when, as he was meditating one day, he noticed a pleasing sensation at the base of his spine.[4] Suddenly, like the "roar of a waterfall," a stream of "light" rushed up his spine into his head, and he became immersed in a "sea of light." For decades, Gopi Krishna would experience these rushes of energy, as well as great mental and physical anguish and tremendous physical pain. The process of dealing with kundalini energy, however, forever changed Gopi Krishna and ultimately made him the embodiment of peacefulness and enlightenment.

Lee Sannella, M.D., has written the most exhaustive book on kundalini in the West in *The Kundalini Experience: Psychosis or Transcendence?*[5] Dr. Sannella describes kundalini as the progression of energy that ascends from the legs to the trunk and the back and then to the head. This energy is said to move through so-called chakras or energy centers, of which there are seven. Some of the chakras correspond to major nerve plexuses in the abdomen and thorax. Each chakra not only represents a center of energy and nervous system function, it embodies a state of consciousness and a variety of qualities. For example, the lower three chakras correspond to our lower, more animal nature, instincts, and feelings. The chakra at the level of our heart is related to love. The chakra at the top of our head is related to transcendent consciousness. These energies lie within us, usually dormant.

For the Chinese physician, the chakras are part of the invisible network of chi. They are the seven major "wheels of energy" through which all of our energy flows. The chakras' energy is actually visible to some people: Buddhist and Hindu masters, from ancient times to the present, have drawn pictures of it.

The sleeping, dormant kundalini energy awakens, as the usually unconscious prana or life-force becomes more conscious to us. It rises through the chakras and takes us through an evolution of consciousness. As the kundalini energy moves through us, a variety of mental and physical "symptoms" arise, change, and dissolve. I hesitate to use the word *symptom,* because it implies sickness or pathology. Although there may be discomfort in kundalini, there is no pathology. When the kundalini process has run its course, the so-called "symptoms" stop, and the individual finds himself much better integrated, mentally and physically.

The person who has progressed through all the stages of kundalini is full of love, so full that others are attracted to him, as if he were magnetic.[6] A great, internationally renowned yoga teacher, Indra Devi, possesses this kind of magnetism. Even people who have never heard of her will walk up to her on the street, hug her, cry on her shoulder—then suddenly step back and say, "Oh, my. I'm sorry. Who are you?"

Some symptoms of kundalini may be physical: cramps in the toes, darkening of toenails (especially of the big toe), vibration, tingling, feelings of heat, and spontaneous body movements. At any point where the kundalini is blocked, pain and a feeling of pressure may develop. The abdomen may contract and be drawn flat. One can have diarrhea or constipation, decreased or increased salivation.[7] One may hear a variety of sounds: bells, flutes, roaring. Chinese Taoist and medical philosophies identify still other symptoms, including itching, coldness, warmth, and feelings of weightlessness or heaviness.

Kundalini energy also produces a wide range of emotions—powerful, ecstatic feelings of joy, as well as panic, fear, and anxiety. People experiencing it may fall into deep states of meditation spontaneously, or they may have extraordinary visions of light, deities, and unearthly realms filled with great love and joy. They may feel themselves surrounded by divine light with an indescribable luster.

Sometimes kundalini energy causes people to assume yoga postures—postures that they have never learned—or they may dance ecstatically. Often people feel no control over their body movements, which may be fluid, dancing movements or wild jumps and gesticulations.

As you can imagine, rising kundalini energy can produce a pretty terrifying state. Many people going through the process wonder if they're going crazy. Certainly most psychiatrists would say they are and would treat them with antipsychotic medications. Even the greatest of saints wonder about their own sanity. When Paramahansa Ramakrishna, one of the great Indian saints of the nineteenth century, went through this process, he asked some spiritual teachers if he was losing his mind.[8]

Mark, age 36, had an experience similar to those of Gopi Krishna and Paramahansa Ramakrishna. He was referred to me by a psychologist who had been working with him—they had not had much progress in therapy, so my colleague asked for my opinion. Mark was anxious and panicky, wondering if he was losing his mind. Although he had once been a very social person, full of love for just about everyone, he had more recently become afraid to be around people and preferred to stay home. But as a restaurant owner, married, with two young children, he couldn't afford to stay home.

Mark was particularly afraid of and upset about the tremendous energy "surges" he was feeling inside. The energy was moving into his head and causing lots of pressure. Its intensity made him shake at night, which made it harder for him to sleep. These surges had started with a chi fast—a diet of Chinese herbal teas, that is used to increase chi, prana, or life-force energy. The fast worked, but Mark had so much energy, it frightened him. He had practiced kung fu for a decade, loved physical activity, and was physically very powerful, but he began having a hard time with kung fu. It stirred up this energy so much, he couldn't stand it.

Once all this energy was activated, it became more and more difficult for Mark to focus on his work in the restaurant. He "saw" energy streaming out of other people's heads and felt that they looked "brighter and more defined." All of his senses were heightened. The world looked almost psychedelic. When he listened to music, he would break down and cry because he would "merge" with the music. He didn't just listen to the music; he *became* the music. "Music sounds like it's from heaven," he said.

Mark seemed like a regular guy. He was very sweet, and he expressed a range of emotions and thoughts. He had had a very angry, dominating father, however, who had put a lot of fear into him, fear that had carried over into his adult life. When his new energy got stirred up, Mark's fear also became much greater. In fact, he was full of fear. He was afraid of the energy, not least because it was making him more distant from his wife. He loved her dearly and was afraid of hurting her emotionally, or losing her and the children.

His medical doctor hadn't been able to find anything wrong with Mark. But in order to be thorough, I asked Mark questions about his physical health and ordered some lab tests. I believed that he was suffering through a kundalini process, but I had to make sure he didn't have a serious physical illness that was causing the anxiety and energy surges.

I evaluated Mark's thyroid. If his thyroid gland were hyperactive, it would be giving him lots and lots of energy, and he'd probably feel euphoric, as opposed to depressed. But his thyroid tests were normal, and he didn't have the usual problems that accompany hyperthyroidism, such as tremors, weight loss, and intolerance to heat. So I was able to rule out hyperthyroidism as a cause of the energy surges.

A much less likely possibility was pheochromocytoma, a tumor usually associated with the adrenal gland. It produces either epinephrine or norepinephrine, also known as adrenaline, the hormones of the fight-or-flight response. A person with a pheochromocytoma will have lots of energy, with a racing, even pounding heart, and sweaty palms. Such a person may be anxious or fearful. But Mark didn't have a pheochromocytoma.

Finally, I checked to see if he had a drug problem. The use of stimulants, such as amphetamines, can make one feel overly energized. But Mark didn't use any drugs whatsoever—except for the ones I had prescribed to help calm him down—and he didn't drink a lot of coffee.

Confident that we were not dealing with a physical problem, I next considered all the mental illnesses from which Mark might be suffering.

At the top of my list was mania. Mark had enormous energy, like a manic person. But he lacked all the other key symptoms of mania. His thoughts didn't race. He wasn't staying up all night. He wasn't spending a lot of money that he didn't have. He wasn't traveling a lot. He wasn't on the phone constantly, or writing letters to everybody he knew. He was neither psychotic nor paranoid, and he hadn't lost touch with reality.

I ruled out serious mental illness as a cause of Mark's problem, but I needed to carefully look at the possibility of an anxiety disorder—a condition much less severe than the others. Mark did have all the symptoms of social phobia. He had "a persistent, irrational fear of and compelling desire to avoid a situation in which the individual is exposed to possible scrutiny by others, and fears that he or she may act in a way that will be humiliating or embarrassing," as the psychiatric guide to diagnosis defines this condition.[9]

Furthermore, he had "significant distress because of the disturbance and recognition by the individual that his or her fear is excessive or unreasonable." And his problem was certainly "not due to another mental disorder, such as Major Depression or Avoidant Personality Disorder."

Mark clearly met all the standard criteria for social phobia, but I wasn't satisfied that that diagnosis covered all of his problems. It didn't explain the energy surges and the paranormal phenomena, for example. But a diagnosis of kundalini process would explain the paranormal phenomena, such as seeing light pouring out of people, and the altered states of consciousness, such as "merging with music." None of these spiritual experiences are caused by social phobia. If anything, I concluded, the kundalini process was producing the social phobia.

Kundalini energy can act like a magnifying glass. Whatever emotional problems we have become exaggerated during a kundalini process. So the fear that had been part of Mark's personality since childhood became greatly magnified, as did his issues with his father. So intense was the energy that he was afraid he was losing his mind.

I wanted to avoid using any medications that would wipe out the kundalini process. But because Mark's suffering was so great, I did prescribe Xanax, a minor tranquilizer, for him to take when he was too anxious. While I was on vacation, Mark called the doctor covering for me and was started on low doses of Mellaril, a major tranquilizer. Mellaril really "snowed" Mark, so he used it only on rare occasions.

In therapy, I helped Mark identify his fears and work through the issues with his father. I also taught him breath techniques to help bring the energy down when it became too intense or threatening. I also referred Mark to an acupuncturist, who helped him gain more emotional control and helped redirect the overwhelming and often chaotic flow of the kundalini energy. The acupuncturist (who is a surgeon) confirmed my diagnosis of a kundalini process.

Mark kept wanting to return to the old Mark, the way he used to be. He had a hard time accepting that the kundalini energy wouldn't disappear quickly. But several things made the process easier for him. I taught him a technique to embrace fear rather than run from it, and I led him through imagery techniques in which he pictured and felt the presence of God right next to him. This was a critical and important part of therapy. To go through a kundalini process without a clear spiritual focus is quite difficult. Mark imagined that God was with him throughout his suffering, guiding and protecting him. Making a deeper spiritual connection through the imagery technique diminished Mark's fears.

I directed Mark in some other imagery and meditation exercises to let go of the energy surging within him, instead of trying to contain it. I asked him to "hold" God's hand and just let the energy flow out of his head. This exercise helped him feel much better.

Mark responded particularly well to "mindfulness meditation," which helped him focus more on the moment, the here-and-now—the moment of cutting the meat, rolling the tortillas, serving the customers in his restaurant. This meditation helped him to experience the present, to live the moment, and to focus less on the kundalini energy.

These mental techniques made Mark better able to allow the kundalini energy to unfold. When he brought a spiritual perspective to his problem, he got past the traditional medical diagnosis of social phobia and dealt with the deep-seated psychological issues in his life. Had he accepted that first diagnosis and the medications usually prescribed for it, he would not have confronted and grown past his fears.

Although this spiritual work of self-reflection and analysis is difficult and slow, Mark is glad that he is following this approach rather than medicating away his anxiety. He will never be the old Mark, but he is becoming a better, happier person. He is regaining his equanimity, is getting closer to his family again, and is overcoming his fears. As the kundalini process works itself out, he is getting stronger, healthier, and happier. When the kundalini energy has completely run its course, Mark will probably be a transformed person, more full of love and peace than the old Mark.

The kundalini experience is an altered state of consciousness and a process that unfolds over time, as it did with Gopi Krishna, Paramahansa Ramakrishna, and Mark. It does pass; the uncomfortable symptoms do go away, replaced by qualities like serenity, love, and forbearance.

## REDIRECTING OBSTRUCTED ENERGY
### *Mental Fitness Technique*

*Human value fostered by this technique: Peace*

Once the kundalini process has started, the person should be encouraged to go through the process, look at the fear, allow the energy to flow, and move into a higher state of consciousness. Once the experience has passed, the person generally has an improved perspective on self, life, and spirit.

To manage kundalini energy, once it has begun to stir,

1. Practice a one-minute imagery ritual four times a day. Visualize a symbol for the human value "peace" and use that symbol as the heart of your one-minute anxiety ritual.

2. Practice breathing deeply and slowly throughout the day. This will help stabilize your energy without stirring it up more. Practice the breath technique that lowers energy and is calming: Inhale to the count of four, hold your breath to the count of four, exhale to the count of eight.

3. Avoid fasting.

4. Get plenty of rest. Avoid sleep deprivation. Fasting and sleep deprivation are likely to cause kundalini energy to surge even more.

5. Avoid any martial art that stirs up chi, prana, or energy.

6. Balance your energy with therapeutic touch, reiki, huna, acupuncture, or yoga. Yoga postures can increase or decrease kundalini energy. Make sure you find a good practitioner—find one who comes highly recommended.

7. Make dietary changes. If your diet has been "light vegetarian," consider adding cheese and other dairy products, then poultry, fish, and beef—in that order. Honey can also lower energy.

8. Find ways to ground the energy. Physical exercise, especially in direct contact with the earth, is helpful. Gardening is another good way.

9. Use the following imagery script to see where the energy may be obstructed:

> Close your eyes and relax. Slowly become aware of the flow of energy within your body. The energy may be a powerful current; at other times, it may be almost imperceptible. The energy may seem to flow from toe to head, head to toe, or from the center on out.
>
> Identify the flow of energy. Let's say, for example, that you feel energy moving from your toes up to your head. In your mind, follow the flow of energy. If you perceive any blockage in the energy, imagine that there is a door at that point. Open the door, and explore the room that lies behind it. Make whatever adjustments are necessary in order to

*allow the energy to flow through the room, then continue on
its upward course.*

An infinite array of images may appear in the blocked rooms. People from the past who have been our tormentors often appear there. Perhaps the room will be filled with memories. If you don't know how to handle the person, place, thing, or symbol that appears in the blocked room, invite your chosen form of God to appear in that room with you. Ask Him for advice as to how to deal with the obstruction. Above all, assume the attitude of "going with the flow." Don't fight stirred-up kundalini. Realize that the kundalini process is an incredible opportunity for transformation. See where the energy is blocked. Practice surrender in whatever way works for you, remembering that surrendering is an active process and does not mean giving up.

# PART II

## *The Lost*
## *Mind*

# 8

## WHAT IS THE MIND?

As we've seen, culture has a profound effect on how people view both illness and consciousness. To distinguish kundalini from madness, therefore, requires a rudimentary understanding of mental illness.

Before we talk about mental illness, however, it's important to know that there is "craziness," and there is "CRAZINESS!" Many medical doctors and lay people use the word *crazy* very loosely. One sweet, intelligent, kind, 15-year-old girl who suffers from severe chronic fatigue syndrome was told by doctors at Kaiser Permanente that she was crazy—that there was nothing wrong with her physically. For eight months she had been running a fever between 102 and 104 degrees. But the doctors had found only one abnormal lab result, an elevation in the level of protein in her urine. "Just pull yourself together. You're just depressed," she was told over and over again.

After Kaiser gave up on Tess as a "loony," her mother, a long-term patient of mine, asked me to evaluate the girl. Amino acid testing and specialized immunological testing showed a severe metabolic impairment, and an immune system quite similar to that seen in AIDS patients. Tess definitely was not crazy, definitely was very sick physically, and I almost certainly could help her. After three weeks on a nutritional supplementation program, she began to feel better.

Medical practitioners have no right to take away a patient's hope, which is what they did to Tess. The moment she felt hopeful, she started to get better. One year after my treatment prescription of "hope," counseling, and amino acids, Tess fully recovered and returned to a normal life. She healed not just because of the amino acids but because of our doctor-patient relationship. The deep sense of trust she felt with me, the hope I was able to inspire in her, and the validation of her illness I provided helped turn on her own inner healing resources.

The medical profession is, and always will be, limited by the current level of its technologies, and as such it has no right to dismiss mysterious symptoms as fabricated or crazy. But all too often it does mislabel as crazy any illness it can't easily explain: "You're just premenstrual, or depressed, or hysterical, or crazy." This lack of understanding and empathy can actually be life-threatening. Tess was dying when I first met her, and I believe that even if she hadn't died, she would have become a chronically sick person if the medical authorities had continued to dismiss her problems. The power of doctors' words is enormous. According to Bernie Siegel, M.D., author of *Love, Medicine, and Miracles,* we can kill with our words—but we can also heal with them. We can make someone feel crazy by telling them they are crazy—even if they're not.

Up until recently, traditional psychiatry has jammed every paranormal phenomenon, every vision, every miracle, every mystical experience into the diagnosis of a hallucination; it has called every accurate premonition "magical or wishful thinking." In the next pages you'll encounter a variety of symptoms seen in mental illness, including depression, anxiety, hallucinations, confusion, manic euphoria, and suicidal thoughts. You will realize that your vision, your clairvoyance, or your kundalini is not a symptom of insanity. Later on you'll find out what it is.

Even if mental illness is the correct diagnosis for what you are experiencing, I want you to know that it can be treated. Powerful medications are available to treat most of the major mental illnesses, in conjunction with psychotherapy. For instance, 50 percent of all Americans will experience a clinical depression at least once in their lives, and there are many ways to work with depression. It's okay to be depressed, and it's okay to be treated for it. There is no spiritual victory in refusing proper medical treatment. It is not "un-spiritual" to treat your depression with medication. It's the practical thing to do.

I want to lift the veil of fear that prevents people from getting help, whether they need help for a mental illness or a mystical experience. Physicians are there to help you, no matter what is wrong. They're there to treat depression and psychosis—and, in my opinion, to accept angels and mystical experiences. Whether you have a case of "angels," "depressive blues," "manic highs," or "mystical union," know that an honest diagnosis will enormously alleviate any fears or doubts you may have about your sanity. Knowing the truth will allow you to get help, no matter what the diagnosis is. Knowing the truth can even help you find meaning in illness.

As we explore the various kinds of mental illness, we'll proceed from those in which real spiritual experience is least likely, such as severe disorders of brain chemistry (organic brain syndrome and schizophrenia), to those in which spiritual experience can occur frequently, such as borderline personality, depression, and anxiety. For people with schizophrenia, spiritual experience is unlikely but possible. People with multiple personality disorder and borderline personality disorder have experiences that are a mixture of imagination, psychosis, and real spiritual influence.

From the standpoint of traditional psychiatry, the human mind is our greatest possession. Eastern philosophy sees the mind as a bundle of hopes, wishes, thoughts, and desires, separate from the intellect. It sees the intellect as "higher" than the mind, and the soul as the "highest." The soul is never lost, although it may be difficult to make contact with it or understand it, and it may be "covered" with layers of mind. The intellect guides the mind to discern with "wisdom and discrimination." Through the intellect, we find our purpose, meaning, and goal in life. The mind carries out the instructions that the intellect gives it.

When the mind becomes lost, the real "I," the soul, seems far away. The mind can become lost in many ways. The schizophrenic's mind is so lost that he cannot tell himself apart from others. The manic's mind runs so fast that her life is ruined. The depressed person's mind may run so slowly and negatively that he thinks of taking his life. The anxious person's mind is so worried about the future that she forgets about living in the present. She is run by fear, forgetting her higher nature. The borderline's mind feels as if he has nothing to hang on to, as if he lives at the edge of a great void.

Most of us have some of the qualities I've just mentioned. We all have a little bit of mania, a bit of depression, a bit of anxiety, a bit of the void. Most of us even have had brief periods during which we wondered if we were really going crazy. The fact is that we all lose our minds to some extent, even in a simple display of anger or a sudden attack of fear. Everyone has lost their mind, if only for a few minutes. It's okay to lose your mind. What is not okay is to suffer over the suffering, to become anxious about being anxious.

The fact that all of us lose our minds from time to time gives us the empathy and compassion to live with one another and help one another. The big difference between most of you and those who are mentally ill is that your "loss of mind" is fleeting and temporary, whereas the person with schizophrenia has permanently lost his mind, and the borderline is always in the void, always experiencing a condition of intense suffering in which comfort from either God or human is impossible.

Mental illnesses appear distinctly different from one another in their early stages. The schizophrenic and the borderline begin their course of suffering in very different ways. However, a person who has been schizophrenic for thirty years may be difficult to distinguish from a person who has been manic or borderline for thirty years. Severe mental illnesses generally start with a bang, then progress to a state of chronic dullness, a state of sameness with other mental illnesses. After thirty years, mentally ill people appear "burned out," whether due to schizophrenia, mania, or borderline personality. The spiritual person, on the other hand, develops his or her uniqueness more and more over time and moves in the opposite direction from the person with mental illness. Spiritual practice brings out the best in us, the best in our hearts, minds, personalities, and intellects.

Some people on the spiritual path, however, become stuck at a certain level of insight and develop a kind of pseudo-spirituality. They appear spiritual but don't act it. The "pseudo-spiritual" start to look alike, just as the chronically mentally ill do. But the "truly spiritual," the great spiritual adepts, the saints, and the sages have all developed their uniqueness. Their personalities are loving, humorous, powerful, and quite distinctive. Like the rest of us, the average saint has lost his mind from time to time and has seriously wondered if he was going crazy. But the average saint differs from the average insane person in one very important way: He doesn't get stuck in his insanity. He witnesses it and then lets go of it. You can do the same with some of the techniques of transformation in this book.

In exploring the "lost mind," remember that saints and sages throughout history have all said that only one thing is eternal—the soul. The soul is never lost. It cannot be lost. It always was and always will be. It is eternal, constant, and never-changing. We are not our minds, and we are certainly not our "lost minds." We are the witness of these changes, all these phenomena, all these so-called states of mind. We treasure our minds and glorify them without realizing that it is the light of the soul that gives the mind any light at all. To quote Sathya Sai Baba, "The soul is infinitely more beautiful than its surroundings."

## ORGANIC BRAIN SYNDROMES: WHEN THE CHEMISTRY ISN'T RIGHT

There are so many ways for the brain to go out of whack: stroke, drug intoxication, fever, medication side effects, drug withdrawal, alcohol intoxication, alcohol withdrawal (DTs), cancer, all kinds of metabolic disorders, infections of the brain, trauma (getting hit on the head), inflammation of the brain tissue or of the blood vessels in the brain, environmental toxins, heavy-metal poisoning, hypothyroidism, and degenerative diseases (such as Alzheimer's disease or AIDS).[1] In all of these conditions, which doctors call organic brain syndromes (OBSs), brain chemistry is extremely abnormal. Brain chemistry may go awry in either of two main ways. Either the brain is under direct attack by trauma, cancer, or stroke—or there is a metabolic problem, in which case the imbalance is affecting the entire body, not just the brain. When we get the flu, for example, we suffer from a minor abnormality of brain chemistry. We can't think straight, and our mind is fuzzy.

In schizophrenia a small part of the brain has abnormal metabolism of the neurotransmitter dopamine. But in an organic brain syndrome (OBS), most of the brain is functioning abnormally, and most of the neurotransmitters are out of balance. Even in the mildest OBS, "diffuse slowing," is evident on the EEG (electroencephalogram). Some kinds of OBS, especially those associated with approaching coma, show epileptic-type bursts on the EEG.

When the brain isn't working right, we get disoriented. We can't remember the day of the week, or the date, or the month, or if we're in really bad shape, the year. Our ability to form new memories begins to fail. Our higher cognitive functions are "shot." We can't think straight or figure out the simplest of problems. Our ability to do simple mathematic calculations falls apart.

Some people with abnormal brain chemistry can fool us into thinking something else is going on. Fritz, a delightful 80-year-old professional musician, is a good example. His sister was concerned about his ability to continue living alone in a mobile home in New Mexico. When she visited him, she was upset to find that he left on the gas stove when he wasn't cooking, and that the house was a complete mess. Fritz himself was finding it more difficult to manage his daily affairs and was developing some strange ideas, believing that his neighbors were plotting against him, for instance.

He was an easy man to speak to, cheerful and gregarious. He had played more than a dozen musical instruments, all professionally. I asked him about his favorite violin pieces—the Beethoven Violin Concerto, and the Mendelssohn Violin Concerto, he said. He could tell me details about his first seventy years of life. But when I asked him about his mobile home, he couldn't even tell me what state he lived in. His short-term memory was rapidly vanishing. He didn't know where he was or what year it was. He couldn't remember my name from day to day—but we had wonderful chats about the various orchestras in which he had played.

Fritz's paranoia, confusion, and disorientation could all have been part of a schizophrenic episode, or even a psychotic borderline break. But Fritz was suffering from advanced Alzheimer's disease, a case of dementia. There is no known medical treatment for this OBS, although nutritional supplements can boost one's brainpower. The best I could do for Fritz was to help find him a nice, safe home, a place with medical supervision that would prepare his meals and take care of his basic needs.

People with organic brain disorders aren't all as sweet as Fritz. They can also behave impulsively and lose control of their sexual and aggressive feelings. Eighty percent of the violent crime in San Diego is caused by people who are on drugs, suffering from an acute drug-induced OBS called *delirium*.

Some patients with OBS develop perceptual difficulties and experience either illusions or hallucinations. Illusions mean "misinterpreting what you see or hear." So a patient might see a pattern on the wallpaper and think that animals are crawling over the wall. They may also hallucinate—see or hear things that are not there at all. For them, visual hallucinations are more common than auditory. Schizophrenics, on the other hand, have many more auditory hallucinations than visual.

People with OBS wax and wane. Throughout the day they go through periods of being much better, then much worse. Schizophrenics and manics don't do that. People with OBS, including those suffering from Alzheimer's disease, tend to get much worse at night. When darkness falls and things become harder to see, their brains go even more out of control. It's what doctors call *sundowning*.

People with OBS are really ill physically. They may have fevers and a whole host of other medical problems, depending on what is causing the brain to get sick. For a psychiatrist, OBS is easy to recognize. Although people with OBS may have some of the same symptoms as schizophrenics, such as hallucinations, they "feel" entirely different to the psychiatrist. Of course, schizophrenics, manics, and borderlines can develop an OBS, in which case it becomes difficult to determine how much of the problem is mental and how much is caused by the physical problem.

Not much about organic brain syndrome can be called spiritual. Probably the most spiritual state associated with OBS comes in the last days of life. A dying person can be in a delirium, an extreme confusional state—and be "visited" by relatives from the other side. In this case, the OBS may actually facilitate the spiritual experience. One patient at the San Diego Hospice, in his final stage of AIDS delirium, went into an ecstatic rapture for almost a day. According to his internist, his eyes were full of light, and even the room appeared radiant. One day after that spiritual rapture, the patient passed away.

But with OBS the real spiritual challenge lies with the patient's health care professionals and family members, since people with OBS can't control their minds because of the nature of their illness. The family caregivers have the greatest challenge, for they must not only face the loss of their loved one, they must cope with an exhausting and often depressing job of caregiving—often twenty-four hours a day. The family needs hope, faith, and encouragement to carry out this difficult task—a task that often ends only when the person dies. The health care professional must pay special attention to the emotional and spiritual needs of the family members, making sure they have sufficient support, alleviating any feelings of guilt that may arise, and providing comfort to those who spend their days providing comfort.

## SCHIZOPHRENIA: WHEN THE BRAIN AND MIND DRIVE EACH OTHER CRAZY

Nick was 36 years old and didn't look out of the ordinary. But his outpatient psychiatrist, Dr. Freeze, was afraid that Nick was about to murder someone. Nick believed that his next-door neighbor had sophisticated computer equipment that was linked to satellites. The satellites were "controlling Nick's mind," and he wasn't the slightest bit happy about it. In fact, he had tried to run down this neighbor with his car. Dr. Freeze couldn't get Nick to take medication. Fearing that Nick was too dangerous to be left to his own devices, he had him committed to a mental hospital—where it became my job to diagnose Nick and get him to take medication, if that was my recommendation.

Nick was hearing voices. "They're real," he told me. And: "I have illegal access to a United States spy satellite. They follow me and track me.

They can make me sick and affect my brain. I am furious with Dr. Freeze, my psychiatrist. He says it's all a chemical imbalance. But my neighbor really has the equipment. I've seen it, but nobody believes me or even bothers to check up on him. I've made lots of phone calls to the police and FBI, but nobody will check it out."

And: "There are satellite beams that come down into my head. They're talking to me right now. They're threatening to kill me. If they try to kill me, I'll kill them."

I wanted to redirect the conversation for a moment, away from the delusions, so I asked Nick about his baseball cap. He took it off and showed me the metallic "chromium" shields he had installed on the inside. "The baseball cap shields me from the microwaves from polarized molecules from the satellites. The satellites are four hundred miles above the Earth." Everything in Nick's life centered on his delusion, and there was no breaking through it. It was solid as a rock, and no matter what question I asked, his answer filled in another piece of the delusional puzzle.

How did Nick know all of this technical terminology? He was in the heating and air-conditioning business and knew electronics quite well. I asked him why the government would be so interested in controlling his life. "Because I know too much!" he replied. "I'm also very psychic. I know when people are lying. I know when someone is trying to drive me nuts."

Much as I trust the diagnostic skills of most psychiatrists, I always resist the temptation to simply go along with their labels and diagnoses without coming to my own conclusion. The reason is that I take into consideration the spiritual side of diagnosis and treatment—a dimension that is almost always lacking in traditional psychiatric diagnosis.

Nick, I decided, could have been suffering from a number of problems. He could have been suffering from an LSD psychosis or the long-term effects of chronic amphetamine abuse. People who have used amphetamines for years think, feel, and act like Nick. But Nick wasn't a drug user. He wasn't sleep-deprived.

Nor had he gone overboard on spiritual practices, meditating for hours a day. Another patient of mine, Chuck, I once admitted to a mental hospital because he had been fasting for three weeks, meditating almost incessantly, and was depriving himself of sleep—intentionally. He "cracked"! He became extremely paranoid, heard voices, and was delusional. His spiritual practice had actually triggered an acute psychotic episode, a schizophrenic episode. He recovered quickly, with the help of Haldol, an antipsychotic medication. Nick, on the other hand, was not suffering from any type of spiritual illness, nor from an illness triggered by spiritual practice.

Nick suffered from paranoid schizophrenia. Most people think *schizophrenia* means "split personality," but that is not the case at all. "Split personality" is actually another name for borderline personality disorder. (We'll get to that later.) Of all the mental disorders besides OBS, schizophrenia is the most biological. Real and permanent physiological changes happen to the schizophrenic's brain, especially problems with dopamine metabolism.

When I was a first-year resident in psychiatry, I dreamed of curing schizophrenics through compassion, wisdom, and intensive psychotherapy. I had been strongly influenced by some success stories I had read about in college, stories in which schizophrenics were successfully treated through psychotherapy alone. The book *I Never Promised You a Rose Garden,* was one such inspiration for me,[2] as was the work of R. D. Laing, a British psychiatrist and author, who claimed to have cured many schizophrenics through psychotherapy conducted in a therapeutic community. For me, it was big shock to discover that love is not enough. The dramatic cures I read about probably involved psychotic borderlines, not schizophrenics. People with borderline personality can be cured, even if they're psychotic. But only over the past twenty years has psychiatry been able to distinguish the schizophrenic from the borderline.

Research into the role the family plays in triggering and perpetuating schizophrenia has been fruitful. But the greatest contribution, in my opinion, to the treatment of schizophrenia has been the development of antipsychotic medications, such as Thorazine, Haldol, and Prolixin.

Nick needed antipsychotic medication. I could work to gain his trust and get him to take medication voluntarily (no small feat!). Or I could take an adversarial approach, file the necessary legal papers, take him to court, and let the judge decide if we had the right to force Nick to take medication against his will. I always prefer the former route, although neither is better or more "spiritual" than the other. Medication was the best, the only effective treatment that would help Nick overcome his insanity and protect his community from his real homicidal potential.

Before I tried to gain Nick's trust, I did my best to center myself. As I sat with him, I silently recited my mantra so that I would be as calm and nonreactive as possible. I mustered as much love as I could. I prayed. "Dear Lord, help me do what I can to give Nick relief." When Nick spoke, I listened without judging. Confronting a paranoid schizophrenic about their delusions is a complete waste of time. I've learned simply to sidestep them and appeal to a "higher" part of the individual. "Nick," I said, "I know your mind is being bombarded by a lot of influences. I know you feel the satellites are controlling your mind. You need to make your mind stronger. This medication, Haldol, will help your mind grow stronger, so that it's easier for you to combat all of those influences." Because he felt accepted and understood, at least to some extent, he took the medicine, and within two weeks he was sane enough to go home. His voices had gone away, as had his desire to kill his neighbor.

Schizophrenia is a biological mental illness, a disorder in which "the brain and mind drive each other crazy." It usually starts during adolescence or early adulthood. Suddenly someone who is fairly normal has a psychotic break. A cascade of neurological changes makes it seem as if a bomb has gone off in their brain, their mind, their consciousness, literally destroying the fabric of their personality. They are almost never the same afterward. They suffer from severe psychotic symptoms: auditory hallucinations (hearing voices), bizarre delusions ("crazy" ideas), dramatically disordered thinking, and incoherent, loose, illogical, rambling speech.

During the psychotic episode the person may be terrified and paranoid. After the episode ends, their mood is flattened or dulled. In fact, this last symptom may be the most important. Nick, like other schizophrenics, had developed such an enormous imaginary world that he became separated from the real world. Unlike ordinary people, who react to people and things in the world around them, the schizophrenic reacts more to his inner world. So Nick had a facial expression that was flat. He was very hard to "read." There was a kind of emotional deadness about him, a feeling that nobody was home.

Schizophrenia is a disorder of thinking, thinking that becomes delusional. Schizophrenics may have religious delusions and believe that they are Jesus, Mary, or John the Baptist, or John Lennon, or Marilyn Monroe, or anyone other than themselves. Or they may believe that somebody whom they've never met is in love with them. They often believe that they're getting special messages designed just for them from the radio and television, or that the FBI had their dentist implant powerful transmitters into their teeth and is monitoring their every move.

Schizophrenic delusions can take just about any form. People may develop body image delusions—feeling that they look like or are an animal, or a member of the opposite sex. Schizophrenics almost always hear voices, but they rarely have visual hallucinations. They may become violent during a psychotic episode, although that is not the rule. Generally, they are completely out of touch with what we call reality.

Schizophrenics' psychotic episodes have a beginning and an end. Nick isn't "crazy" all the time. Like other schizophrenics, his episodes are usually brought under pretty good control with medication. In between psychotic episodes, the schizophrenic goes home, maybe works, maybe has a relationship. But the psychotic episodes come back, and the person's personality gets more and more eroded through the years. Schizophrenics get burned out. The voices, which initially occurred just during psychotic episodes, often increase in frequency until they are present all the time. Over the years the voices usually become fainter. They become whispers or background noise, but the individual retreats more and more from society. The world becomes too frightening and too hard to fit in to.

Schizophrenia progresses from an acute disturbance of the norm to a chronic dullness. Eventually the "abnormal" state becomes the norm. Loud and clear voices become distant, muffled, and unclear. The person on the spiritual path, in contrast, is moving in the opposite direction. She is learning to listen to the one "voice," not to many. Her voice of conscience becomes louder and more distinct as she quiets down the mental noise and can listen to it. She learns how to distinguish the real voice from the mumbles of the noisy mind, and she uses that knowing as an anchor and a powerful positive force. The schizophrenic, on the other hand, is overwhelmed by the voices.

Not only does the schizophrenic lose his emotional center and his sense of self, he usually struggles to regain that which is forever lost, namely "who he was." The schizophrenic may have been a talented straight-A student in high school with a number of hobbies. But after his illness has progressed, he probably is no longer even able to attend school and has lost interest in most of his hobbies. Still, he remembers who he was and holds on to that image as a safety net. This difficulty in "letting go" of "who they were" is a big problem for schizophrenics, as it is for others whose mental illness has severely compromised their functioning in the world. The fact is that 99.9 percent of schizophrenics are worse off than they were before their illness, and it's very hard to come to terms with this reality.

For the average person, however, the memory of our past successes can serve to inspire us to even greater achievements. And our memories of spiritual experiences remind us that if we keep putting one foot in front of the other and continue with our spiritual practice, we will reap the rewards of more spiritual experiences and have a richer, more meaningful life.

On paper, schizophrenia and mystical experiences come very close to looking the same. But the two are very different. Even a schizophrenic patient who says he is psychic usually is not. Clairvoyance and extrasensory perception require an openness to the environment and to other people. Schizophrenics, especially those who are suspicious or paranoid, may be aware of their environment, but only insofar as they believe danger lies there. Nor, in general, are they open to the feelings and thoughts of others. They are buried in their own inner world. The schizophrenic lives in a tragic, lonely state of fearful separateness. By contrast, the mystic lives in a state of union, experiencing a conscious oneness with all of life.

The severe confusional state called schizophrenia is primarily caused by a chemical imbalance. It is not a mystical state. But can schizophrenia be explained entirely by abnormal brain chemistry? Or does something unseen, something as yet immeasurable, contribute to the chemical cascade in the schizophrenic's brain? That, I believe, is a question that will challenge psychiatrists of the future. Is it possible that something both physical and metaphysical actually *is* going on with schizophrenics? Is it possible that their brains are chemically so out of balance that they become *tuned* to a different frequency? Are they sensitive to vibrations of thought and energy that are inaccessible to the rest of us? And if so, are their delusions the result of misinterpreting those vibrations, those energies? Can part of the schizophrenic's abnormal brain chemistry actually be attributed to invisible demons? The doctor of the future will have to face these questions in order to understand the schizophrenic's brain chemistry and the possible influence of unseen forces.

From a genetic-evolutionary-cultural perspective, schizophrenia may have been a healthy adaptation at one point in human history. Schizophrenics, especially paranoid types, tend to be night owls and loners. In early indigenous cultures, the paranoid schizophrenic would have been a good night watchman. He liked the night, preferred to be alone, and was hypervigilant. As we saw in Chapter 6, the schizophrenic does in fact do much better in indigenous cultures but deteriorates after moving to the large modern city. From this perspective, schizophrenia could be an evolutionary step that humankind has outgrown.

But the schizophrenia gene may still serve a purpose today as well. After working with mental patients for many years, I was able to sense schizophrenia in a patient even before being told about his voices and delusions. I felt more deeply and appreciated the extraordinary emotional distance, the aloofness of the schizophrenic. Eventually, I developed the ability to diagnosis schizophrenia almost instantly. A few years later, I noticed on several occasions that some relatives of schizophrenics gave me a bit of the same "schizophrenia feeling." I mentioned to a friend, Sandy, that I believed her cousin, Lee, carried the schizophrenia gene. "That's ridiculous," she responded. "He is so gregarious and funny. He loves people, has hundreds of friends, is brilliant, and works hard."

"I still think he carries the gene," I replied.

Several months later, Sandy casually mentioned that Lee's brother, Maynard, wasn't doing so well. Not knowing anything at all about Maynard, I asked what was wrong with him. "Oh, I thought you knew," Sandy replied. "He's schizophrenic. He's been in and out of mental hospitals."

Lee himself has never had any mental problems, yet I still believe he may carry the schizophrenia gene. If my theory is correct, the gene is being expressed only to a minor degree in him, not enough to cause problems. Perhaps a small "dose" of it can even do something good. That may be the case with Bjorn, another person I know whose brother is schizophrenic. Bjorn has that dreamy faraway look, like what I perceive in Lee. But Bjorn, in my opinion, is highly advanced spiritually. He is loving, courageous, and a powerful dharmic leader, and he has frequent mystical experiences.

I have no proof, but I would suggest that a strong dose of the schizophrenia gene creates the brain biology that causes schizophrenia, a confusional state. Perhaps a very small dose of the same gene opens us up to spiritual awareness and mystical experience.

## MANIA: WHEN THE BRAIN GOES ON OVERDRIVE

I met Alexia during my first year of psychiatric training. Her brain had too much of the neurotransmitter norepinephrine, which caused her to have too much energy, too much aggression, and too much sexuality. She entered the mental hospital dressed in silky black pants and a heavy black cape. Her Grecian black hair and blue eye shadow were dramatic, and her pink lipstick was subtle. As I first approached her, she was rifling through her purse, sorting out pills and handing the nurse a five-hundred-dollar bill for safekeeping. Alexia believed she was being poisoned by her former husband, and she wanted everything, including her money, to be kept in a safe place, away from him.

My first interaction with her was the obligatory physical examination. In between looking in her eyes, ears, nose, and throat, I asked her what problem necessitated her hospitalization. "Doctor, nothing necessitated my hospitalization," she replied. "You see, my husband—that is, my former husband—has been poisoning me and tearing my house apart. I'm in the hospital to run up a big hospital bill that he'll have to pay. That bastard will have to pay for it! Anyway, I don't *have* to be here. There's nothing wrong with me, and you know it. You and I know the real reason for my being here."

Alexia made total sense about 75 percent of the time; the other 25 percent I wasn't sure. At any rate, I did not know the same "real" reason she thought I knew, but I did know that she had been racing all over town in a taxi. She had been buying a vast number of expensive art objects. She had been staying up around the clock, making phone calls around the world, and writing letters to anyone and everyone. Did she look like a mentally ill person? No. On the surface she was warm and engaging, a young 45-year-old, albeit a bit extreme. She spoke a mile a minute, gushing a barrage of coherent, upper-middle-class, educated phrases. She seemed to have boundless but frenetic energy and felt high as a kite. She wasn't the least bit upset about her mania, but everyone else in her life was upset with her.

As I continued with the physical, Alexia asked, "Doctor, what kind of vagina do I have?"

"Female type, Alexia. Female."

She laughed uproariously. "You're fabulous, doctor. Is it large, medium, or small?"

"I stick to my original statement—female type." I struggled to maintain my perfect medical objectivity—no easy task for a first-year resident. "Your physical exam is entirely normal."

"Great physical, doctor!"

I checked out Alexia's story, reviewed it with her family, and discussed the case with the medical director of the hospital. She was clearly manic—a most unfortunate condition, in my experience, because manics usually don't want to be treated, although they respond well to treatment with lithium combined with an antipsychotic medication like Thorazine or Haldol. They like being "naturally high," even if the high is destroying their life, as Alexia's was. Everything moved too fast for Alexia. She became grandiose and began to lose touch with reality. She stayed up night after night, writing long letters to everybody she knew. She traveled around the country, blew most of her money, and ran up her credit cards in a hurry. A manic can blow through a lifetime of savings in a month, destroying a marriage and friendships at the same time.

I tested Alexia for a number of physical problems that can produce symptoms like those of mania, including an overactive thyroid gland, a pheochromocytoma (a tumor that produces adrenaline), Cushing's disease (an excess of cortisol, a steroid hormone), and amphetamine addiction. She did not suffer from any of them. Nor did she have any of the psycho-physiological or spiritual prerequisites for a kundalini process. She had no conscious spiritual practice and was neither meditating nor fasting. And she was not experiencing the huge surges of light and energy that pour up the spine of someone in a kundalini process.

With the diagnosis clear, the treatment seemed clear: Get Alexia to take lithium. I wrote the orders for her medication on a Friday, explained to her its actions and potential side effects—and headed home for the weekend. On Monday I learned that Alexia had been taking her lithium religiously, but that she took her Thorazine only when she wanted to. She felt that it made her too tired (which it probably did)—"and besides, I don't need medication anyway." I didn't worry about her situation, figuring that in a short while, once the lithium took hold, all would be well. I tried to forget that lithium sometimes needs several weeks to take hold.

As the days progressed, Alexia became more and more paranoid. (She felt that I was mistreating her and lying to her, and I thought the opposite!) She couldn't find her contact lenses or her underwear; she kicked a nurse who tried to give her medication.

Working with Alexia became more and more frustrating and confusing. Manics have an ability, which may be psychic, to zero in on others' weaknesses, their Achilles' heels, with deadly accuracy. Usually they can do it instantaneously. The moment they meet you, they can size you up and somehow, sorting through the millions of impressions, know the one item that will throw you off guard. They take one look at you, shake your hand—and know your weakest point. The more I talked with Alexia, the more she understood my weaknesses and the better she was able to "play the manic game."

My Achilles' heel is that I was a late bloomer. When I was 18, I looked 13. When I was a medical student, some patients wouldn't let me touch them because I looked like Doogie Howser, a high school student. As a psychiatrist in training, I was still sensitive about my maturity. Manics had a way of getting to that issue immediately—by calling me Dennis. I would introduce myself as Dr. Gersten, but they would look at my name tag and say, "Nice to meet you—Dennis!" Alexia quickly began calling me by my first name, which drove me nuts. Here I was finally practicing psychiatry, wanting the ego-gratification and respect of being a "real doctor." Being called by my first name hit me really hard.

For years every single manic patient I had would call me Dennis. In fact, it was so predictable that I stopped responding defensively to it and used the information to help me diagnose mania. That may sound like a strange way to diagnose, but the "feel" of the patient is actually critical to diagnosis.

I finally succeeded in getting Alexia to take the Thorazine, but not for very long. She decided to leave the hospital AMA (against medical advice) and prepared to say her good-byes at the community meeting on the ward. As Alexia waited to say farewell, I was impressed with how serenely she was sitting through the entire meeting. During her first community meeting, she couldn't sit still for longer than thirty seconds. Now, clad entirely in white, in stark contrast to her black entry outfit, she arose from her chair and took a position in the center of the room, assessing the peasants below her, glancing from one face to another. She looked no less regal than when she had entered, cloaked in black.

"I would like to say good-bye to this fine establishment. My care has been . . . extraordinary." She whirled around to Pat, a pleasant and shy nurse whom I had never heard utter an unkind word. "You have been the perfect bitch. No, I take it back—the imperfect bitch." She hovered over Pat like a great bird. Pat turned various shades of red and remained speechless. Alexia proceeded around the room. I anxiously awaited my own coronation/crucifixion. My stomach was making loud grumbles, intermixed with knotting and twisting that nobody could see. As she approached me, she smiled and glared at the same time.

"Dr. Gersten, you could make a fine physician someday. In my forty-five years, I have never had such a thorough physical exam as the one you gave me, but you have a long way to go. You've been a perfect ass and an expert at mistreating me." She continued to berate me, but the impact of her words passed over me. I had fully expected to be slaughtered by something, some exposé, some public revelation of my weaknesses. Alexia must have sensed how much I dislike having to perform complete physical exams on new patients. But she didn't mention the physical at all.

After the community meeting, I approached her one last time. "Alexia, I think that coming from you, I've just been paid a backhanded compliment."

"You have. I told you, you give a damn good physical—but that's all you do well." By the time Alexia left the hospital, I wasn't angry with her. Even though she had beaten me at her game, exposed some of my weaknesses, I still respected her. I respected the fight in her, even if she took it out on me. I had used all the psychiatric skills available to a first-year resident. And I was happy that she had made significant improvement in her mania.

I even respected her need for control, her need to fight the dark depression that had sent her to the depths for five months back in New York City. In retrospect, I would deal with Alexia much differently today, but I would have no illusions about how hard it is to treat a manic.

At the extreme of mania, the Alexias of the world become psychotic, paranoid, and grandiose. In fact, when they are acutely psychotic, it may be hard or impossible to tell them apart from schizophrenics. But apart from the personal history, there are a couple of ways to distinguish schizophrenic psychosis from manic psychosis. The schizophrenic says "Satellites are controlling my mind" and seems totally crazy. Manics who are too high can look just like paranoid schizophrenics. They can hear voices and have paranoid delusions. But the manic almost always has a grain of truth, a grain of reality in her story. She may, in fact, be a millionaire businessperson who just went off the deep end. And her grandiose ideas may have started from a place of logic, fact, or truth.

While the schizophrenic mentally arms himself against you in order to protect himself, the manic disarms you in order to protect herself, to maintain a sense of control, to keep her fragile ego from breaking into pieces. She seems half crazy and half sane. The feeling she gives her physician and the people around her is very different from the feeling a schizophrenic gives. The manic even made me question my own sanity!

The manic is a perfect teacher of spiritual lessons for the psychiatrist, because the spiritual path requires a conscious desire to detach from one's ego. When I was able to stop feeling defensive with Alexia, she became a terrific teacher for me, zeroing in on my weaknesses, my ego defenses, and exposing them. This kind of painful experience can accelerate one's psychological and spiritual growth, if one can keep an open mind about it. Alexia revealed my overattachment to my identity as a doctor, for which I am grateful to her. She revealed to me my discomfort in performing physical exams, and my disappointment at not dealing with the "perfect" open-minded patient with malleable attitudes. The ego-destruction Alexia blessed me with prepared me to be a better doctor, a more humble doctor, to every patient I had after her.

The ego blows that I received from Alexia arose out of her ego hyperinflation, a state that is opposite to the ego deflation that a depressed person experiences. The manic's ego is huge and unrealistic. She believes she is the greatest, the best, the richest. Her ego seems to get harder and harder and less available to constructive criticism. In fact, if one actually got through to a manic and forced her to realize her true state, she might immediately plunge from a manic high to a depressed low. In my opinion, ego rigidity is the psychological basis of both mania and depression.

In general, mania sounds pretty crazy, but we can understand its psychology by remembering the nature of the mind. In Chapter 3, I explained that the average person has ten thoughts every minute. The average manic, on the other hand, probably has thirty thoughts every minute. The manic mind behaves the same way as the normal mind, but it is racing, full of desires, quests, and dreams. It is racing so fast that the manic can't implement any of her thoughts.

Where the spiritual person's mind becomes ever quieter and more one-pointed as a result of spiritual practice, the manic's mind becomes less peaceful and more scattered. In many ways, the manic and the spiritual aspirant are traveling in opposite directions. Where the normal person and the spiritual aspirant make plans that are appropriate to their dreams and talents, the manic's dreams are much greater than their talents. As a result, the manic fails in both secular and sacred pursuits. In order to reverse this downward spiral, the manic requires lithium to stabilize brain chemistry, and meditation to slow down the mind.

## BORDERLINE PERSONALITY DISORDER: WHEN SPIRIT AND MIND COLLIDE

If there is a hell on earth other than war, my patient Rosanne has lived there. Having undergone the torment of a tortured childhood, she carries that pain with her every day and every night, although she is now in her forties.

As a child, Rosanne was the victim of mental, physical, and sexual abuse. Home was not safe, and at age 14 she ran away and was kidnapped by a serial killer. During the year that he was holding Rosanne hostage, he murdered twenty people. Rosanne was raped and beaten daily. At the end of her year as a prisoner, Rosanne was sold into white slavery. At 15 she was a "high-class" Hollywood prostitute, owned by the Mafia.

Finally, at age 16, she managed to escape from her tormentor and retreated into the woods. There she lived for twenty years in deserted cabins, walking miles a day to fetch water from the river, living off the land. Her mountain friends were also refugees from society. At last she had some peace of mind.

When she moved back to the city, she couldn't cope very well. She fell apart emotionally and sometimes would go through twenty different moods in one day—from elation to suicidal depression, from rage to serenity. She went from one chaotic relationship to another, often with men who beat her and threatened to kill her. She could not stop herself from repeating the abuse with which she had grown up. She attempted to kill herself many times. Yet Rosanne is immensely gifted, a talented singer, writer, painter, and yoga instructor, and she has held many jobs. She is also tremendously intuitive.

Rosanne gets so overwhelmed by her emotions, however, that she is constantly acting out, constantly engaging in behaviors that temporarily relieve her anguish but undermine her safety and security. She comforts herself with alcohol, speed, or men. She can never seem to handle the basics of her life—food, clothing, and shelter. Her emotions, finances, housing, and relationships are always in a state of flux.

Rosanne suffers from borderline personality disorder. I regret having to use such an awful label—it doesn't sound like a real diagnosis—but I'm afraid we're stuck with it for now. Many patients who are neither neurotic nor psychotic but something in between are labeled borderline.

The first impression one has of a borderline personality may be that they are very depressed. A common mistake in psychiatry is to treat this depression with antidepressant medication. It rarely works. An important factor in distinguishing borderline personality from depression as such is the length of the depression. Borderlines usually feel that they have been depressed their entire life. It's not something they can compare to a time or a feeling of happiness. Depression is not an aberration for them—it's the baseline.

Rosanne's inner world is filled with all shades of emotion. She feels torn to pieces inside, as if she were standing at the edge of a great void and terrified of falling into the void. Her void is "wider than the Grand Canyon—and is a bottomless pit." She has many unpleasant mood states that simply don't have names. Patient and doctor often call all of that intense emotion "depression" for convenience's sake.

Although Rosanne does not get psychotic, other borderlines get just as psychotic as schizophrenics. The predominant feature of their psychosis is confusion and auditory and visual hallucinations. They tend to have visual hallucinations much more often than schizophrenics do, and they also tend to get frightened and paranoid more readily.

Unlike almost all schizophrenics, borderlines can appear quite normal and often can function quite normally. They may have terrifying episodes of depression, despair, suicide attempts, or psychosis, but when they are well, they may be able to feel well, look well, and perform adequately both in the working world and in relationships. They may sustain long-term relationships—but there is almost always a lot of chaos in those relationships.

Borderlines have "sliding states of consciousness." They readily go in and out of different states of consciousness. They can be depressed in the morning and elated in the evening. They can attempt suicide the next day. They can "slide" in many directions. They may slide into a state of psychosis that is similar to schizophrenia—and they may develop something that looks like mania. Or a panic disorder. There simply is no foundation to their personality, so they live as if they were in quicksand, constantly struggling to get out and constantly being dragged back into the mud.

Borderlines are the real "split personalities." They are fire and ice—Jekyll and Hyde. When they are good, they are very very good, and when they are bad, they are horrid. Their problem originates in childhood. Their parents would not love and accept them unconditionally, through good times and bad. When Rosanne was angry as a child, her parents despised her, so she "disowned" her anger, split it off, and tucked it into some corner of her mind—until it broke loose decades later. She didn't receive a healthy message, "I love you even when you're angry."

Unlike most schizophrenics, borderlines can be very psychic and can experience a wide range of supernormal states. The reason is that they have *permeable ego boundaries*. They don't seem to know where "they" stop and "other" people begin. So they are often open to the universe and receive information easily. Many of my borderline patients have had psychic experiences while I was with them—they knew the phone was about to ring—or they had a precognitive dream. They may have experiences of divine light into which they blissfully merge.

The downside to their openness, however, is that they are also terribly open to their own unconscious minds, and they can't seem to keep the flood of the unconscious from pouring over them. When Rosanne tells me that she sees auras around me and around many people, I believe her. When she tells me that she sees "entities" and "negative thought-forms" hanging out in the mental hospital or stuck on the walls, I believe her. And when she tells me that for two years as a mountain woman she was frequently in a state of samadhi or nirvana—I believe her. (In Chapter 10 you'll read about samadhi, or divine ecstasy—Rosanne fits those descriptions to the letter.)

Borderlines can be extremely difficult to work with because their anguish is so severe and they are so desperate and needy. The mental health professional usually perceives the borderline in one of two ways. The first is that the patient is like a black hole. No matter how much you give, they want more. In fact, if you don't set very clear limits with them, you will feel sucked dry. I don't mean this in any disparaging way. The second way is that the patient is like tar or taffy. While working with them, the psychiatrist feels stuck to them, and it doesn't usually feel good. If the psychiatrist is not aware of his own internal reactions, he is likely to be manipulated by the patient, or get angry, or reject them. But a psychiatrist who can simply be aware of how he feels in the presence of the patient, and simply observe that feeling, is in a position to diagnose accurately and be of service.

I personally enjoy working with Rosanne. I like her as a person, and I am not easily pulled into her borderline "split." In this "split," her inner battlefield is projected out into the world. For her, there are "good guys" and "bad guys." Frequently a borderline in a mental hospital will be adored by one nursing shift (say, the morning shift) but will be highly frustrating to the evening shift. A borderline will idealize one person and denigrate the next. The Rosannes of the world can drive their psychiatrist and everybody else crazy—in a hurry. But one can work with them by being very open, loving, compassionate, and nonjudgmental. At the same time, by setting very strict limits and boundaries, one can help them stabilize themselves. A borderline will test limits like a three-year-old trying to see what she can get away with—and the adult borderline can't help doing it any more than the three-year-old can.

Rosanne's complete diagnosis is extremely complex. Before I give you a quick rundown, let me add one more piece: She is absolutely exhausted. She's been exhausted for so long, she's forgotten that she's exhausted. She's so tired, she can't always concentrate or think straight. Not all borderlines are exhausted, but many suffer from a compromised immune system, which can lead to exhaustion. Rosanne's immune system is shot. Her muscles ache. She runs a low-grade fever. Her exhaustion makes it that much more difficult for her to maintain any mental or spiritual balance. She has a severe case of chronic fatigue syndrome.

Her physical suffering is so great that when I referred her for treatment with a chiropractor, Dr. Glenn Frieder, he told me that she "carried the suffering of at least ten people put together." Dr. Frieder also said to me, "There is something very special about this woman's energy. While working with her, I felt as if I were in some kind of energy field. It was really a good feeling. I worked on her for three hours, and at one point her psychic energy seemed to explode. It was as if the room lit up with her energy. Pretty weird for someone who is that sick and exhausted, don't you think?" I told Dr. Frieder that Rosanne has more psychic power than any professional psychic I know of and that I too have experienced dramatic energy shifts around her, as well as within myself, while working with her.

People are drawn to Rosanne. They sense something unique about her. People approach her out of the clear blue and ask, "Are you a psychic or something? Can you give me a reading?" Even in the mental hospital Rosanne is approached in this way. One of the nuns sat down with Rosanne every single day during her hospitalization and asked her for spiritual advice. Sister Ann would say, "Please, Rosanne, tell me what you know. You're the only person I can talk to about spirituality." Rosanne was happy to share her wisdom with Sister Ann, but I advised her to protect herself from the general public. "When someone asks you if you're a psychic, tell them 'No. I'm an artist.' And that's not a lie—you are an artist."

Every year or two in her life is so full of change and drama that it is as if she has lived twenty lifetimes already. Not all borderlines share Rosanne's complexity, but they do share her basic emotional makeup and her inner turmoil.

Rosanne's condition is an extreme case resulting from childhood abuse. Almost all of us, as children, suffered from a degree of abuse or neglect, either physical or psychological. We all experience an inner void from time to time; its depth depends on the severity of our abuse. Our addictions, our compulsions, our workaholic lifestyles often arise out of the void. Recognizing the void inside is part of the process of self-healing. We can all explore it in our imaginations. But we should do so only with the assistance of a mental health professional, who can help us as we "jump" into it or "climb" down the sides. Also, we should take God or a Higher Power along, because the void cannot be healed without faith and surrender to something greater than ourselves. There are not many black and white statements I make as a psychiatrist, but in my twenty years of working with the void, with abuse, I have come to know that the void can be healed only in a process where the spiritual focus is central.

Rosanne may sound as if she has little in common with the average person, but we can empathize with her better if we realize that the core of her problem is a lack of deep trust in herself and in others. Almost all of us know what it feels like to be betrayed by someone we love. A powerful emotional bond is severed, perhaps irreparably. The borderline experienced such a dramatic rupture in trust as a small child. Continued episodes of abuse or neglect deepened the lack of trust, until the void became a permanent internal state. It is very important to understand that the teen years are also critical to human development. An individual who enters the teen years on emotionally shaky ground can become emotionally strong if those years are filled with loving and trusting relationships. But if that shaky individual encounters a series of betrayals during the teen years, he or she may grow up to be a borderline. Therefore it is critical that society pay special attention to teenagers.

As adults, most of us can deal with breaches of trust. We can choose to avoid our betrayers or maintain a healthy physical and psychological distance from them. But on rare occasions, a "normal" adult who had a "normal" childhood develops a profound lack of trust in the world, like that of the borderline. That is the case with many Vietnam veterans. The death, destruction, dismemberment, and seeming meaninglessness of the war broke the spirit of many of our fighting men and women. Many surviving prisoners of war were tortured until they broke. But almost anybody can be broken emotionally. At the breaking point, we lose faith in ourselves, in others, and in God.

Perhaps saints are those who are able to resist the breaking effects of torture. Joan of Arc, inspired by the voice of God, became a valiant soldier for the French, handing the English one defeat after another at the end of the Hundred Years War. She had visions and heard voices, and she claimed that she took her directions directly from God. When the ecclesiastical court asked her about her "alleged" religious experiences, Joan replied, "The angels? Why, they often come among us. Others may not see them, but I do." Joan was not willing to retract her statements, even on pain of death. Found guilty of being a "heretic and idolater," Joan was sentenced to burn at the stake. On May 29, 1431, at the age of 19, she was burned to death. As she went up in flames, she prayed that God would forgive her tormentors. Five hundred years later, in 1920, she was canonized as Saint Joan of Arc.[3]

Almost all of us would have been emotionally broken by the experiences that Joan had to endure, but she died with a smile on her face and the name of Jesus on her lips. Like other great saints, Joan was moved by a profound trust in God and in her spiritual experience—a trust so great that renouncing her beliefs would have been more agonizing than physical pain. But where a great spiritual adept like Saint Joan follows the path of trust to the extreme, the borderline feels betrayed over and over again. This is not to say that a borderline cannot become a saint. But the borderline must overcome enormous doubts, fears, and feelings of mistrust in order to follow his or her heart.

Rosanne is an example of a person who is emotionally challenged and saintly at the same time. In order to understand better this complex individual, I have used the Psycho-Spiritual Assessment (PSA) with her on numerous occasions. I'll illustrate two PSAs, one that dealt with her visions, and another that dealt with more profound challenges.

In the first PSA, Rosanne's "main concern" was her visions—a genuine spiritual experience. She was seeing angels. She also had a host of paranormal experiences, involving clairvoyance, clairaudience, telepathy, and seeing auras and thought-forms.

When someone's main concern is a spiritual experience, it is helpful to clarify it in greater detail than one would for a nonspiritual problem. Did she experience the angel while in normal consciousness or while in an altered state of consciousness? I asked. In fact, many of Rosanne's paranormal phenomena occurred while she was in an altered state of consciousness—*samadhi,* healing trance, and out-of-body experiences.

For step two of this PSA, we assessed how Rosanne felt about her spiritual and paranormal experiences. She felt a mixture of peace, love, and even ecstasy—along with fear. She was afraid of her abilities because when people sensed that she had psychic powers, they would bombard her with questions. Even in the psychiatric hospital, patients and staff alike frequently asked Rosanne for spiritual and psychic advice. She gave too much of herself and found herself depleted rather than energized by her hospital stays.

For step three of this PSA, we assessed how Rosanne's experiences affected her belief systems or sense of meaning in life. At a profound level, they gave her an ongoing sense of divine connectedness, as if she were being guided through her mental and physical suffering. In fact, shortly after we met, Rosanne confided to me that one week prior to our first meeting, she had prayed intensely that she would find someone who could help her along her spiritual path. Her random discovery of a spiritual psychiatrist, she felt, was a direct answer to her prayers. Of course, I served only as a guide, and not a guru. During the course of her psychotherapy, however, she found her true spiritual guru.

Once we had completed this PSA, we proceeded with action steps that acknowledged the validity of her spiritual and paranormal experiences. My main task was to help Rosanne set limits on others so that they would not drain her. I taught her how to create a "force-field" around herself. To her amazement, once she put up the force-field, people would approach her, then seem to bump into a wall about ten feet away from her and walk away. I also taught her an imagery technique called "the figure eight," in which she pictured others with a golden circle around them. This technique helped Rosanne clarify her own boundaries and dramatically slowed down the energy drain she had previously been experiencing.

Far more significant than the spiritual and paranormal phenomena were Rosanne's mood swings, mental confusion, physical exhaustion, and pain. Here's how the PSA for these problems came out:

1. Rosanne's *main concern* were her serious mental and physical problems, which were caused by childhood abuse and by chronic fatigue syndrome with fibromyalgia.

2. She *felt* terrified of and overwhelmed by the great number of her problems, as well as by their intensity. The pain alone devastated her life. The extent of her mental and physical suffering would have been enough to provoke many others into suicide. Lack of money was an additional problem, for it is almost impossible to recover from chronic fatigue syndrome without spending hundreds of dollars a month on nutritional supplements. Rosanne was on welfare.

3. Rosanne's serious mental and physical problems held great *meaning* for her. One of the great spiritual lessons she learned was simply to hang on for dear life. But she was also able to find a specific meaning in each catastrophe, and she managed to keep going because she felt that life had a purpose. Even in her darkest hours, she remembered God and prayed that she could better surrender. Another great lesson from her illness was forgiveness. Rosanne was actually able to find meaning in those years of mental and physical torture at the hands of her kidnapper. Even if she didn't fully understand why she had had to suffer so greatly, she believed that God knew why.

For her mental and physical problems, my treatment plan involved physical, mental, and spiritual exercises. The physical steps included nutritional supplementation, medication, chiropractic treatment, and breath techniques to help quiet the anxiety. The strategies aimed at alleviating her mental suffering included finding a structured spiritual living arrangement, continuing her psychotherapy, practicing imagery and meditation techniques, and chanting a variety of mantras. The spiritual steps included reading sacred texts, attending religious services, and praying fervently.

One of the main action steps we undertook was a thorough exploration of the void. In this guided imagery technique, one "jumps into the abyss" while "holding the hand of God." We worked on the void for

months, with the result that her inner emptiness became filled by feelings
of peace and love.

## MULTIPLE PERSONALITY DISORDER:
## WHEN DIVIDING IS SURVIVING

Multiple personality disorder (MPD) is actually a severe form of borderline personality disorder. Where severe abuse and neglect in childhood give
rise to borderline personality disorder, the trauma that gives rise to MPD
is nothing short of true torture.

Like borderlines, multiples often experience a host of mystical and
paranormal states—depending upon which subpersonality is the active
one. When my patient Ann was crazy, she was very, very crazy. But some
of her forty-five personalities were balanced, intuitive, creative, and psychic. And yes, some of these personalities can experience mystical bliss.

Multiples experience another amazing phenomenon: Their different
subpersonalities can have different physiologies. One personality can have
full-blown diabetes mellitus, while another is completely free of diabetes.
This incredible example is proof of the reality of the mind-body. Subpersonalities are not only different mental states, they are truly separate
mind-body states.

MPD is very rare. The only reason I am including it in this book at
all is because so many people ask "What's wrong with me? Is this just a
memory of abuse? Do I have multiple personality?" I want to show you
that, whatever is going on in your life, the chances that you suffer from
MPD are almost zero. Some professionals don't believe that MPD exists.

I have worked with only two true MPDs in my life, but there was
no question in my mind from the first time I met with Ann that she was
one. She was admitted to a psychiatric hospital after having been instructed by one of her multiples that she was going to the hospital for a
union of the multiples.

Hers is not a story of successful therapy. Rather, it's a tale of one
woman's incredible ability to survive psychological and physical torture.
The only way she had been able to survive was to create multiple personalities—more than forty-five of them.

During our initial session and during the half year that I worked with
her, I saw her subpersonalities come and go in a flash. She could be coherent one minute, then furious the next. She would get very angry one
moment and ask, "Why did you call me Ann? My name is Mary." Sud-

denly, she would plop herself on the floor and become five-year-old Jenny—cute, smiling, and innocent.

Ann, now in her late forties, didn't realize she had MPD until about ten years ago. Slowly, the memories of her trauma had been coming back to her, and she had identified one personality after another. She keeps a three-ring binder with a section for each of her personalities. Each section includes a diary of that personality, a personal history. Each personality has relationships with different people. One personality acts "normal" in public. Another has a boyfriend. Each personality has a different voice, a different gait, a different posture, and different handwriting.

What stunned me most was Ann's inner landscape. She lives in a three-dimensional world of her own making, inside her head. I learned about it from using guided imagery with her. I had been trying a variety of techniques to facilitate the expression of each personality and ultimately to integrate them into one solid person. I asked Ann to select a mantra that had meaning for her, and then I asked her to close her eyes and imagine that she was sitting at the center of a large circle. I asked her to invite her subpersonalities into the circle, one at a time, and teach each one the mantra. My hope was to have all the personalities chanting the same mantra at the same time. In fact, about ten of them entered the circle and joined in the process.

Then Ann stunned me by saying, "Oh, Beater-Killer is stuck in the pipes." Discussion of this remark revealed an imaginary inner world, with a well-structured inner landscape, where Ann "lived." Her different personalities lived in different parts of the landscape.

I asked Ann to draw a picture of this inner landscape. As she gazed into the distance, she described a barren area, a no-man's land, that stretched for two or three miles. Beyond that were huge panes of glass— "flexible, organic glass, almost like skin"—that some of the multiples could penetrate. Beyond, a huge desert stretched for miles—and then there was the Wall, which was "high as a castle." Giant ropes were part of the Wall—and some of the "alters" could emerge through the ropes. Then came another desert. Then came a complex system of underground pipes. One pipe led to the forest—a place where the friendlier multiples "lived." Another pipe led to a series of buildings. There were blocks of land, interspersed with rivers and lakes. The far reaches of Ann's landscape included: the Jungle, Quicksand, Hades River, Mirror Walk, the Labyrinth, the Dormitory, and the Mausoleum. When I asked her what lay beyond all of that, she would always grow silent and depressed and would say no more.

It was astonishing that anyone could have such a well-developed inner landscape. It was as if she *lived* in those deserts, walls, forests, and rivers. Her imagery never went away, and it was completely real to her. Equally fascinating was the fact that within her landscape she could still practice the guided imagery techniques that I introduced. Most of us bring up images on a blank, inner screen, but Ann brought them into her existing landscape. One could not alter her inner landscape, any more than one could make a real lake appear or disappear.

When Ann was in the hospital (which she was many times, while she was under my care), she was extremely lucid about her inner world. She was able to remember the real torture that caused her agonized existence and was able to tell me which of her multiples was active at a particular moment. But when she was in my office, she was always terribly frightened, and I had little access to the multiples except by observing her extraordinary personality changes. Apparently the structure and safety of the hospital allowed her to feel secure enough to share her inner world. Outside that safety, she fought for survival on a daily basis, driven by her multiples but unaware of their activity, hardly aware of her sudden and dramatic personality changes.

Here's an example of such a change. One day she came into my office looking depressed, hunched over, and anxious, as usual. After we talked for a few minutes, she noticed the Kermit the Frog on my desk. She picked up Kermit, then sat on the floor and instantly became a five-year-old personality. She laughed, giggled, and had a good time with Kermit. Slowly she "traveled" through several other personalities. When she became more adult, she wondered how a frog had ended up in her hands. At the end of the session, I asked Ann to put Kermit back where she had found him. She looked around the room, bewildered, then put Kermit on the floor beside her. She had virtually no recall of how, when, or where she had found the toy. Many of her multiples simply had no communication with other parts of herself.

For someone so fragmented, Ann could do some astonishing things. One day she arrived at my office having absolutely no idea who or where she'd been for the past forty-eight hours. She had taken a long bus ride to get to my office, but only when she got off the bus in San Diego had she realized that she was coming to her appointment with me. On another day she brought in a tape recording of a song she had written and recorded in a small home recording studio. One personality had written the lyrics, another the melody. She had recorded the song by playing a keyboard and singing at the same time. One personality played the keyboard, and another handled the engineering of the equipment. When I asked her who sang, she said, "Oh I guess I do the singing—except I can't hear myself sing at all. I have to play back the tape to hear what it sounds like." Her songs are amazing. She also draws and paints, creating astonishing works of art. But most of the time she just gets by. She often gets lost in the small community in which she lives. The police know her and will pick her up and take her back home. She has attempted suicide many times.

What keeps her going? "If I kill myself, it will be a victory for those horrible people." What horrible people? Her father, grandfather, brothers, and friends of her brothers. What did they do to Ann? I will not write about this—for the protection of you, the reader. The gruesome details of her years of torture, as she told me about them, are emblazoned on my mind. Even the pain of listening to her describe them is almost unbearable—I can't imagine what it must have been like to live with those memories every day.

An image has to be pretty powerful for a therapist to be traumatized from hearing about it. Ann's images are an awesome and terrible force for her. Her multiples arose very early in her life, to help her keep some sanity—multiples that hold the memory, that do battle with each other, that hold the rage, the guilt—the joy and creativity.

I am no longer seeing Ann. When I made the commitment to work with her, I knew it would last at least ten years. I don't know why she stopped coming. She didn't kill herself, and I hope and pray that something from the work we did will help ease her pain. Life is indeed strange. It is inexplicable why terrible things happen to good people. Ann is a good person, a kind and absolutely brilliant person. A person who once held jobs and sang in bands even while the multiples were splitting her apart.

Although I said that this story doesn't have a happy ending, that's not entirely true. From my own perspective, I would have liked to see Ann improve more. But she did have one joyous and momentous experience shortly before she left therapy. She visited New Mexico for her son's wedding—an event that was very scary for her because her childhood tormentors were going to be there. Not only did she handle the situation well, but she had some very good fortune. Her daughter-in-law is Native American, so there were two weddings—one Western style and one Native American style. After the Indian wedding there was a special ceremony to which Ann was invited—a rarity for a white man or woman. In fact, it was the first time it had happened with this tribe. A lot of attention was focused on Ann at this ceremony, enough that it made her quite uncomfortable. To her astonishment, she learned that this ceremony was in her honor, as the mother of the groom. A number of rituals were performed, and Ann was made a formal member of the tribe and of the family into which her son had married. She was overjoyed and came back to California literally with a new family—a functional, loving family.

Shortly after her return, Ann asked to be hospitalized again because she was becoming suicidal. But her new family remains for her. She has been drawn into a circle, a tribe of people who love and accept her.

I wish her well on her journey, and I hope that her beautiful new outer landscape will slowly dissolve the inner landscape that has been both her protection and her prison.

Many of us "normal" folks have a variety of sides to our personality. We can be happy, sad, angry, jealous, compassionate, greedy, and joyous all in one day. This normal variety of mood changes is nothing like multiple personality disorder. What the average person experiences is much less severe than what the borderline personality experiences, and what the borderline experiences is much less severe than what the multiple personality experiences.

## 9

# WHEN THE SPIRIT
# CAN HELP THE MIND

It is most unlikely that you suffer from the mental illnesses that you've just read about. It is far more likely that you, like most of us in the West, get depressed or anxious from time to time, or are stressed out and overworked, or are in emotional pain about some real-life loss, such as divorce, loss of a job, or death of a loved one.

For some of us, the small depressions can accumulate into a big, incapacitating depression. And the everyday wear and tear, the stress of modern life, can lead to a more severe anxiety disorder if not handled properly. While psychiatry can treat both depression and anxiety with a variety of medications, mind-body techniques and spiritual approaches can alleviate or eliminate them as well. By asking the deeper spiritual questions and seeking spiritual solutions, you can discover and heal the real heart of the matter, the source of the problem.

## DEPRESSION: WHEN THE PAST WON'T LET GO

Paul is an extremely successful priest, well respected in his community, a spiritual powerhouse. But when his energy fizzled out, he came to me, at the suggestion of the Mercy Hospital chaplaincy service. Affable, lovable, brilliant Paul had plunged into a depression on the anniversary of his father's death. It was also the anniversary of his own diagnosis of osteosarcoma (bone cancer), from which he had fully recovered. He had just completed an important and lengthy job assignment, and now he felt a big letdown. It wasn't the first time he had been seriously depressed; it had happened twice before.

Paul felt like a slug: slow-moving, tired, exhausted, and listless. As he came into my office, he shuffled his feet across the floor. He spoke slowly. He spoke of an "emotional heaviness," a huge weight on his shoulders. He was despairing, both helpless and hopeless. He was doubting everything—even his worth as a priest. "Maybe I'm just not cut out to be a priest anymore. I'm no good. I can't concentrate. I can't make decisions. I'm all washed up. I'm worthless. I don't want to disgrace my church, my parish." Because he was very depressed, he could no longer work his usual eighteen-hour days—giving mass and communion, performing weddings and funerals; visiting his parishioners in their homes; taking care of emergencies in the lives of literally thousands of people.

Although it was hard for him to tell his story, I could tell, even from our first meeting, that Paul had nothing to be ashamed of. I was convinced that he was a very good man and a superb priest. At the end of our first session, I tried to make two things very clear to him. I assured him he could be helped—and I told him point-blank, "Paul, you *are* a priest, a good one. Being a priest is your life. You're not at all confused about that. You have never had any other desire than to serve your community as a priest, and you still have no other desire. *You* are a *priest*." We shook hands. He looked me in the eyes, mustered a smile, and said, "Yeah, I am a priest. Thanks, doc. I really needed to hear that."

Fifty percent of Americans will experience at least one very serious clinical depression in their life, similar to Paul's episode. Depression is caused by inner and outer stresses, by genetics, by brain chemistry, even by the amount of sunlight we get. Paul was not a victim of a "bad childhood," or bad mothering or fathering. He loved and respected his parents. They were the salt of the earth and, like their son, brilliant. But some of the stresses in Paul's life needed to be fully worked through, lest they combine to make for some bad brain chemistry. And Paul had the genes for depression—they ran in his family.

The neurochemical basis of clinical depression is the neurotransmitters, the chemicals in our brain that allow one nerve cell to communicate with the next one. There are numerous neurotransmitters, but the most common are serotonin, the catecholamines (which include norepinephrine), acetylcholine, and GABA. When there is not enough of these chemicals in our brain, we become depressed.

I prefer to rebalance brain chemistry using the least drastic means possible. In Paul's case, I started with amino acids. When I performed amino acid testing on Paul, I found him to be deficient in tyrosine and phenylalanine—amino acids that turn into norepinephrine in the brain. But amino acids work slowly, and Paul grew impatient with them. So I started him on Prozac. He continued to get more deeply depressed, however, and so at his own request, I hospitalized him. For this kind of clinical depression, it's important to break the descent as early as possible, because once the depression "sets," the person believes his situation is absolutely hopeless, and the risk of suicide is high—it must be treated as aggressively as the risk of heart failure after a heart attack.

Upon admission, Paul requested treatment with ECT (electroconvulsive therapy). ECT has been much maligned by Hollywood, and I am not a big fan of it, but it does have its place. In the past, Paul had received acupuncture treatment for pain, and he had responded well to it. In his mind he found a connection between ECT and acupuncture, feeling that both boosted his electricity. After only two treatments with ECT, Paul began to recover. After six treatments he left the hospital and continued to improve steadily thereafter.

Paul is a "normal" American, with a normal, if severe, depression. After his release, he felt whole again rather quickly. His thinking cleared up. He regained his hopeful, cheerful, and inspiring attitude. I taught him to use a mantra: *Jesus Christ.*

I never shared with him anything about my personal spiritual path, but we talked about God a great deal, and about the spiritual meaning of his illness. Paul did, in fact, learn deep spiritual lessons from it. He became much more balanced after his depression than he had been before. We talked about love, service, and forgiveness, and I did my best to help Paul grow closer to Jesus.

Paul's illness seemed more than a biochemical abnormality. It seemed more like a confluence of environmental, psychological, and biological factors. We took a broad look at his life, from the moment he woke up until he fell asleep. And I got a picture of a man who had not set proper boundaries in his life. He had been available to his community twenty-four hours a day. I convinced him that even with his normally huge levels of energy, he still had to learn some limitations. So he stopped taking phone calls after nine P.M. He stopped doing work that he could delegate. He gave up doing things that drained him and that he did not find meaningful. I discovered that he did not eat breakfast but began eating heavily around lunchtime, ate through the afternoon, and then ate double and triple por-

tions for dinner. I suggested that he eat breakfast and cut down on the huge
dinners. "You need to fuel your engine on a more steady and regular basis.
This is part of the problem you've been having. You're plunging into a full
schedule with no fuel in your system." Paul corrected all that, and his energy grew stronger.

Perhaps eight months after he had been hospitalized, we uncovered
a spiritual cause of his depression. Paul had gone to a mountain retreat
for a week, during which period he had contemplated the pain and anguish of two of his parishioners—a couple who were about to give birth
to an anencephalic baby, a baby with no brain. Because their emotional
pain was so great, Paul prayed intensely during his week of contempla-
tion, "Oh, Lord, their pain is so great. Please let me take on some of their
pain." When Paul returned, he went to visit the couple, who by now had
given birth to the child. Mercifully, it had died after six hours. Before he
left their house, Paul felt the first wave of the depression, which grew into
a tidal wave.

When he told me this part of the story, I replied, "Well, you see,
your depression does go much further than just an imbalance of neurotransmitters. You actually got what you prayed for. You took on some of
their pain, some of their illness. You'd better be more careful what you
pray for."

Paul pondered my words for a minute. "You're right. I did take on
their pain—and their baby's pain." The insight sank deep into him. He
began to see the bigger picture. His illness wasn't just an illness. It was
part of his spiritual journey—and it actually *was* the answer to his deepest prayers. He had traveled from darkness back into the light. A few weeks
after he and I discovered the spiritual roots of his depression, he received
a card from the couple he had prayed for. The card, which was mailed on
the anniversary of their child's birth—and death—expressed their gratitude to Paul. They were grateful not only because of his loving care during their time of grief, but also because they believed that he had taken on
their suffering.

Paul's depression was clinical—and as such it was very different
from the feelings experienced by someone on a spiritual path. Although
Paul's depression may have been caused, at least in part, by his loving and
meaningful act, the depression itself took him further and further away
from meaning. In fact, as his disorder progressed, life seemed to become
utterly futile and meaningless. The person who is making slow, steady spiritual progress, on the other hand, gains more and more meaning in life.
In fact, even those things that previously had seemed meaningless or ir-

relevant—such as stopping to smell a rose or watching the sunset—become more precious and meaningful. To the person who is evolving spiritually, the little things in life become treasures and joys, but they lose all meaning to the depressed person and feel like a burden.

After I had helped correct Paul's brain chemistry, set limits on his accessibility, and changed his diet, I did a complete body-mind-spirit diagnosis. Paul's physical diagnosis of "history of bone cancer," and his mental diagnosis of "major depression," gave us the information we needed to get started. It took some time to flesh out his spiritual diagnosis and to complete his Psycho-Spiritual Assessment.

We worked with the three questions in the PSA, which dramatically accelerated his recovery. Let's review his PSA.

1. Paul's *main concern,* at the time I met him, was a profound, painful feeling of depression. Although he was clairvoyant and could go into healing trances to help his parishioners, these phenomena were not his main concerns during the time I worked with him.

2. Paul *felt* terrified about his depression. He was afraid that his life would be ruined and that he would remain depressed forever. He felt hopeless and helpless.

3. Paul's "sympathetic suffering" (taking on the pain of his parishioners) helped him realize that his depression had *meaning* beyond a biological disorder. He felt that it was triggered, at least in part, by prayers that actually were answered. He had prayed that he could take on the suffering of his parishioners, and he did.

Traditional psychiatry believes that abnormal brain chemistry can explain every aspect of major depression, but I disagree. I believe that each kind of personality is prone to a particular kind of suffering and a particular kind of mental illness. Some of us are prone to depression, others to anxiety. The combination of brain chemistry and a depression-prone personality is the cause of depression.

From a spiritual standpoint, the depressed person's ego is being harshly confronted by real-world reality and is being chiseled away. Paul suffered from this, what I call *ego deflation.* The good news about ego deflation is that each time we pass through the chiseling process, we have less ego, and, as a result, we become better able to resist depression.

Although the spiritual process of ego deflation can be painful, it should be openly embraced. Every one of us is faced with ego deflation on a regular basis, and so it behooves us to develop a strategy for dealing with it. Like everyone else, I have experienced innumerable instances of ego deflation. One powerful instance happened in 1976, when I auditioned to study with classical guitarist Celin Romero. I played "Romance," a classical guitar piece that I had practiced for ten years. I had played no more than fifteen seconds when Celin interrupted me, leaned back in his chair, and said, "I will teach you under two conditions. First, you must give up everything you ever knew about how to play the guitar, and second, you'll have to practice a half hour a day." The second request was an easy one, but giving up everything I knew about guitar was shocking. Still, I knew I was dealing with a world-class master of guitar, and I agreed to his terms after only a few seconds. The ego deflation was swift in this case, and I totally surrendered to Celin. Over the following few years, I was privileged to be taught by one of the greatest music instructors in the world.

Many people become depressed after receiving constructive criticism. Although we prefer to be praised most or all of the time, those who offer genuine criticism are our real friends and helpers.

The concept of ego deflation helped me make a more complete diagnosis of Paul's depression. His abnormal brain chemistry had not only biological and mental causes, it also had a spiritual cause, a spiritual component, a spiritual meaning, and a cure that involved spiritual practices. When we focused on action steps, Paul decided he would never again pray to take on another's suffering. He made a conscious switch in attitude, from fearing ego deflation to welcoming constructive criticism. He had weathered the storm, his ego had been chiseled down, and he was much happier than he was before he became severely depressed. Before I met Paul, he believed he "could do it all," working eighteen hours a day, and being available to his parishioners twenty-four hours a day. This was an unrealistic belief, based on an inflated ego. He took this "ego-deflation" well and made the necessary changes in his life, giving up the idea of being "superhuman."

Later Paul wanted help with other secular and sacred issues. He wanted help with a host of "secular" problems, such as losing weight, boosting his energy, dealing with difficult staff members, taming his temper, and charting a long-term career vision. His "sacred" issues included his desire to deepen his faith, learning to surrender to God more completely, and learning how to serve more selflessly in his capacity as priest. I asked him to picture God in the room with him and to connect with Him at the deepest level he could imagine—and then at an even deeper level.

We did guided imagery work in which I asked him to imagine himself walking up to a cathedral that had five pillars in front. On each pillar was engraved the name of one of the five core human values (truth, right action, peace, love, nonviolence). I asked Paul to meditate on the five pillars and then "walk" into the cathedral. Once he was seeing himself inside the cathedral, I asked him which human value he needed more of in his life. "Nonviolence," Paul replied. "Sometimes I feel a little edge of anger behind my own words, and I'd like to work on that."

"Okay, Paul. Simply allow nonviolence to pour into you. Imagine that the cathedral is an embodiment of nonviolence. Imagine that nonviolence is a kind of energy, and then allow that energy to fill you up."

During another session, in which Paul was troubled and worried, I asked Paul which passages from the Bible were most relevant to his current main concern. He replied, " 'Therefore I say to you, do not worry about your life, what you will eat or what you will drink; nor about your body, what you will put on.' 'Look at the birds of the air, for they neither sow nor reap nor gather into barns; yet your heavenly Father feeds them. Are you not of more value than they?' 'Consider the lilies of the field, how they grow. They neither toil nor spin.' 'Now if God so clothes the grass of the field, which today is, and tomorrow is thrown into the oven, will He not much more clothe you, O you of little faith?' 'Therefore, do not worry.' "

I asked Paul to picture himself among the lilies of the field, and feel the serenity of that scene. "Notice how well-cared-for the lilies are, how the Lord provides for them. And then allow yourself to feel the same kind of care. Allow yourself to deeply experience a sense of peace. There is no room for worry," I said.

Over and over again, Paul and I used Psycho-Spiritual Assessment to help him understand what he was experiencing, how he felt about it, and what it meant, so that we could figure out what to do about it.

Science has begun to understand the mind-body connection only in the past decade. Physical illness affects the mind, and mental illness affects the body. Spiritual illness affects both mind and body. Paul's brain chemistry was way out of balance; others with depression may have more of a psychological imbalance. When psychiatrists can diagnose problems of body, mind, energy, and spirit, they will better be able to treat their patients with approaches that are physical, mental, energetic, and spiritual.

Here is a powerful spiritual technique, which I have found to be very effective in treating depression:

## SMILING BUDDHA
### Mental Fitness Technique

*Human values fostered by this technique: Love and Peace*

> *Picture your chosen form of God (Jesus, Buddha,*
> *Krishna) and imagine that He is very happy. He is smiling,*
> *radiant, and overjoyed. He is happy with you.*

That's all there is to it. Depressed people often experience God as a critical, elderly, guilt-inducing patriarchal figure. By simply imagining that God is happy and smiling, and is with you, all aspects of depression can be alleviated, including the biological and psychological symptoms.

## ANXIETY DISORDERS:
## WHEN THE FUTURE TAKES OVER

Caroline's life was being ruined by one powerful emotion—panic. On two separate occasions she had gotten stuck in elevators. Not just stuck—on one of these occasions the elevator had gone into free fall for several stories. A decade later, she still had not recovered from the experience but had become even more terrified of elevators—and other enclosed spaces, such as subways and airplanes. She suffered from the anxiety disorder called claustrophobia, which, in the early days of psychiatry, would have been called a neurosis.

The panic Caroline experienced in elevators was crippling. Her heart would race and pound so hard, it felt as if it were going to "jump right out of her skin," as she put it. She would sweat profusely, shake, tremble, grow short of breath, and come close to fainting. She would have a sense of impending doom, feeling that she surely was going to die on the spot. She would feel so overwhelmed, she was afraid she was going insane.

For years she completely avoided elevators, refusing to enter any building more than one story high. As the owner of a successful jewelry store, this self-imposed limitation caused her some difficulties—but she was able to work around them. Her physical problems (rheumatoid arthritis with chronic pain, and generalized candidiasis with mood swings) made it harder to cope with her anxiety and added to the intensity of her panic.

Caroline weighed about 250 pounds and stood five-foot-four, but she was an attractive woman, always stylishly dressed, in keeping with her professional image as a jeweler. One day her doctor told her that she required surgery for an umbilical hernia and a large benign tumor. She was terrified both of the surgery and of the elevator she would have to take to get to the operating room. She kept postponing the surgery because of her anxiety, but she knew she had to have the operation soon, because her health insurance was going to be switched to a new company, and the new company might not approve her elective surgery. Fearful of this possibility, she grew more and more panicky. Finally she realized she could no longer delay and scheduled the surgery right away, while her insurance would still pay for it. That was when she called me for help.

I said to her, "You have two big issues here that you need to look at separately. One is your fear of elevators. The other is your fear of surgery." Caroline was very anxious about the surgery, afraid that she would die on the table or experience terrible problems with recovery. "Caroline, you need the surgery. Tell your doctor you insist on having your surgery in a hospital that has an operating room on the first floor. That way you can focus on the surgery, and we can deal with your fear of elevators at a later date. If your surgeon won't or can't comply with this request, get another surgeon. It's that simple."

That piece of advice was liberating for her. Her surgeon was able to obtain temporary privileges at a suitable hospital. To help her get through surgery, I worked with Caroline using a combination of meditation, relaxation, and guided imagery techniques.

"Caroline, your fear of surgery is a spiritual issue," I told her. "I'll explain that in a minute, but first tell me about your faith." She replied that she loved God deeply and trusted him completely, and she said that deepening her spiritual life was a prime goal for her.

"This is an issue of trust and surrender," I explained. "Once you've done everything you can do, you have to surrender. You've decided on the best surgeon. You've decided on the best anesthesiologist and the best hospital. There's nothing more to decide, and nothing more to do. You just need to leap into the void and trust God. Trust that God will work through the surgeon. Trust that the situation is now beyond your control and must be surrendered to. You see, I don't believe you fully trust that God is going to be there for you. We could talk about how your brain chemistry makes you anxious, and we could continue working on imagery and relaxation. But the bottom line here is much deeper."

Caroline began to cry. "Maybe God is just too busy to listen to me." She paused. "Do you believe in reincarnation?"

"Yes, I do. Why do you ask?"

"I have an actual memory of being Jewish in a past life. I was be-headed. God wasn't there for me. Maybe he's not there for me now."

I encouraged her to express her fear, her disappointment, her lack of trust, and her anger toward God. I asked her to picture God in what-ever form He presented Himself and to share all her feelings. "Tell God how you feel. If He can't take it, he's not God!"

I told Caroline that her primary spiritual diagnosis was "crisis in faith," and for several weeks we worked on faith. I taught Caroline a mantra, *God the Father*, as well pre-operative imagery techniques.

Caroline let the hospital staff know about her claustrophobia, and virtually everyone she came in contact with treated her with love, respect, and understanding. After her pre-op visit to the hospital, the director of nursing called her on the phone, asking if they had made her feel com-fortable—and if there was anything further they could do to make her surgery go even more smoothly. Her anesthesiologist was an "angel." "He put my mind completely at ease," she said. "Even when they took me for an EKG [electrocardiogram], the staff was concerned about my claustrophobia. They asked me if they could close the door or not during the EKG. It was just incredible."

The night before surgery Caroline was very jittery, so she practiced the pre-op imagery techniques I taught her and meditated using her mantra. The morning of surgery, she was so calm that her serenity star-tled her anesthesiologist.

The operation was performed with a local anesthetic, so Caroline was awake the entire time. The surgeon offered to play music she liked—Pavarotti. Throughout the operation she silently chanted her mantra, keeping herself calm and centered.

When the surgery was over, it was more than just "over." It was a real success for her. It was a healing experience, a coming together of the best of Western medicine—a good surgeon, a good anesthesiologist, com-passionate and competent nurses. "God was really with me all the way—but Dr. Gersten, I couldn't have made it without the mantra."

Caroline's panic disorder had physical, mental, and spiritual com-ponents. There are many angles from which a doctor could look at her situation, and each would lead the doctor toward a different treatment. Here's what gave me my view of her mindscape. Her predisposition to anx-iety could have originated either in her past life, when she was "beheaded," or in her childhood, in situations where she felt abandoned, betrayed, or trapped. The fear slowly rose to the surface in her late teens, when she first noticed a slight discomfort in elevators, and then became fully conscious after her two traumatic events in elevators. Her physical problems (rheumatoid arthritis, chronic pain, and generalized candidiasis) contributed to "anxiety physiology," to a brain predisposed to panic. Caroline's system was easily triggered into a massive adrenaline rush—a severe fight-or-flight physiology. In my opinion, the adrenaline rush was not the ultimate cause of her suffering but rather was triggered by a combination of psychological, physical, and spiritual factors. In effect, Caroline's brain and mind were driving each other crazy.

Surgery confronted her with her crisis in faith, a fear that God would abandon her, bringing a spiritual dimension to her anxiety. In fact, I believe that her crisis in faith was the main cause of her anxiety. Surviving the surgery was a healing for her—a healing of body, mind, and spirit, a renewal of faith.

Anxiety, with its spiritual cause, a crisis in faith, is so much a product of Western civilization that many of us take it for granted—and most of us experience anxiety from time to time. Most of us don't need medication for it. We need meditation. Anxiety arises out of a failure to live in the moment. It exists because most of us think far too much about the future and about things over which we have no control. Most of us can alleviate our anxiety by becoming aware of these causes, by bringing our attention back to the present. Practicing meditation can anchor us more firmly in the present, be it Mantra Meditation or all-day mindfulness meditation, in which one pays attention to each bite of food one takes, each step one takes, each breath one inhales.

Anxiety is further alleviated by surrendering to God as one understands Him, and by realizing that anxiety, from a spiritual standpoint, is a crisis in faith. Ask yourself what you don't trust about God, and then have a heart-to-heart talk with Him. Many of us believe that we must first have spiritual experiences before we can have faith, but the opposite is often true. Make a leap of faith, and spiritual experiences will follow. Making a conscious effort to develop faith will diminish anxiety.

A severe mental illness, such as schizophrenia, is extremely unlikely to occur in a highly advanced spiritual adept. But we all experience anxiety to one degree or another. A person with anxiety disorder may find that a specific type of anxiety is fixed in the mind and returned to over and over again, but the mind of the spiritual aspirant passes over annoying experiences. The person who suffers with anxiety—or panic disorder, as Caroline did—finds it impossible to stop replaying the frightening scene in her mind. She simply doesn't know how to escape the mental prison in which she finds herself.

The anxious person and the spiritual aspirant also handle stress differently. Suppose you're an anxious person, and your work space is small and cramped. Far too many people walk in and out of it. If you're claustrophobic like Caroline, that small work space will drive you crazy. You'll keep saying to yourself, "I wish this were larger. I feel as if I'm going to explode. I wish my boss would do something. I wish people would leave me alone." The spiritual aspirant, on the other hand, would see the cramped work space as a lesson to be overcome. She might, as a result of that attitude, turn that small work space into a small temple. She might place a flower on her desk, along with a picture of a saint. She would say to herself, "I know that God wouldn't give me more than I can handle. I'm here, so I must be able to handle it." Given a choice between worrying and creating a temple, it's obvious which one makes for a happier life, happier work, and even more productive work. The spiritual aspirant rarely feels trapped, for she realizes that obstacles are only lessons. Caroline's therapy involved helping her act more like a spiritual aspirant and less like a prisoner of her own mind.

In my own personal life, I have learned some important lessons about anxiety and fear, and I have shared those insights with Caroline and others with panic disorder. Although fear makes us want to run away from whatever is scaring us, it actually holds a key to our power. My biggest fear was once stage fright. Public speaking terrified me, as it does most Americans. After I completed my psychiatric training, I thought I'd never be "trapped" into doing it again. But several years later, one of the psychiatric hospitals in which I was working asked me to give a lecture to the staff, on any subject I chose. I refused, but I was told I had no choice: "Give a talk, or we'll kick you off the staff!" The six weeks leading up to that presentation were anxious ones for me. When the talk was over, I joined Toastmasters, a public-speaking organization, so that I could come to grips with this panic that was limiting what I could do in life.

For well over a year, I continued to feel nervous about public speaking, even at Toastmasters. After several years, however, I overcame the fear and grew to love it. I've been speaking in public now for years. Interestingly, in all that time, the beeper that I always carry with me has never once gone off during a presentation. But on at least ten occasions, it has gone off at the exact moment when I've concluded. It feels like a divine reward, as if, having faced the fear, I am more deeply connected with a higher reality.

I've shared this experience with many patients, so that they might appreciate that their fear is actually a window to their power. By finding a way to face the fear, they can get through it, and by getting through it, they will be transformed for the better.

Finally, remember that if you are experiencing panic like Caroline's, you are not going crazy. Panic is not insanity. It is immense suffering, triggered by biological and psychological factors, and it can be healed.

Now let's look at some mental fitness techniques that all of us can use in order to relax.

## LEARNING TO RELAX
### Mental Fitness Technique

*Human value fostered by this technique: Peace*

In order to learn to relax, I recommend you practice two techniques. First, do Mantra Meditation or some other form of meditation. And second, follow that meditation with one of the following imagery techniques. If stress is a big problem for you—as it is for most of us—I strongly advise that you practice all four of them. Then you can select the one that best suits you.

1.   THE FEATHER

*Imagine you are a feather floating in the air high above the earth. You become more and more relaxed as you slowly float downward through the air. You finally glide to the ground . . . gently and softly touching down. Lying on the ground, you are totally and completely relaxed.*

2.   THE CLOCK

*Imagine a clock with only one hand. The hand at twelve o'clock high represents the most intense stress you have ever experienced. It's electrocution time, and every hair of your body is standing on end. But when the hand is at the six, it represents no stress whatsoever. You're just floating in a tank of Jell-O, or you're a wet, limp noodle lying on the floor.*

*Now get in touch with the level of stress you are under right this second, and set the pointer appropriately. Inhale a deep breath, and as you exhale, imagine the pointer moving down toward six. As you continue to exhale, drop your shoulders and let go.*

*If necessary, reset the pointer, repeat the breath, and let the pointer sink down even further toward six.*

The clock imagery was developed by David Bresler.[1]

### 3.  PEACEFUL PLACE

One of the simplest and most powerful ways to relax is to use peaceful place imagery.

*Imagine yourself in some setting in nature—perhaps high in the mountains, or on a beach, near a lake, or in a desert. Find yourself walking along a path in this setting. Notice what the sky looks like, how the air smells, and what the ground feels like beneath your feet as you walk. With each step along your path, allow yourself to grow more and more relaxed.*

*As you look ahead, you see a little cottage. It's there just for you. Walk up to this cottage. What does it look like, and what is it made of? Go inside, and walk around your cabin. Decorate your perfect cabin to your own taste, with your own artwork. Everything about this place is peaceful. If you like lots of sunlight, imagine that your cabin has lots of windows with an incredible view.*

*Sit down in a comfortable chair in your cottage, and soak in the relaxation. This is your place . . . a million miles from nowhere—if that's where you want it to be.*

Of course, if the words *cottage* and *cabin* doesn't suit you, call your dwelling whatever you like.

### 4.  FOOTPRINTS OF STRESS

Millions of Americans leave work feeling stressed out, and they bring that stress home with them. Here's a simple way to leave stress at the office.

*When you've finished your work for the day, before you leave your office, take three deep breaths, allowing yourself to let go of tension with each breath. Then, as you walk toward the exit, imagine that tension flows down your body and out your feet. Imagine that you are leaving behind footprints of stress. Imagine that with each step, you are leaving behind one percent of your stress. By the time you reach the front door of work, you have left most of the stress behind.*

Now go back over these four relaxation techniques and put a star by those that you liked best. Number them from one to four. Number one is the technique that works best for you. Number four is the one which works the least well for you.

## NEUROSIS AND SUFFERING: WHEN THE SAME TROUBLES HAUNT YOU

We all yearn for the intense love about which poets write and singers sing. We all want to be "standing inside the fire." Yet too many of us are afraid to enter the fray of life, to give our all with heart and soul, with reckless abandon, to give with no thought of return, to dare to fully live our own dreams and not someone else's. We "stand outside the fire."[2]

Those who stand the farthest from the fire, who find it the most difficult to live fully in the moment, are often those whose childhoods were missing love, who were abused or neglected. Being fully loved as a child allows one to become whole, to be at peace with oneself, to have a sense that all is right with the world, and that it is safe to stand inside the fire. Almost anyone can learn to live completely and happily if their yearning is strong enough. But those who have suffered from abuse, neglect, and inadequate parental love have the greatest challenge, the most obstacles to overcome, in order to live a fuller life.

When we're "standing outside the fire," from a psychiatric standpoint, we're neurotic. The lives of saints, sages, philosophers, poets, and even country singers show us what life *is* and what living *is*. Here we'll look at how emotional suffering interferes with life.

I once understood a great deal more about neurosis than I do now. Strange as it may sound, most of psychiatry doesn't understand neurosis. In fact, we don't use the word *neurosis* anymore as a diagnosis. It's not in the *DSM III,* our diagnostic manual. Perhaps psychiatry has become so slanted in the direction of biological diagnosis and chemical treatment that it neglects the true psychological disorders, the neuroses.

A lot of the people who we once thought suffered from neurosis we later diagnosed as having a borderline personality disorder, a mood disorder, or a phobia. In fact, the "neurotics" with whom Sigmund Freud worked and about whom he wrote twenty-six books, were probably people suffering from borderline personality disorder.

Back when "neurosis" existed as a diagnostic reality, we thought of neurotics as people whose sense of self was fundamentally well-formed. And neurotics do have a solid foundation of self-identity, of conscious selfhood. This is in great contrast to people with borderline personality disorder. Because these people suffered severe abuse or neglect as a child, they grew up without a solid foundation. As adults, they stand at the edge of a great void. Their sense of self was never formed.

In this era of HMOs, PPOs, and increasingly complicated billing procedures, psychiatrists no longer can bill for "neurosis." Insurance companies won't pay for the treatment. Still, it's worthwhile to take a look at what used to be called neurosis.

Freud believed that man was doomed to neurosis because his *id* (sexual and aggressive impulses) would always be at odds with the *super-ego* (society's restriction, limitation, and regulation of his impulses). The *ego* was the mental function that makes compromises between the id and the superego and that allows us to function in the world. We always live in a mental battlefield, Freud believed, where sometimes the id is victorious and sometimes superego wins. We survive by channeling our impulses in productive ways, such as by building bridges or having babies.

*Neurosis* is one of those words, like *spirituality,* that is difficult to pin down. Although psychiatry has thrown out *neurosis,* that hasn't stopped millions of people from neurotic suffering. Suffering is part of the human condition, and neurotic suffering can be best understood by adding a spiritual perspective to the traditional psychiatric perspective. Neurosis is mental suffering that is self-perpetuating. It is the act of getting stuck in an emotion. We all suffer when a parent or loved one dies. We go through grief, which includes sadness, pain, anger, guilt, and confusion. Grief is "normal" suffering. Neurosis is a failure to move through these thoughts and feelings. We get stuck in a mental loop in which we can't let go of the anger, sadness, or guilt. We get stuck in neurosis and continue to repeat the same thoughts, words, feelings, and actions. When we can welcome, embrace, and examine each thought and emotion without judgment, we have moved through our grief. We grow stronger and don't develop neurotic suffering.

From a spiritual perspective, neurosis is the failure to recognize right action or moral conduct—or the lack of will or courage to carry it out. The Sanskrit term for right action is *dharma,* and it has no adequate translation in English. Nonetheless, it is an important idea. Every living creature has its own dharma. The dharma of the tiger is to hunt and kill; that of the koala bear, to eat eucalyptus leaves; that of the monkey, to leap from limb to limb. Animals rarely develop neuroses because they live their dharma. Each person has his own personal dharma, as well as the general dharma of a human being. If it is your dharma to be a musician but family and societal pressures have driven you to be an accountant, you are likely to suffer, for you have not followed your dharma—or as Joseph Campbell put it, you have not "followed your bliss." Neurosis is living someone else's life, someone else's dream. It is the failure to identify and claim your unique role in the world, to identify how you fit in to society, and to carry out that dream to its fullest potential. Neurosis is the failure to "stand inside your own fire."

Why would anyone choose wrong action over right action? They do so out of fear, out of a lack of self-confidence, or out of ignorance. Buddha said that ignorance is the root of all suffering. From Buddha's perspective, we all suffer until we develop sacred awareness—awareness of the unity of creation and of the divinity that permeates all things, living and inanimate. Neurosis is born out of the belief and identification of our separateness. Neurosis is ignorance—and a misguided attempt to deny life's uncertainty and unpredictability. None of us knows what life will offer us one minute from now, whether we will face good news or bad news. Life is a complete mystery, a mystery that most of us don't like. In an uncertain world, we like to create the illusion of certainty, and the only way to create that illusion is to cling to old habits and rigid thought patterns. We will all suffer from life's uncertainty until we learn to embrace it and stop fighting it. It is as if we were floating downstream on a powerful current but denying the direction of the flow and trying valiantly to swim upstream.

From this wider spiritual perspective, we can expand our definition of neurosis. Neurosis is the inability to live in the present, to surrender to the moment, to live one's personal dharma. It is the inability to let go of one's preoccupation with control, whether conscious or unconscious. It is the need to struggle to maintain the status quo, which results in struggling against the flow of life. It is the failure to let go of pain and grief, that lock sufferings in place by ruminating on "What if?" and "If only."

The spiritual perspective on neurosis is clearly quite different from the psychoanalytic view. According to Freud, religious belief is itself a sign of neurosis, a way to deal with the unresolvable conflict between our own impulses and society's restrictions. Freud labeled mystical experience as "infantile helplessness" and a "regression to primary narcissism." But from the spiritual standpoint, neurosis is ignorance of spiritual truth.

By this spiritual definition of neurosis, it is obvious that all of us suffer, and most of us suffer neurotically. When we stop clinging, when we stop controlling, we move from neurotic suffering to "normal" suffering, and in the process, our suffering decreases.

Let's look at a few examples of neurosis. René is a psychologist who is conflicted about money. It's hard for her to tell her clients how much she charges. It's hard for her to know how much a particular patient can afford. It's hard for her to ask for payment. Her neurosis is caused by confusing her urge to help with her need to be paid for her work. Many psychotherapists feel uneasy about money and feel unworthy of charging the going rate. That's a very simple example of neurosis: a repetitive pattern of suffering over money.

Understanding dharma was quite helpful to Robert, a patient of mine, a policeman, who had killed a man in the line of action. Robert had prided himself on never having fired his gun once in fifteen years of police work, even though he works in one of the most dangerous parts of San Diego County. But that changed one night when Robert arrived at a dangerous crime scene. He is so intuitive that he often arrives at crime scenes before the dispatcher has even put out the call. And the dispatchers ask him, "Are you psychic or something? You're always the first one there—and half the time, you're there before we call you!" "Just doing my job," Robert replies. His life is full of synchronicity, and he knows it.

That night Robert had to arrest a fellow named Billy. As Robert approached, Billy reached into his pocket and put his hand on a weapon. Robert coolly said, "You really don't want to do that. Right now I have to arrest you for a very minor charge. Don't make it worse." But Billy pulled the shiny weapon out of his pocket, and for the first time in his professional life, Robert pulled his gun and fired one shot, aiming at Billy's shoulder. But just as he pulled the trigger, Billy spun. The bullet severed his spinal cord and killed him.

Robert's action was not that of a cop-gone-mad. "I was in the zone. It was as if it all happened in slow motion. I was perfectly still inside."

But Robert felt bad about the shooting. He knew he had carried out his duties carefully and properly, but he had wanted to complete his career as a cop without ever having shot anyone.

I had to work on that one with him. "You know, Robert, you did what you had to do," I said. "Your ego is attached to the idea of never having to pull the trigger, but that just wasn't in the cards for you." I talked to him about dharma, and about how no jobs are better or worse than any other jobs. Every society has a warrior class. Robert's dharma was that of being a good cop, a good warrior, and sometimes that dharma calls for the use of overwhelming force. Robert felt reassured when he understood that he had upheld dharma and had not violated it. By applying an understanding of dharma, I was able to help Robert overcome the doubts, sadness, and confusion that the shooting had caused in him.

Robert had experienced a kind of neurosis—he had been "suffering over his suffering." The symptoms of neurosis are broad and include anxiety, depression, insomnia, obsessive thoughts, compulsive behaviors, and irrational fears. The obsessive-compulsive neurotic, who has a lot of unresolved feelings of anger, may "have to" wash his hands forty times a day. He doesn't know why he has to do it, but if he doesn't, he becomes anxious. Millions of people have minor compulsions, such as forgetting whether they've locked the front door and returning to the house to check.

Elizabeth, a 25-year-old graduate student in mathematics, has neurotic conflicts about her spiritual teacher, Sathya Sai Baba. "I used to see Baba in a different way than I now do, and I try to make my mind see him the way I used to. I want to let my mind go, but I'm making it do something it doesn't want to do. I force myself to see Baba the way others see him. Sometimes I'll feel so happy when I'm thinking about him, and then I'll wreck the feeling by obsessing. Deep down I want my ego to die, and I know that love allows the ego to die, but the ego says, 'I don't want to die,' so my ego fights for survival. I'm afraid to give up this game I know I'm playing. Even though my ego fights so hard to stay in control, when it's gone, I feel so comfortable and don't feel I have to try to control things."

Spiritual pursuit in itself does not free us from neurosis, as Elizabeth's story shows. She has an obsessional neurosis focused on her spiritual teacher. But anything or anyone can be the focus of an obsession. Elizabeth suffered from a spiritual neurosis. Locked into a fixed view of God and her spiritual teacher, she was afraid to abandon her preconceived ideas and just let things be, let things develop naturally.

My spiritual description of neurosis may seem at odds with traditional psychiatry, but it's not. I believe the root cause of neurosis is ignorance, the failure to recognize and follow right action, and the struggle to make life certain instead of going with the flow. Freud answered the question, "What mechanisms in the mind produce neurosis?" He showed us that powerful mental conflict leads to suffering.

When internal conflict arises in our minds that we cannot satisfactorily resolve, we develop "symptoms." Let's say your boss has made you so angry that you want to strangle him. But this boss is not open to communication, so you swallow your anger because you can't afford to lose your job. You're not going to walk around angry indefinitely, so eventually you may develop a symptom, such as depression, anxiety, or headaches. The anger is still inside you, but it has gotten "buried" and been converted into a symptom. Now if, as a child, you were taught never to express your anger or even to feel your anger, you are likely to suffer all the more in this situation. You may not even be aware that you're angry at your boss. The anger never even reached your conscious mind. Since you're not aware that you're feeling angry, you don't talk out the anger with someone, scream, ventilate, or exercise as a way of burning it off. So you develop neurotic symptoms—you can't sleep, or you're irritable with your husband or wife.

If spirituality is sacred awareness, neurosis is spiritual ignorance. Neurosis is at the heart of suffering. That psychiatry has dropped the label *neurosis* does not diminish the fact that all of us suffer, and some of us suffer neurotically. To suffer is part of the human condition until we become enlightened. To suffer is normal. All of us have hang-ups, conflicts, and struggles that we handle either well or poorly. Sometimes we do it better than at other times. But no one is free of conflict. Being conscious of our feelings and the situations in which we find ourselves makes us better prepared to deal with life's ups and downs. If we can find a way out of the "box of conflict," we will grow and not develop symptoms. If we can't find a door out of that box, we'll suffer more.

Now that you know the cause of neurosis, you also know the cure. If ignorance is the cause, awareness is the cure. Become aware of your suffering, and stop pushing it away. Embrace it as you embrace joy. Welcome victory and defeat equally. Practice service or volunteer work, for it helps dissolve the illusion of separateness—the neurosis of separateness. Awareness that everyone is your brother and sister will awaken your heart to respond immediately to others' suffering. By opening your heart to your own and others' suffering, you are healed.

Become mindful of each waking moment. Be aware that you are eating when you're eating, walking when you're walking. With practice, you'll become anchored in the present moment, which is the place and time where suffering does not exist. Only when the mind dwells on the past or is pulled into the future do we suffer. Reenter the moment, realize the unity of all living beings, and your burden will lighten.

Most of us have a problem with anger, to one degree or another. Indeed, perhaps the greatest plague of humankind, greater than the black plague and greater than AIDS, is the plague of rage. The United States is the most violent country in the world. Murder, rape, spousal abuse, and child abuse have become so ordinary, we merely watch the body counts go up. We grow numb to the reality that each person has but one life to live—and one life to die.

By overcoming anger, we become more peaceful and loving, and those around us benefit from our serenity.

Without subjecting the entire population to years of therapy, how can we deal with this general anger? Let's take a look at some general principles as well as some simple techniques.

The very first question that must be asked, regarding a given person, is whether his anger needs to be expressed or reined in. Those of us who carry repressed anger need to practice taking the lid off, blowing off steam, expressing our anger in appropriate ways. Others explode on a moment's notice, getting angrier and more out of control with time. So first figure out if you need your lid taken off, or put back on and screwed on tight.

## ABCS OF ANGER CONTROL
### *Mental Fitness Technique*

*Human values fostered by this technique: Nonviolence and Peace*

For those who can't keep the lid on, whose rage is at a dangerous level, I advise the ABCs of Anger Control:

**A.**  Avoid loud speech.
**B.**  Breathe.
**C.**  Curtail swearing.

The logic here is simple. Loud speech and swearing are like gasoline thrown on the fire. They cause an explosion rather than a resolution. And by taking a series of deep breaths, you'll begin to cool down. These ABCs are so simple, you might think they couldn't work. But imagine what would happen if everybody in the world practiced their ABCs of Anger Control.

Now let's continue with our alphabetical treatment:

**D.**  Drink a glass of cold water. It will help cool you down.
**E.**  Exercise. Burn off the anger. Run, walk, swim, bike, or dance.
**F.**  Find a friend, and talk it out.

What else can you do?

- Sit quietly and collect your thoughts.
- Practice buying time. Find a space between the feeling arising and the mouth or fists expressing that feeling. Live with the feeling for one or two seconds. Expand that to 60 seconds. Live with the anger, and just experience it.

- Lie down until the anger passes.
- Look in the mirror. When you see what you look like when you're en-raged, you will want to let go of the anger. It's not a pretty sight.
- Beat on a pillow.
- Roll up the windows in your car, go for a drive, and scream.

### Roots of Rage

The ABCs of Anger Control are designed to prevent real physical violence. But remember: a violent slip of the tongue can last a lifetime (or lifetimes!). These techniques are also for self-defense—defense of others and yourself. These are emergency procedures and are not meant to substitute for in-dividual or group psychotherapy, settings where one can safely look at one's anger, release it, and resolve conflict. That's longer-term work. The techniques in the ABCs of Anger Control are about putting out fires and helping people stop from even striking the first match.

Why do we get angry? It's clear to me that anger is a product of both heredity and environment. I've seen young children who came into the world with a chip on their shoulder. It's hard to believe, but I've seen rage even in a baby's eyes—and I know it's in the DNA, not in the milk.

But given the nature-and-nurture roots of personality, let me explain the Vedanta theory about anger. According to Vedanta, we are driven by desire within the lower self. Once we have acquired our object of desire, we want to multiply it. When the desire is not fulfilled, when it is dimin-ished or taken away, we get angry. It's that simple. So how do you deal with desire? If the desire that arises in your mind will not harm others or yourself, proceed toward it. But remember the lessons of the Temple of Delphi: (1) Know thyself, and (2) Nothing in excess.

Realize that your anger is *your* responsibility. Your partner doesn't make you angry. Your partner does something, and your reaction is anger. Give up any idea of ownership. Nobody owns anybody. Examine the root of the anger. Examine your desire, and realize that the anger comes from your fear of losing the desired person.

Taking responsibility for one's anger is easier than most of us think. Rather than saying, "You really infuriate me when you gossip for hours on the phone," try this approach instead: "I'd like to talk to you about the hours you're spending on the phone. I feel angry when you do that. I know I have a problem with anger. I'm not blaming you, but I'd like to tell you how I feel so I can get it off my chest. Then, after I've calmed down,

I'd like for us to sit and talk about this problem and come to a better understanding."

## TAKING THE LID OFF ANGER
### *Mental Fitness Technique*

*Human value fostered by this technique:* Nonviolence

If your problem with anger is that you need to take the lid off, this imagery script may help you learn to express, release, and overcome anger:

> *Imagine yourself sitting on the ground facing the person with whom you are angry. He or she is also sitting on the ground. From the bottom of your heart, tell this person how you are feeling. Share all the nasty details. You don't need to be polite. You can yell and scream. Notice if you're speaking in soft, controlled tones. If you are, let go of that style and really blow off some steam.*
>
> *Now imagine that you have three buckets next to you. One is filled with water, one with honey, and one with rice. Which one would you like to pour over the other person? Go ahead. Pick up that bucket, and pour it all over him. Doesn't that feel good?*
>
> *Has he learned his lesson, or do you need to pour one of the other buckets? Pick up one of the other buckets, and empty that one on him. You may have something special in mind that you'll want in that bucket. It's your bucket. Fill it with whatever you like, pour it over him, and feel yourself releasing anger as you do.*

You can probably guess which bucket most people pick first—the honey. People just love to imagine pouring a bucket of honey over the person they're mad at. And they almost always like pouring something else over the honey, such as rice, confetti, feathers, pebbles, or leaves.

### *Nip Anger in the Bud*

If you can identify the precursors of your anger, you can put out the fire before it ever gets lit. Every day stress shortens our fuse. Identify your stress, and deal with it. Don't let yourself get too tired or too hungry. Protect your own personal space. Find a way to have time alone every day, if you need it. Become aware of how much physical space you require, then mentally claim that space. Failure to deal with these precursors to anger will lead to loss of control.

### Spiritual Approaches

1. Just as we have dark archetypes, we also have angelic archetypes. Call on your angels, your angelic side, your connection with the Absolute, when you are filled with anger. Picture that divine angelic form standing by you.

2. Read one passage of a spiritual or inspirational text, and reflect upon it.

3. Silently chant the holy name that resonates within your heart.

4. Practice forgiveness.

5. Try to love your enemies.

With this arsenal of techniques, anyone can gain better control over their anger. They can learn to pour water on it if they're fire-setters, and they can learn to express it if they tend to suppress it.

If you're like most people, you periodically face decisions that leave you straddling the fence. You weigh one choice against another and discover that they seem equal. We face such dilemmas throughout all parts of our lives. For some, indecisiveness is such a severe problem that it becomes a neurosis. The following technique will help the neurotic sufferer, as well as the rest of us, who need assistance, from time to time, in making decisions.

## DECISION-MAKING
### Mental Fitness Technique

*Human value fostered by this technique: Right Action*

This powerful technique was developed by Don Crawford, Ph.D., psychologist and contributing editor to *Atlantis: The Imagery Newsletter*.

*Picture in your mind a scale. This scale is calibrated from zero to ten. Now imagine that this scale has a needle or arrow that can point at any number on the scale.*

*Think of something, someone, or some experience that you absolutely love or loved. That's a ten, so picture the needle on the scale going directly to ten. Now, let the scale return to a neutral position. Think of the worst experience in your life—the most painful experience. That's a zero, so picture the needle on the scale going to zero.*

*Now that you've practiced using the scale, think of one of the choices you are contemplating. Then allow the needle to settle wherever IT chooses. If it lands on ten, that means you are 100 percent in favor of that choice. If it lands right in the middle on five, you are 50 percent in favor of that choice; and if it ends up on zero, you do not want this choice at all.*

This exercise is so simple, you may wonder how it can work. The scale directly accesses your unconscious mind, providing information that your rational mind couldn't find.

I have seen this tool used successfully by business executives making difficult corporate decisions. My daughter has also found it very helpful in buying presents for her friends. On one occasion, when she was a teenager, she was torn between buying two presents. I asked her to picture the scale. One of the presents "came in at nine," and the other at eight. She immediately felt comfortable buying the nine.

Don't forget to brainstorm, think, plan, reason, and research when you're trying to make a decision. Using the scale imagery dramatically increases your decision-making abilities, because you are using both right- and left-brain functions.

### Using Symbols

Imagery is instantaneous. You can get feedback from your symbolic unconscious mind in seconds. It's not only doctors, nurses, business executives, and Olympic athletes who can use it. Anybody can tap into imagery on a moment's notice to help solve any dilemma or make any decision more easily. Nor does imagery have to be a long process that requires an hour of deep work. If you're stuck and don't know whether to turn right

or left, so to speak, and you still need more clarification after practicing
the scale imagery, just close your eyes for a minute.

> *Ask your unconscious mind to provide an image that*
> *clarifies the situation and shows what is best for the highest*
> *good of all concerned.*

Here's an example. A friend of mine and his 12-year-old son were
asked to be part of a family gathering, a gathering that the son had mixed
feelings about. They both did this exercise, and here's what they "saw."
The son saw himself comfortably being part of the gathering. The father
told his son, "I saw a five-pointed star, and it means I'm supposed to be
the sheriff. I'm the protector. I'll make sure it's safe for you." The decision
was easy, and at the gathering a good time was had by all.

# PART III

## *Getting*

## *Enlightened*

# 10

# HIGHER STATES
# OF CONSCIOUSNESS

Part III is filled with amazing stories of spiritual and paranormal phenomena, involving angels, ghosts, auras, and miraculous cures as well as higher states of consciousness. By understanding these phenomena and altered states, we will be better able to answer the first question of Psycho-Spiritual Assessment, namely, "What is your main concern?" Once we have named, examined, and embraced these experiences and integrated them into medicine and into our own lives, we won't have to push mystical experience back into the shadows. Rather we will be able to follow the advice of the roshi.

Spirit, or soul, is beyond words, ineffable. All the saints, sages, and holy men and women who have directly experienced the light of the soul or who have had overpowering spiritual experiences reported that these experiences could not be adequately described in words. Words can only be like signposts that say, "There is a light in the distance." Beyond the last signpost, the last word *is* the light. The love, the peace, the awe of spiritual experience cannot be done justice through words.

As you open the door to the light and explore higher states of consciousness, keep in mind a few key principles. First, altered states of consciousness can arise either spontaneously or as a result of a conscious spiritual discipline. Two, higher states of consciousness are not a sign of mental illness. Rather, they are a great gift, an opportunity for self-discovery and spiritual growth. Three, after years of practice one can go in and out of higher states at will. And four, higher states almost always transform the individual in a positive way.

Once we find the door to the Light (or it finds us), we can learn to walk in and out of the Light or stay in it forever. Throughout recorded history, men and women have become capable of voluntarily entering the highest states of consciousness. Some of these great souls, such as Jesus and Buddha, will be forever remembered, while others remain unknown. Even today such great souls exist. These enlightened ones feel a sense of oneness with everything at all times, and they are able to go about their work in the world without retreating to a cave. The enlightened ones live in a state of perpetual peace and happiness.

In the following pages, you'll read about specific altered states of consciousness. Keep in mind that these "enlightening" experiences are not reserved for the few but are available to all.

## OUT-OF-BODY EXPERIENCES

There are two major classes of out-of-body experiences (OBEs): simple and complex. In a simple OBE, the person simply drifts out of his body. In a complex OBE, the person may also experience flashing lights, feelings of divine bliss, angels, dark tunnels, and celestial kingdoms that are characteristic of complex OBE's. I once had a simple OBE while lying in bed. Suddenly I drifted out of my body, right up to the ceiling. I could touch the ceiling with my hand—or so it seemed, even though my body was still lying in bed. That was it. After my short flight into space, I simply drifted back into my body. Mind you, I was fully awake. There was absolutely nothing—no event, no stress, and no drug—that could have triggered this event. And it's only happened to me once. I've stayed in my body the rest of the time. Other people who have had simple OBEs soar far out of their bodies. They feel as if they are connected to their body by a cord, which is often felt to be of "silver."

The most humorous out-of-body experience (a complex one) I've heard of happened to the late Dr. Benito Reyes. When he was 16 years old, he suddenly flew out of his body. He was quite exhilarated and frightened as he "flew around." When he reentered his body, he landed upside down, with his head in his feet. I can't comprehend what that means, but that was his experience. At that moment, he heard a voice—a voice that would become his spiritual teacher, his guru. The voice said, "Now do that again, but land right side up." Dr. Reyes spent the rest of his life (when he wasn't working, teaching, driving, and so on) taking astral journeys. In fact, he and his wife "traveled together." These journeys were not just for pleasure—Dr. Reyes and his wife had work to do. Both were able to go to realms of consciousness in which they could see disembodied souls. In particular, they met countless souls killed in World War I, souls who had died so suddenly and so violently that they got lost on their journey from this plane of existence to the next. The Reyeses spent their lives "traveling" to help these lost souls make their excursion to a higher plane—to take them to the other side.

If this sounds crazy, I can vouch that when I met Dr. Reyes and heard him give a two-hour lecture (without notes), I found him to be of solid character—an absolutely brilliant, loving, and grounded human being. His credentials were most impressive: he was the founder of two highly regarded universities, World University in Ojai, California, and the University of the City of Manila in the Philippines. His degrees included a Ph.D., an Ll.D., a Litt.D., and an L.H.D. He lectured at Harvard and Brown, was a Fulbright-Smith-Mundt professor at Boston University, and authored seven books.

In my clinical practice I frequently hear about out-of-body experiences, usually from people who have been severely abused. Rosanne was kidnapped and raped every day between the ages of 14 and 16. She coped with the agony by "leaving her body." Traditional psychiatry would say that Rosanne was "dissociating," but it could not say where consciousness goes when it dissociates. I believe that "dissociation" may often be an out-of-body experience. Rosanne's consciousness had separated from her physical body, temporarily vacated its confines. In fact, she learned to "leave her body" at will and would often go into states of ecstatic bliss while out of her body.

Dozens of other people who survived extreme abuse have also told me that they had left their bodies during the abuse. Unfortunately, leaving the body does not immunize one to the effects of the abuse. The pain, the memory, the thoughts and feelings are deeply registered in the person's heart and mind, and years of inner work are required to recover emotionally.

Out-of-body experiences often lead people onto a spiritual path, onto a quest for God—a search for meaning, truth, and peace. Rosanne is a case in point. The pain of her abuse was outweighed by the ecstasy of her out-of-body experiences. That joy kept her going through depressions, suicidal feelings, and physical exhaustion and pain. Eventually, her frequent psychiatric hospitalizations were no longer necessary, and she moved into a Buddhist mountain retreat. From this retreat, Rosanne, who had long since decided that spiritual reality is more valid than material reality, wrote me: "Spirituality usually begins with an earnest grasping directed toward the outside world in what too often proves to be a vain attempt to locate sacredness, a sound sense of connection, value, and meaning in our lives. Encouraged by a culture that trains us to be good consumers, we search for ways to purchase and possess something ineffable, formless, and vast that can't be acquired with any amount of external exchange." Rosanne's experience of the light helps her remember what is most important to her—her spiritual quest.

Some people with cancer report that they leave their bodies when the physical pain becomes too great. In this instance, the OBE serves a dual purpose; it not only alleviates severe pain, it expands awareness.

Another kind of out-of-body experience, the near-death experience (NDE), has been extensively researched by Raymond Moody, M.D., author of *Life After Life,* and by Melvin Morse, M.D., author of *Closer to the Light.*[1] NDEs are common occurrences in emergency rooms. Upon awakening, people who have suffered near-fatal heart attacks often report leaving their body and drifting above it or into a corner of the ER. They observe the doctors and nurses frantically working on "the body," and they feel a sense of detachment and tranquillity. Normally we can see only what's in front of us, but they have a full 360 degrees of vision. They often later report exact details of what was done and said while they were "unconscious." They may even know the exact amount of time that has passed.

During an out-of-body experience, the person may find himself flying through a tunnel and emerging into a realm of light, where he is met by deceased relatives and friends, divine personages, God, or beings of light. He often feels an indescribable sense of peace. Before returning to his body, he may have a "life review," in which his life flashes before him. Upon returning, he may feel or hear a "click" as his consciousness reconnects with his body.

Most people are dramatically changed by near-death experiences. They have less fear of death than before, or none at all. They feel full of love and peace and may have an urge to share that love, to serve others, and to make the world a better place. Above all, they report that the NDE was super-*real*—more intensely real than any other life experience.

In his second book, *Transformed by the Light,* Dr. Morse showed, through extensive and careful research, that children who have near-death experiences are also transformed.[2] When they grow up, they show significantly less fear of death than people who have never experienced an NDE, more zest for life, and greater psychic powers. His subjects' psychic abilities were four times greater than normal people's and twice as great as those who call themselves psychic. They scored better on a whole host of personality issues, too, including less drug use, better income management, fewer psychosomatic complaints, better nutrition, and more exercise, personal growth, social activity, and spiritual awareness. Oddly, twenty-five percent of Morse's subjects who had NDEs were unable to wear watches. Watches simply wouldn't work for them, inexplicably working in fits and starts or stopping altogether. Yet the same watch would work for someone else. Dr. Morse's study showed that people are indeed "transformed by the light." But having the experience of *light* during an NDE is essential for the transformation. Simply being out of your body does not provide the impetus for life transformation.

## DEATHBED EXPERIENCES

Deathbed experiences (DBEs) have not been studied as thoroughly as NDEs, but they tend to be characterized by a sense of peace and tranquillity, a divine light, visitation of angels or God in some form, and a visitation of deceased relatives.

It is a testament to the San Diego Hospice that they take these experiences seriously. When a patient is given pain medication to ease her terminal suffering, the hospice staff considers the possibility that too much medication might prevent her from having a profound spiritual experience in the hours or days before her passing. If a terminal patient is displaying unusual symptoms, the hospice physicians try to determine, in the spirit of true medicine, whether the patient is having a delirium (an organic brain syndrome) that is caused by a metabolic disorder, the illness itself, medication, or other purely organic cause—or a deathbed experience.

Celedonio Romero, the classical guitar master whose son, Celin, was my teacher, suffered a painful death from lung cancer. During his final days, he found it increasingly difficult to breathe, and he encountered extreme physical pain whenever he moved at all. Yet despite his physical suffering, he exuded love and peace as death approached. He remained so in love with life, with his family, and with music that even on his deathbed he continued to instruct students, including his three sons, who are all classical guitarists. He laughed and smiled through the entire ordeal.

Because of his breathing difficulties and his poor oxygen perfusion, he was asked to wear an oxygen mask. Periodically, however, he would take off the oxygen mask and smile at his children. Pepe, one of his sons, naturally panicked and told his father to put the mask back on. Celedonio, with sparkling eyes, replied, "Don't you see? I don't need this. I'm doing this for you, not for me." Then he would put the oxygen back on—only to make his children happy. In spite of his physical agony, he remained in a state of mental and spiritual bliss.

Minutes before he took his final breath, he said, *"La guitarra . . . la guitarra."* According to Pepe, "At the moment my father died, his love became so vast that it felt as if his love blew through me. Never in my life have I experienced such a profound love. My father was a saint. He lived like a saint and died like a saint." As a good friend of his father's, I agree with Pepe.

After Celedonio died, his mouth stayed wide open for four hours in a fixed position. While his mouth was still open, his wife, Angelita, who had not been present at the moment of his death, opened the door to his hospital room. Before she had fully entered, his mouth suddenly closed and turned into a smile. Angelita was therefore greeted by a sweet smile rather than a cold, rigid expression. I am sure there is a good physiological explanation for how this change occurred. Electrical activity does remain in the body after the spirit departs. It is possible that a sudden electrical discharge in his nervous system caused his mouth to close. But even if the physiology was human, the timing was divine. (Of course, this experience was a bit terrifying for Celedonio's children and grandchildren, who were present and observed his mouth suddenly close.)

Death is often a time of great, conscious spiritual opening. The person departing this world may have a profound spiritual experience, as may those around him. The period after death remains a time of psychic opening, in which the dead can make contact with the living. But the great lesson in watching a loved one die is in observing that how they die is directly related to how they lived. Celedonio was a modern-day Zorba who lived and died with gusto. We in the West need to learn more about both the art of living and the art of dying, for one does not exist without the other.

## HEALING TRANCES

Lenora, who works as an office manager for a large surgical group, can enter higher states of consciousness at will. She has done so for years. But sometimes she just slips into this state without willing it. And sometimes, while in a higher state, she feels she is able to connect with other people and heal them at a distance. Her healing trance is a kind of out-of-body experience, a genuine spiritual experience. Here is one of her remarkable experiences, in her own words.

"Monica, the 20-year-old niece of a friend of mine, was in a serious automobile accident. She had a serious brain injury that the doctors in the hospital weren't able to cure. Monica was semicomatose. She could talk, but nothing she said made any sense at all. When she spoke, it was non-sense. She wasn't aware of her surroundings and couldn't recognize or re-spond to anybody. After a couple of weeks in the hospital without progress, Monica's doctors felt she wasn't going to recover, at least not very soon, so they were making plans to transfer her to a long-term re-habilitation center. In the meantime, they had decided that they would soon have to put in a feeding tube (a nasogastric tube) because Monica wasn't able to eat or drink.

"I spoke with Jamie, her mother, on the phone, and she was quite distraught about the situation. I had met Monica a couple of times because her husband was a patient of one of the doctors I work for and Monica had come into the office a few times. So I could picture Monica in my mind as Jamie spoke about her.

"After I spoke with Jamie, I lay down to go to sleep, and I slipped into a state that I've entered many times. I've been told that this state is called chidakash. All of a sudden I was visualizing the area in Monica's head where I was perceiving the damage to be. I was not in my physical body, nor was the area I was looking at a physical body. And Monica didn't have a physical body during this experience. I wasn't seeing her in the hos-pital. There were no surroundings.

"But I knew exactly where I was going, and I knew exactly what my intention was. I scanned her very well and focused in on the back part of her head, and suddenly I found myself saying to myself, 'She has a hole there. How can she heal herself when she has a hole there?' My percep-tion was that there was damage in a particular part of her brain.

"As I was focused in on that part of her head, I suddenly became aware of Monica's consciousness—not her physical body, but her con-sciousness. Her consciousness wasn't focusing in on me being there, but she started to focus in on the area that I was looking at in her physical body. At that point I said to myself, 'I wonder if she can heal herself now.' Because neither of us was in our body but were rather consciousness meet-ing consciousness, I didn't need to speak with her in words. I simply needed to help her become aware of herself and of the hole in her brain that I was seeing. That was all I felt I needed to do. From there, it was her choice to go back into her body or not. So that was my experience—and then I fell asleep.

"The very next day I got a call from Jamie saying that Monica had awakened and was completely normal and healed. Shortly thereafter, Monica came into our office to pick up some medication for her husband. I was so happy to see her, and I said, 'Monica, how are you?' She responded, 'Oh, I'm fine.' Initially we had a normal, friendly interaction until I said, 'Do you remember anything at all about when you were in a coma?' At that point she kind of shook her head, stopped talking, took a step backward, and her face got red—and she sat down in a chair. I again said, 'You don't remember anything at all?' And she said, 'No, I don't.' But the whole cadence of her voice was changing.

"Now, I don't really know what was happening. I don't know if she was remembering the interaction we had had on some level—or if it was my feeling toward her that was throwing her off. I was feeling an incredible love for her. When you connect with someone in an altered state, as I did, you develop an incredible bond with that person. Once you connect on such a deep level with another human being, you're not limited to just the physical senses. You've connected completely. So I felt such love for her, a kind of deep love you usually don't feel for another human being. But from my experience with her, I touched something deep inside both of us. I don't know if Monica was aware of that connection. As I spoke with her in the doctor's office, I was trying to stay balanced and not get absorbed into my own feelings. I was amazed at the consuming love I felt for her—a very spiritual love, probably the way we should love one another all the time.

"I didn't want to press her. It really didn't matter to me whether she remembered it or not because I felt that I should stay detached from something like that. I couldn't take credit for doing anything, any more than I would have taken the blame if she had died. I believe that when you have an injury of her severity, consciousness can literally get knocked out of the body. I simply pointed it out to her."

In this remarkable story of love, compassion, and inspiration, Lenora is very matter-of-fact about her abilities. She shows no pride or ego; she makes no claims about being a psychic or a healer, and she does not view this experience as special or extraordinary.

Imagine how Lenora would have felt if she had had no understanding of consciousness. She might have felt as if she were losing her mind. She could not have even entertained the notion of "consciousness meeting consciousness."

## IDENTITY TRANSFORMATIONS

In her "healing trances" Lenora is deeply aware of the other person and is able to interact with them in a realm of consciousness that is quite out of the ordinary. In the state called *identity transformation,* one goes even further. Not only is the person deeply aware of the other, he believes that he temporarily *becomes* that other person. Identity transformation is almost the opposite of possession, in which a "foreign entity" takes over the personality. In identity transformation the individual feels as if he has become someone or something else. He has taken on a new identity. Nor does he feel terror at losing his own personality.

Most American Indian shamans can assume the form and identity of animals and convey messages through them. This shamanic practice is widespread among the Kwakiutl and Nootka of the Northwest, the Lakota, Crow, and Blackfoot of the Plains, and the Maidu of southern California. Identity transformation is least common among the Pueblo Indians—the Navajo, Hopi, and Acoma. Aztec and Mayan cultures also relied on shamans who could assume the identity of an animal. A good friend of mine, Shama Smith, an internationally recognized psychic, has had countless experiences that involve altered states of consciousness, including identity transformation. She tells me that on one occasion she left her body and literally became a friend of hers, whom we'll call Jane. While she was in that state of "being Jane," she had a fight with Jane's husband. Several days later, Jane told Shama that she had just had a terrible fight with her husband. The argument she recounted to Shama was exactly the same, word for word, as the one Shama had had with him when she "became Jane."

A restaurant and hotel owner in Oregon, a woman of incredible good cheer, told me that she once stopped her car because a mountain lion was sitting very near the edge of the road. She gazed into the mountain lion's eyes and temporarily "switched places" with the animal and experienced "mountain lion consciousness." She had the same experience again with another mountain lion and then with a bobcat.

Now how is this experience different from that of the schizophrenic who tells me that he is John the Baptist, Jesus Christ, Napoleon, or Elvis Presley? The story of "Shama becoming Jane" may sound as if Shama and I are both crazy—she for reporting the experience, and I for believing her. But you have to look at these experiences in context. The schizophrenic has a destroyed personality. He is usually unable to work, sustain relationships, or enjoy life. He is full of fear and may be quite frightening. His whole world is a fiction of his psychotic imagination. This is not the case with someone who experiences an identity transformation.

I don't want to imply that there are certain states of consciousness that "normal" people can have and that sick people can't. Borderlines, as I've mentioned, can be very psychic and go into mystical ecstasies. Their consciousness is fluid. They can leave their bodies. I'm sure they can experience identity transformation. But they can also become psychotic, hear voices, and become so depressed that they attempt suicide. The extreme fluidity of their consciousness allows them to experience a broad range of states of consciousness.

In identity transformation, consciousness merges or becomes one with the consciousness of another, be it human or animal. Like other spiritual and paranormal phenomena, it often transforms the individual for the better. People who have experienced an identity transformation usually find deep spiritual significance in it. Let's review Shama's experience of "becoming Jane." Months after she shared her story with me, Shama called to make a further point. "You know," she said, "I know why I had that experience. It wasn't just for the fun of it. You see, Jane had really been bugging me. She had been clingy and demanding, and I had to put some distance between us. She was driving me crazy. For a while, most of my thoughts about her were negative. However, after I became her, I developed tremendous compassion for her. I knew what it was like to *be* her. Afterward, I didn't just let her walk all over me again, but I felt incredible love for her. I really knew what made her act the way she did."

Identity transformation, although it is a profound state of expanded consciousness, provides just a glimpse of what saints and holy people consider to be the goal of spiritual practice—the attainment of the "highest" spiritual states, known variously as ecstasy, unity consciousness, nirvana, or samadhi.

## NIRVANA

A person in a healing trance is experiencing an altered state in which his consciousness is detached from his physical body—and he feels immense compassion for another being. A person in identity transformation is not only "out of" her body, she has temporarily "become" the other person. But in nirvana, also called samadhi or unity consciousness, one's entire consciousness merges with God, Nature, or Universal Spirit. It is a state of supreme bliss, of unspeakable joy, of complete peace and tranquillity. One loses all identification with the physical body and with all separateness. In nirvana, consciousness expands to its ultimate limit, merging with everything. There is no "other" to feel compassion for or even to merge with. There only is—one. All is One. Nirvana is not a trance or unconsciousness, states that may be caused by hysteria or imagination. Nirvana is the ultimate experience, a heaven on earth that one can experience without dying. In the state of nirvana, only the ego dies.

Here is a mystical experience, nirvana, that was reported to me by Joy Thomas, author of *Life Is a Game, Play It; Life Is a Dream, Realize It;* and *Life Is a Challenge, Meet It.*

"One morning I was sitting on my bed meditating. After reaching a place of deep stillness, I began to see small pinpoints of light. They were of different colors and seemed to be whirling in and around each other within a boundary. That boundary, I realized, was my body. I seemed to be seeing my own body as a form made of moving atoms, and I was also aware of the feeling of a limited body mass.

"As I watched, the little specks of light began to move faster and spread wider. Looking beyond them, I saw the sliding doors of the closet begin to dissolve into similar dots of light. Gradually the atoms of my body began to merge with the atoms of the doors, and it felt to me as if the boundaries of my body had expanded. The expansion continued through the closet to the outside wall, and as the specks of light blended into each other, the front yard became visible to me.

"There in the front yard was a large boulder I had recently purchased to beautify our yard. It began to break down into beautiful varicolored lights, each whirling and turning until the boulder and I were one. The expansion continued slowly down the street, with trees, houses, and cars all becoming a part of my body. Sun, moon, stars, and galaxies finally joined in, and I felt the boundaries of my body expand until I included the entire universe.

"Then the vision of the whirling lights began to fade, the sense of my body gradually dissolved completely, and I was aware only of being in infinite bliss. How long this sense of boundless being continued, I don't know. The moment I thought, 'Isn't this wonderful,' I began to return to normal consciousness."

The feeling of being at one with nature is nirvana. So is the state of oneness that Pepe Romero often experiences when he is performing. During many of his concerts, he loses all sense of personal identity, all sense that he is playing the guitar. There is no Pepe, and there is no audience. In his words, "There is only the music—and really, there is only love." It is a state of oneness with everything, a state where the sense of "I" has vanished. Pepe says, "It is as if I have one foot in this world and one in the other. Except the normal, ordinary world becomes just a memory. It's not real for me anymore." At these moments Pepe is more than "in the zone." He *is* the zone.

Call it nirvana, samadhi, or unity consciousness—they all mean the same thing. This state of perfect peace, boundless love, and indescribable joy is not a "high" in the usual sense. Because it may sound like a "high," we need to contrast it with the "highs" of drug use and mania. In Sanskrit, *samadhi* means "equal-minded" and *nirvana* means "without a trace of mental agitation." In this highest state of consciousness, the mind is absolutely still. It is as if the individual spirit or soul has merged with the vast ocean of Infinite Wisdom or God. The soul is no longer yearning to find God, yearning to be with God, or yearning to merge with God. Rather, one's consciousness has expanded so completely that there is only the experience of One. There is only peace, only love, only joy—only One.[3]

The euphoria of mania, by contrast, is caused by a flood of norepinephrine throughout the nervous system—a massive adrenaline rush. It's a fragile "high," an unstable state that rapidly gives way to anger, fear, and depression. The manic person is speeded up—talking fast, walking fast. His thoughts are racing. He is so irrational that he is making terrible business decisions and may be destroying his marriage. That certainly is not the case with nirvana. In nirvana thoughts do not race. There are no thoughts at all.

Nirvana is also completely unrelated to the events of the physical world. It is not the happiness we experience when things go right or when we get what we've been desiring. It arises out of the fulfillment of the soul, not fulfillment of material desires.

# 11

## VISUAL PARANORMAL
## EXPERIENCES

One sure way to get the attention of your loved ones is to tell them that you just had a vision of an angel. This is the kind of strange experience that makes people wonder if they're losing their minds or getting enlightened. Some visions are indeed caused by schizophrenia, mania, or borderline personality, but others are spiritual in nature. In fact, among spiritual and paranormal experiences in general, visions are particularly common.

In writing about visual paranormal experiences, I am in a real bind about what terms to use. The word *hallucination* implies psychosis or insanity; *vision* implies a positive, beneficial experience of a spiritual or mystical nature—a revelation; *apparition* and *ghost* seem occult or metaphysical; *perception* is too neutral.

I'm going to use the term *hallucination,* but I'll use it to refer to a wide range of experiences, only some of which are psychotic and others of which are normal or supernormal. A hallucination is the experience of a sight, sound, smell, or taste in a situation in which there is no verifiable physical cause of or evidence for that experience. A vision is a visual hallucination, seen with the eyes of something or someone outside of oneself. It's not the same as an image or a fantasy, in which one "sees" something in one's mind's eye, mentally. Visions are seen *outside* oneself.

Because so many strange experiences are related to vision, I have devoted this entire chapter to the subject. We'll look at angels, ghosts, and

191

visions of the departed, but we'll also look at psychic attack, possession, thought-forms, artistic hallucinations, and the human aura. It's obvious why I have included the first three in this chapter. But psychic attack, possession, and thought-forms are visible too—to those with advanced psychic sensitivities.

## VISIONS VERSUS HALLUCINATIONS

A spiritual vision is usually a very pleasant, uplifting experience. One may "see" God, angels, saints, or indescribable light. The vision usually brings a new direction to one's life and leaves the person with a "lighter" countenance, a greater joy in life, and more love to share with others. Visions may occur spontaneously, in a normal state of consciousness, or they may occur during an altered state, a mystical union, or a kundalini process.

Visions are common in the lives of saints and great mystics and others who are spiritually advanced. Artist and poet William Blake wrote of his visions, "A vision is not a cloudy vapor or a nothing. It is organized and minutely articulated beyond all that the mortal and perishing nature can produce. I assert that all my visions appear to me infinitely more perfect and more organized than anything seen by the mortal eye."[1]

Visions of deceased loved ones happen all the time. Whether or not it is "objectively" true that people are regularly visited by the departed, in non-Western societies such visitations are considered the normal experience. Even in Western society, grief counselors commonly reassure bereaved people that seeing and talking with departed loved ones is part of the grieving process.

People who are approaching death often experience visions in which deceased relatives appear in order to help them in their transition. Karlis Osis and Erlunder Haraldsson studied this phenomenon in a variety of cultures and found that such "deathbed visions" are nearly identical from one culture to another.[2]

Schizophrenics tend to hear voices much more frequently than they have visions, but when they do have visions, they are almost never pleasant. They feel controlled by their visions. Their visions are part of a psychotic process. This may sound odd, but they will have a psychotic relationship with their hallucination. Most psychiatrists would say that hallucinations in themselves are psychotic, but I disagree. The "normal" person who has a vision doesn't have a psychotic reaction to it. She may be frightened by a ghost—or even by the sight of the Virgin Mary—but she is not likely to feel that her mind is being controlled by the vision. On only one occasion in all my years in clinical practice, have I heard a schizophrenic describe a vision as spiritual. She hears voices as other schizophrenics do, but she also has glorious visions of saints and holy men—visions that bring her great peace. But she is quite the exception to the rule.

People with borderline personality disorder can have any spiritual experience, and they can "rotate" through all states of consciousness. They can also be floridly "crazy," which makes a psychiatrist's job very difficult. I have found that borderlines can have "split images," in which they see an angel and the devil at the same time. It's a function of the general split—the inability to integrate "good" and "bad"—inside their personality. The image is as split as their heart and soul. Borderlines, who may have either spiritual visions or psychotic visions, experience visual hallucinations much more frequently than do schizophrenics.

A psychotic hallucination is a projection from one's unconscious mind into the outside world. For example, a borderline may be filled with conscious and unconscious murderous impulses. He may project those impulses outside himself. One borderline patient of mine hallucinated Godzilla. Godzilla joined her in the shower, ran around her house, and even ran across the highway while she was driving. It wasn't a very safe situation for anyone concerned. Godzilla was a projection of her own murderous and angry impulses.

On some occasions, borderlines see "creepy crawly" things—bugs, ants, snakes, and small birds. But those occasions are very rare. The more fragmented a psychotic person's vision is, the more likely it is that that person feels very fragmented inside. Someone who sees a single benevolent angel is better integrated mentally than someone who sees and feels hundreds of bugs crawling all over himself.

A hallucination of bugs crawling all over one's skin may be a delirium—a disorder of the brain chemistry. People in DTs (delirium tremens) while withdrawing from alcohol often have this kind of hallucination, which should be checked out right away by a doctor. Delirium is fatal in ten percent of cases. In delirium, not only does one have visual hallucinations but the entire visual field is distorted, both foreground and background. In contrast, a schizophrenic hallucination is not accompanied by a distorted background.

In order to know for certain if we're experiencing a vision or a hallucination, we first must be sure it's not an illusion. An illusion is a distortion (almost always visual) of something that is already there. For example, at dusk, we may see a rope lying on the road and think it's a snake. That's not a hallucination—it's an illusion. A mirage of a lake in the desert is an illusion. Our brain and mind are misinterpreting sensory information, because they're not being provided with all the information they need to make an accurate image.

In a sense, magic tricks are a form of illusion. Using sleight-of-hand, the magician pulls a rabbit out of his hat. Nothing metaphysical is going on here—it's just that the magician's hands are faster than our eyes, and he fools us by directing our attention away from the place where the deception is going on. Watching magic tricks, we're not hallucinating, we're just misinterpreting the sensory input.

One of the only things that saints and schizophrenics have in common is the fear of being ridiculed and called "crazy" for their visions. Saint Hildegard of Bingen experienced so many visions, she felt overwhelmed by the task of trying to remain silent about them.[3] A vision of divine light instructed her to speak about her visions, however, saying to her, "You shall proclaim [them] as you have heard and seen [them] in the miracles of God." Saint Theresa of Ávila was also troubled by her visions. She saw angels, cherubim, bright lights, Jesus, and many other visions, but she had few people in whom she could confide, at first, because she was afraid she would be called "crazy." Still, because she was unable to conceal her "raptures," she was also unable to conceal her spiritual experiences from the world. After she was regarded as a saint, she disliked the special attention showered on her, and she especially disliked people looking upon her and talking about her as a saint. She had no interest in sharing her visions with the world. To her, her visions were not the point of her spirituality. Her contact with the spiritual world made her better prepared to work in the "real" material world. They taught her how to live with one foot in each world.[4] Unlike Theresa, the schizophrenic becomes isolated from society and often very attached to his hallucinations, even to the point of being ruled by them.

In this age in which many believe that a deeply spiritual life is synonymous with mental and physical health, it is important to remember that many saints suffered physically, sometimes throughout their entire lives. Such was the case with Theresa. The nineteenth-century Indian saint Paramahansa Ramakrishna also endured tremendous physical suffering. Although he was of Hindu origin, Ramakrishna worshiped many forms of God. In fact, he worshiped the forms of God so intensely that each one of them appeared to him. When he worshiped Jesus, he forgot about everything else in the world and was visited by Jesus. When he worshiped

Shiva, only Shiva was in his mind, and Shiva too would appear to him. But Ramakrishna's main love was Kali, the Hindu divine mother. Ramakrishna "saw" Kali and spoke with her often. Toward the end of his life, he developed cancer of the throat, which made it difficult to him to eat or drink. His devotees couldn't bear to see their guru in such pain, and they begged him to ask Kali for help. Ramakrishna didn't feel that it was appropriate to ask Kali for help with a problem as "mundane" as his physical health. This attitude of detachment from the body is common among saints and sages.

Suzuki-roshi was the great teacher who brought Zen to the West earlier in this century. As he was dying of throat cancer, he said to his students, who were worrying about his comfort, "This is only suffering Buddha." There are more aspects to us than our bodies.

The visions of the great ones are part and parcel of their lives and works. Because of their love, compassion, courage, and great works, the saints have gone down in history. The visions of the saints remind us to examine all visual paranormal experiences with an open mind. When we keep an open but critical mind, we can embrace our own visions.

If you've had an unusual visual experience, you'll know what to call it by the time you've finished reading this chapter. Here are some ways to determine the nature of your experience:

1.   Decide whether your visual experience was a spiritual vision or a hallucination of some kind.

   A. If it was a drug-related hallucination, go to a doctor and get treatment.

   B. If it was a genuine spiritual experience, you need do nothing further. Be grateful for the divine gift you have received. Take the inspiration from the vision and try to live a more noble life. Follow the advice of your angel.

2.   If your vision involves a visitation by a deceased loved one, and you don't like it, you can quickly turn the situation around with this four-step process:

   A. If you are being visited on a regular basis, figure out what the pattern is. Let's say your deceased uncle visits you in the evening shortly before you go to sleep at nine o'clock. Rather than being frightened about your "uncle's" random appearances, you can turn the tables by waiting for him between nine and nine-fifteen every night. That's all you have to do. Whether or not the vision appears, you now control that fifteen-minute block of time. If your "uncle" visits you, he will be coming on your terms.

For most people, this first step will radically cut down on visitations, and frequently it will eliminate the "intruder" completely.

B. If the visits continue, begin to communicate with your "uncle" beginning the second week. Ask him why he's visiting. Simply chat with him. Your fear will continue to drop, and your relationship with the vision will change.

C. If your "uncle" is still visiting you, and you still don't like it, beginning the third week, say the following words to him: "Why are you late?"

Don't be fooled by the simplicity and the humor in this last technique. It evolved out of my intensive study of the great American psychiatrist Milton Erikson.[5] Not only does it work—it works 100 percent of the time, given the following conditions.[6]

1. The vision is a single figure—in other words, your uncle visits you over and over again. This technique does not work as well if multiple people "visit" at the same time or if the cast of characters in the vision changes.

2. The vision is whole and intact. In other words, the vision is of your uncle's whole body, not just from the waist up.

3. Your vision is not ghastly or overwhelming.

There are few guarantees I can make as a doctor, but this technique, given the right conditions, has a 100 percent success rate. (Of course, you may not want your deceased "uncle" to stop visiting. That's a different story.)

The reason this technique works is simple. No matter what name you give your vision, your relationship with it is one in which you probably feel out of control. This technique turns that relationship around by 180 degrees, so that you move from fear to curiosity. When you can ask "Why are you late?" you simply have no more fear.

Now, here is the fourth and final step:

4.   If the visitations stop, you may miss them. If that is the case, grieve the loss as you would any other loss.

Now that you know how to deal with an unwanted "visitor," you can more happily embrace all of your visions, especially angels.

## ANGELS

Don, a likable, soft-spoken, outwardly tough fireman of few words, was referred to me by his oncologist. Don had lung cancer, and six inoperable tumors had appeared in his brain. The oncologist wanted to fight the cancer with every technique he could find, and he thought it would be good for Don to learn some imagery skills to help him cope.

In our first session, I asked Don the twenty-five spiritual questions psychiatrists are afraid to ask. At one point Don volunteered, "I don't know if you'll believe this, but as I was coming out of surgery after the first cancer operation, I had a real vision. I saw this giant eagle that swooped down and picked me up in its claws. It carried me over hills and valleys, finally landing at the top of a great cliff. It dropped me into its nest. I wasn't scared at all, even when the eagle began tearing out my guts. I knew it meant he was eating the cancer. Suddenly a beautiful angel appeared over me, hovering in the air." At this point Don broke down and sobbed. "Why me?" he asked.

"What do you mean?" I replied.

"Why would I deserve an angel? I've never done anything special." He was trying to regain control of himself.

"Don," I said, "you're asking the wrong question. The question isn't 'Why me?' The question is 'Why *not* me?' "

"Why do I deserve an angel?"

"That's exactly my point, Don. Everybody deserves an angel. To think you aren't worthy of the love this angel brought you is incorrect. Now, I don't know if we can save your life through imagery, but I can tell you that to be open to healing your cancer, you're going to have to open yourself completely to love. You're going to need to let go of old ideas that you're not good enough, that you're not worthy, or that God doesn't love you. The angel came to you. That's proof in itself that you deserve the experience."

This was a new way of thinking for Don, one that he needed. I told Don, "Whether you live or die soon, connecting with this deep love is the real healing. We're going to be working with your angel a lot from now on."

Psycho-Spiritual Assessment was quite helpful for Don:

1.  We clarified his *main concern:* He had experienced an angel, a genuine spiritual experience, while he was in an altered state of consciousness called *twilight state*.

2.  We looked at Don's *feelings* about the experience. He felt happy, ecstatic, tearful, doubtful, and confused all at the same time.

3.  We explored the *meaning* of the experience. Don's realization that he had been visited by an angel made him rethink his entire spiritual belief system. God and the angels were no longer far away or reserved for the few. He accepted that every one of us, including himself, can have a direct experience of God.

The PSA allowed us to move quickly with his therapy. In this first session, I encouraged Don to deepen his spiritual practice by giving himself permission to accept the gift he had received—the gift of the angel. Over the course of several weeks, I had him imagine himself with the angel over and over again, allowing himself to connect ever more deeply with the angel, with love, with God, and with the deepest levels of healing.

Sixty percent of Americans believe in angels. According to Sophy Burnham, author of *A Book of Angels* and *Angel Letters,* every culture and every major religion in the world, with the single exception of Shintoism, describes angels.[7] It is my belief that "helpful angels" are *real*—and that they are significantly different from psychotic hallucinations.

Although some believe that it's very difficult to tell an angel from a visual hallucination, it's really not. Angels come with a simple and universal message. They teach people to love and forgive everyone, friend and foe alike. They inspire great hope and almost invariably cause a positive and permanent transformation in a person's life. Angels may look like "regular folk," or they may look like divine beings of light with wings. They may be solid or translucent. If an apparition is telling you to hate, to kill someone else or yourself, it's not an angel.

According to Burnham, angels do not relate to terms like *angel,* and in fact they may be confused if you ask them if they're an angel. As beings from another realm, they are beyond labels. It's we who have the need to label. Angels don't. Nor do angels necessarily appear to "religious" people. Actually, they are more likely to appear to "regular" people. They either appear at particular times of great stress and rescue us; or they serve as a source of strength throughout our lives, to help us through hard times. They may or may not appear to more than one person.

These stories were reported to me by good friends:

Mary, age 80, was driving her old Buick when it got stuck on some railroad tracks. She and her two friends in the car were terrified—a train was bearing down on them. But she couldn't get the car off the tracks. Suddenly she saw two powerful brown arms grab the steering wheel and turn it powerfully, dislodging the tires from the tracks. A moment later the car lurched forward, out of danger. Mary's friends were startled beyond belief, and they asked her how the car had moved. They had seen the miracle—they hadn't seen the angel.

Sometimes people have a vision that they think is an angel but isn't. Jack, age 35, was a U.S. Navy man with sixteen years of experience on the high seas. But what he saw during Operation Desert Storm, he had never experienced in all his years at sea. As his ship was passing into the Persian Gulf, he and all on deck saw a rainbow of pure white light arch across the waters and the gulf in the distance. It was like a rainbow, but the archway was pure white and glowing. As the ship passed under the arch of light, Jack and all the others on board got the feeling that they would be in God's hands during the ensuing battles. Jack felt that an angel was showing the way and saying "Don't worry. Everything is going to be okay."

I heard the following story twice, from two people who don't know each other and, as far as I know, have never spoken with each other. Carla Jones was driving on one of L.A.'s freeways when she was startled by the presence of a "nonhuman being" in her back seat. This casually dressed being, whom she felt was an angel, told her that there was going to be an earthquake the next day. Carla looked back to the highway to regain her bearings, then looked again to the back seat. Her "angel" was gone. The apparition rattled Carla, and her driving became quite erratic—enough so that she was pulled over by the police. When the officer asked her what was wrong, Carla replied, "Officer, I don't think you're going to believe me."

He said, "Go ahead. Try me. I'll listen."

After Carla told her story, the officer replied, "You are the seventh person today who has told me the same story."

(In another version of this story, the officer said the driver was the ninth person to tell him the story.)

That night, Nicole Simpson and Ronald Goldman were murdered. A week or so later, Americans were glued to their televisions, watching the famous chase of O.J. Simpson along the freeway. Perhaps Los Angeles, the city of angels, is so much the city of earthquakes that even social upheavals are earthquakes to angels.

History is full of angel sightings. The Prophet Mohammed's vision of the angel Gabriel provided the inspiration for an entire new religion, Islam. The best-known sightings in the West are visions of Mary, mother of Jesus, who first made her appearance to James the Apostle in Spain in A.D. 40. Then and in her frequent visitations since then over a two-thousand-year period, she appeared in a long dress, wearing a head cover, and surrounded in a globe of light. A mist often surrounds her feet. Her most famous appearances include those of Guadalupe, Lourdes, Knock, Fatima, and Medjugorje.

In 1531, an Aztec Indian, Juan Diego, had a vision of Mary. She said to him, "Are you not under my shadow and protection?" Initially frightened by the vision, Juan Diego soon felt immense love and comfort in her words. This appearance of Mary came to be known as Our Lady of Guadalupe.

In 1858 in the French Pyrenees, Mary appeared to a 14-year-old girl, Bernadette Soubirous, her sister, and a friend. Over a six-month period, Bernadette was visited by Mary eighteen times. In 1862 the visions were declared authentic, and the site of those visions, Lourdes, became world renowned as a pilgrimage site, offering hope for mental, physical, and spiritual healing.

Thirteen Irishmen standing near the church of Knock, in 1879, experienced a vision of Mary wearing a large radiant crown. On her right stood Saint Joseph and on her left, Saint John the Evangelist. Although the other citizens of Knock did not see Mary, many reported seeing a bright light illuminating the church and its surroundings.

The twentieth century has seen an ever-increasing number of visits from Mary. The miracle of Fatima, in Portugal, occurred in 1915, when she appeared to three children and said, "Don't be afraid. I will not hurt you. I am from heaven. I come to ask you to come here for six months in succession, on the thirteenth day at this same hour." Mary's final visit was "set" for October 13, 1917. Seventy thousand people stood in the rain awaiting her final appearance and were not disappointed.

In 1920, a vision of Mary hovering in the sky apparently stopped Russian soldiers "dead in their tracks." Instead of crossing the Vistula River and then invading Warsaw, the soldiers withdrew.

In 1981, Mary appeared to six children in Medjugorje, in the former Yugoslavia. She promised to give each child ten secrets, ten prophecies. Her vision and her words are consistent with the legendary sightings at Fatima and Lourdes. The children report that she said, "Children, darkness reigns over the whole world. People are attracted by many things, and they forget about the more important," and, "By means of the messages, I wish to make a beautiful mosaic in your hearts."[8]

Divine visitations are nothing new. Rather, there has been an unending flow of the miraculous into everyday life throughout recorded history. What may be new or at least of special import is the rise in worship of the goddess. In *Woman as Healer,* Jeanne Achterberg, Ph.D., speculates that historically the decline in worship of female forms of God went hand-in-hand with decline in respect for the environment, as well as the decline in civilization as a whole.[9] When worship of the pre-Christian goddesses, such as Diana and Ishtar, was banned by the church in favor of an "all-male cast" of gods, society soon plunged into the Dark Ages.

Worship of Goddess is not better than worship of God. The reemergence of Mary and other forms of the Goddess indicates a restoration of balance. In Chinese philosophy, life is a balance of yin (female energies) and yang (male energies). We in the West have been out of balance for a long time. Body, mind, and spirit have been split apart, as have God and Goddess.

Whether or not we choose to believe that "Mary sightings," and angel sightings in general, are real, it is a grave mistake to write off these experiences as hallucinations, imagination, or attempts by psychologically unstable people to get attention. Although we may never be able to put every angel and every vision into a neat box, the way we can with different types of pneumonia, we can receive messages from many altered states of consciousness, and we can allow angels to alter our consciousness.

If we remember that we are not alone in our angel sightings, we can grow in hope and faith. Angels have been reported for thousands of years by people in a great variety of cultures. Spiritual masters, gurus, saints, and shamans from every religion and every culture all agree on the existence of angels. We each must decide if we believe angels exist, and then, if the situation presents itself, we must decide if we have had a genuine vision of an angel or not. Here's how to deal with your "angel."

1. Decide if you saw an angel or were hallucinating. If your "angel" left you feeling inspired, full of tears of joy and love, you most likely really did see an angel.

2. There's nothing more you need to do about it, other than feel grateful for the experience and do as the song advises: "Fall on your knees. Oh, hear the angel voices." Rejoice if you've seen an angel. Express your gratitude to God and the angel.

3. If you believe the angel was trying to convey a message, but you aren't sure what it was, write down any words the angel spoke. Meditate on those words. Angels never present themselves for no reason; nor do they speak for no reason. If no words were spoken, meditate on what the angel was doing, how he or she was dressed, and the feeling he or she inspired in you. Continue meditating on the meaning of the visit until the message is clear.

4. Do not lose hold of the power of an angelic visit. Write down the experience in all its detail, then revisit the angel in your imagination on a regular basis, so that you can continue to receive the inspiration the angel intended to bring you.

## VISIONS OF THE DEPARTED

Approximately 105 million Americans believe they have had messages from dead people or visions of them. In many cultures, visitations from the dead are an expected and normal part of the grieving process. All Hopi widows receive visitations from their deceased husbands, who return in order to complete unfinished business. If the marriage was peaceful and well-adjusted, the husband visits a few times and then leaves for good. If the marriage was conflicted, the husband visits frequently, and the experience is emotionally upsetting.

A patient of mine who is a Lutheran minister tells me the following story. Reverend Thomas routinely consoles grief-stricken parishioners. On one occasion he was consoling the mother of a young man, Steve, who had suffered an epileptic seizure. As they sat on a couch outside the emergency room where her son was being treated, Steve's mother suddenly gasped and said to the reverend, "Did you see that?"

"Did I see *what*?"

"Did you see my son? His spirit just walked out of the operating room—hand-in-hand with the spirit of his deceased father. [Steve's father had died six years previously.] They both looked so happy, so content, so full of light. Steve and his father smiled at me and then walked away together." Reverend Thomas hadn't seen it, but he certainly believed she had.

Moments later, the emergency room doors swung open, and the surgeon sadly told them that Steve had just died.

Stephanie, a travel agent and a friend of mine, had a vision of her departed grandmother, Helen, six months after her death. "I came out of a deep sleep and was startled to see that the room was incredibly bright. At first I thought it must be morning and the sun was streaming in through the window. Then I saw my deceased grandmother, Helen. She looked absolutely beautiful. She was just glowing. I was so happy to see her, and in my usual gregarious manner I said, 'Grandma, it's so good to see you!'

"She was very happy to see me and replied, 'Something wonderful is about to happen!'

" 'Really!' I said. We communicated for a while nonverbally. I could see her only from the waist up. She was completely engulfed in light. Although she had died in her nineties, she appeared to be about 50, although her hair was still white. She was dressed in a white tunic or robe.

"I fell back asleep, and when I woke up again, the sun was just beginning to rise. It was then that I realized that Grandma had visited me in the middle of the night, when it was pitch black. It wasn't the sun that was illuminating the room. It was Grandma.

"I was so excited and curious about her saying 'Something wonderful is about to happen.' I expected some dramatic thing in the family—but maybe the news was on God's plane or about something of a spiritual nature.

"When the family was at the breakfast table, I shared my vision, and my son said that he had been visited by Grandma in a dream that same night."

Spirits of the dead can visit us in a variety of ways, not just by standing in front of us. My friend Pepe Romero had an unusual visitation from his departed father. Shortly after Celedonio died, Pepe saw him lying on a "sheet of light," with his head pointing toward Pepe and his feet pointing away. Pepe saw that he was not only lying on the sheet of light but was part of the light.

Physicians would be doing serious harm if they told people like Pepe, "You're just seeing things. I'm going to put you on some Valium for a few days until you're feeling better." When someone is being visited by the dead, they are not denying reality or avoiding the pain of grief. Nor do visitations from the dead interfere with the grief process. In fact, they're part of the grief process, and they help us find meaning and purpose in life. Like angels, visions of the departed usually bring hope and inspiration. They help us awaken to our higher nature, offering us comfort in times of pain and suffering and direction when we are confused. Such visitations help us face our own mortality—for those who have had such experiences develop a firm belief in the continuity of life after physical death. Those who have fully embraced their mortality are the ones who can best give themselves to the moment, to life, and to living. Experiences like these should be shared with one's physician, and physicians should be asking patients about them. In so doing, the doctor-patient relationship will grow stronger, and we will all be better able to face both life and death.

## GHOSTS AND HAUNTINGS

Some people have a highly developed sixth sense and can peer into other dimensions, escaping the grip of time and space. Shama Smith, an extraordinary professional psychic and a friend of mine, is one such person. As a psychiatrist, I can vouch for her sanity. As a friend, I can attest to her solid character, her loving, compassionate nature, her sense of humor, her solid business sense, her strong desire to be of service to others, and her deep love for God.

Shama has solid credentials as a psychic. She has worked with a team of psychics in the UCLA Parapsychology Department, in conjunction with the Metropolitan Los Angeles Police Department, the California Highway Patrol, the Santa Barbara Sheriff's Department, the Westminster Police Department, and other municipal police departments in California, as well as the FBI and Interpol. Shama was researched, examined, and trained through the UCLA Parapsychology Department of the Neuropsychiatric Institute (NPI), before becoming part of its team of consultants. She also has advised and consulted for four heads of state. Because psychics are not part of a recognized profession in the United States, she has always worked for the government for free. Although the FBI may call her for an assignment, taxpayers would throw a fit if they learned that their tax dollars were going to a psychic.

It took Shama between five and six years to differentiate clearly a bona-fide psychic impression from an imaginative image. For her, a psychic impression is clear, without being dramatic, and is not accompanied by thunder or lightning.

With Shama's assistance I have gained some understanding of the differences among ghosts, nonhuman entities, and other "weird" phenomena. On several occasions she and I have gone "ghost-busting" together, each of us bringing our particular outlook and skills to dealing with people who think they are "haunted." Shama is able to enter a realm that exists outside of time and space, a "place" that is actually no place, but from which she can obtain information.

Before we dive into the story, you'll want to know the difference between ghosts and entities yourself. *Ghosts,* according to Shama and the vast literature on the subject, are souls of the dead who remain attached to a physical place. Often that place is a house, but a ghost may also be attached to a place that existed long before a house was built on the site. Hauntings are very long-lasting, sometimes persisting for hundreds or even thousands of years. Ghost don't really care who's in the house. It's "their house"! Metaphysically speaking, the ghost still believes he or she lives in the house. A ghost is really a lost soul that has gotten stuck on its way out of death's door and has not found its way to the light.

An *entity* is the soul of a dead nonhuman or human being. But it is a very "low" kind of consciousness, the mental and spiritual remnant of an individual who was quite violent, abusive, promiscuous, or addicted. An entity attaches itself to a specific person, not to a place. Entities require "two to tango" and are usually attracted to an individual who has intense sexual or aggressive desires. They are attracted only by our strong impulses and cannot coexist with us unless we are feeding them with the energy of our desires. When a person afflicted by an entity has overcome his addiction to anger, sex, power, or drugs, the entity automatically leaves. Fortunately, entities don't hang around for very long—they almost always disappear within a few years.

Exorcism is of little value in these cases, unless the "victim" can let go of his or her subconscious attachments that keep the entity around. An entity may periodically attack someone in what is called *psychic attack*. If the entity has entered the individual's life so completely that the mind and behavior of the living person are completely comingled with the entity, we call it *spirit possession* (more about that later).

*A word of caution:* The rest of this section and the following one— "Psychic Attack and Spirit Possession"—contain some potentially frightening stories. If you do not want to delve into this somewhat dark, strange, and scary territory, feel free to go straight to the section on the human aura. The end of this chapter tells you how to live in a way that will not predispose you to psychic attack.

Here is an extraordinary story Shama shared with me about how she dealt with a ghost that was haunting her own house: "When my husband, Cass, and I moved into a house in southern California, I was standing in the kitchen the first day and said to him, 'Honey, the house is haunted.' He said, 'Oh no, please don't tell me that.' I replied, 'It is, and I know it is.' 'Well, how do you know it is?' he asked. 'Number one, I can smell it, and number two, I can feel a presence around me here.'

" 'Why didn't you realize it was living here when we first looked at the house?'

" 'Because, Cass, I wasn't tuned in to it, and it wasn't making its presence felt. Besides that, we needed to find a new place to live quickly, and I was feeling pressured. Now that we're settled in and the stress of finding a new place and moving in is over, I'm relaxed and can feel this presence.' "

According to Shama, sometimes if there's been a grotesque death on the premises, the house will smell, no matter how much cleaning you do. In her new house she knew she was perceiving an odor from another realm—a perception that would definitely be called "crazy" by most psychiatrists.

"Once I had the house in order and had things put away, I made myself an office. I was finally settled down in my office, doing my work, when I began perceiving the presence more clearly. I was perceiving a 'woman' who would walk into the office and stay close to the door. The vision, the ghost, would stand there and watch me work. The ghost appeared to be in her late twenties and of medium height. I knew she was the presence I had felt the first day.

"The ghost *followed* me around the house everywhere. This went on for weeks. I wasn't frightened because I've had a lot of experience with this kind of thing—although most people would sense that their territory has been invaded. I talked about the ghost with my husband. After we were in the house for a few weeks, Cass came down with bronchitis. He was coughing so badly, I couldn't sleep in the same room with him because he was keeping me awake all night. So I made up a bed in the office, the room where the ghost most frequently visited me.

"I went to sleep and woke up to the sound of a child violently screaming. Then the child was struck dead—struck dead by surprise. The child, a young girl, had been killed without any warning. Then I saw blood in the rugs, and I saw myself with blood up to my ankles."

For any of you who think being a psychic is fun, this story may make you reconsider.

"I came out of a deep sleep by the scream, but I then entered an altered state that was neither asleep nor awake. In this other state I was able to perceive the story of what had happened in the house. The information I receive in that state is received in a unit. It's not linear and sequential like the information exchanged in day-to-day conversation. So I experienced the whole story in one instant."

Certainly Shama was not in a normal state of consciousness; she was not in linear, time-and-space-bound consciousness. Shama feels that she wasn't just an observer in this experience but was also a participant, actually feeling the blood coming up to her ankles.

"When I became fully awake, I knew that whatever had happened there was so gory that there was tremendous bloodshed. Psychiatrists perceive an object from the outside, walking around it, making notations, recording data, and making decisions. In a psychic's line of work, the idea is not to walk around the object but to enter into it, so it's a coexistence. And that's the only way a psychic can ever experience how another person really feels. Even though I was fully experiencing what was going on, there was part of me that knew that it was okay. I was not terrified, upset, or feeling victimized. I was in the experience but also witnessing it.

"At that point, I ran into the bedroom, woke up my husband, and told him, 'Now I know someone was murdered in this house—a child. It must have been a savage murder, because the child lost all of her blood. Tomorrow I'm going to speak to the landlord and tell him that I know.' Cass said, 'Please, honey, don't go tell the landlord that.' "

The next morning she did go to the landlord's house and said, "You can be honest with me. I'm not going to move out. I'm not upset, but I want to tell you what I saw in the house, and then I want you to tell me what happened." She told him the story, and he said, "By law I don't have to tell you anything about the house—but I will. A woman named Kendra had lived there with her daughter. It was Monday. Kendra's daughter didn't feel well and stayed home from school. That morning while her daughter was watching television, Kendra struck her daughter over the head with a baseball bat and then stabbed her countless times with a butcher knife. Then Kendra stabbed herself to death. They both lost all the blood in their bodies. The carpet was literally soaked with their blood. We couldn't hire anybody to take out the carpets, so my wife and I had to take the rugs out ourselves. My wife has never returned to the house."

As Shama tells the story, "After I heard the actual history, the presence of Kendra continued to follow me around the house. It was as if Kendra wanted to talk to me and was reaching out to me. I told Kendra that she was dead—because she didn't know that she was, in fact, dead.

Many psychics, myself included, believe that if you die suddenly, you are so disoriented that your spirit may remain around the premises where you last lived or worked.

"I sat down in a chair and began talking to Kendra as you would talk to a friend. I thought that if Kendra had any religious background, she probably had been exposed to Christianity, so I spoke to her about Jesus and told her that Jesus *does* forgive and that she had to forgive herself and ask God to take her into the Light. She needed to head to the Light to go on to a new life. Kendra understood me. She understood her own confusion and her death."

Consider how frightened most of us are to even think about death. It takes great courage, in my opinion, to actually face death and *talk to the dead.*

"I told Kendra that she was dead and did not live in this house anymore. I told her that she had committed the murder while she was not in her right mind and that she needed to see it in that light and forgive herself. I spoke with her very compassionately as opposed to screaming at her, 'Get out!' Most people, of course, would scream at a being like Kendra if they could sense her, because they experience the presence as an invasion of their privacy, and they're terrified."

Their *conversation* continued for about an hour, and then Shama burned frankincense, lit candles, and prayed for Kendra for several hours, to "purify body, mind, and spirit—including spirits of the dead."

That night, after Shama had gone to bed, she was awakened when a candle began burning spontaneously on its own. It was a brand-new candle, one she claims she had never lit. "But it lit itself. I woke up to the illumination of the entire room. It was so beautiful and the illumination was so strong that it felt like more than the light of that one candle. That intense spontaneous lighting of the candle made me feel that Kendra had finally gone into the Light. And she never came around our house again."

Many people see ghosts, and how they choose to deal with them is important. By realizing that a ghost, unlike an entity, is attached only to a physical location, any of us can be better prepared to cope with the situation. When we're dealing with an entity, it is essential that we discover the part of ourselves that is attracting it. But when we're dealing with a ghost, the love and compassion that Shama displayed are the key to defusing this potentially frightening situation.

Ghosts have probably been around as long as has the human race, and they have been researched and written about for centuries. The Brown Lady of Raynham Hall is one of the most reliably photographed ghosts in history. She is usually seen dressed in a long brown dress or cape and carrying a lantern. She was first seen in 1835 and was last seen in 1936. During the early period of her visitations, a Captain Frederick Renée intentionally went to sleep in the room where the Brown Lady was most often seen. That night the captain was awakened by the ghost. Startled, he pulled out his pistol and fired at point-blank range. The bullet had no effect on the ghost, which continued its haunting for another hundred years.

The Borley Rectory is considered to be one of the most haunted houses in England. The rectory was initially inhabited by Benedictine monks. In the late 1800s, Reverend H.D.D. Bull tore down the old rectory and built a new one on the same site, at which point the hauntings commenced. One of the ghosts frequently seen at the Borley Rectory was that of a thirteenth-century nun, who according to legend had fallen in love with one of the monks. The monk and the nun tried to escape in a horse and carriage but failed. The monk was hung, and the nun was imprisoned in the rectory, where she later died.

The Tower of London has a long history of hauntings. In 1483 two princes were murdered there. Their ghosts were repeatedly seen until 1674, when their bones were removed from the tower and were given a proper burial. Anne Boleyn, beheaded by her husband, Henry VIII, in 1536, is the ghost most frequently seen in the tower.

Hauntings are not limited to Western cultures. The trampled burial sites of indigenous peoples are another source of ghostly visions. In Hawaii native burial sites that have been moved or destroyed by the booming tourist industry have become fertile ground for ghost sightings.

Regardless of time, place, or culture, the reason for hauntings appears to be the same. The spirit of the dead remains attached to a physical place, such as a house, a tower, or a burial ground, instead of leaving the material world behind and moving on to higher planes of consciousness.

## PSYCHIC ATTACK AND SPIRIT POSSESSION

A great many of you will have visions of departed loved ones, which you should experience as a gift. A few of you will see or feel ghosts, but you should not be bothered by them. A very, very small number of people will experience *psychic attack,* or its more severe manifestation, *spirit posses-*

*sion.* These latter two phenomena are included here merely for the sake of completeness. The average person need have no concern whatsoever about them. (But it is a good idea for medicine to become familiar with these phenomena, so that physicians can be of assistance in these rare situations.)

In 1974, Barry Taff, Ph.D. (Doctorate in Psychophysiology), part of the UCLA Parapsychology Department, came in contact with Mrs. B., a 35-year-old woman who claimed that her house was haunted.[10] Dr. Taff, who has examined more than 3,300 cases of ghosts, hauntings, and poltergeists, visited Mrs. B. in her home. She reported that she had recently been raped by a ghost. Dr. Taff later told me, "I felt like rolling my eyes. I thought she was hysterical and had an overactive libido. I was convinced that she was psychotic, and that was that."

Ten days later, Mrs. B. called him again, asking him to please come see her again, and he agreed to do so. When he arrived, he was surprised to find that the house was icy cold inside. The house had no air conditioning, and it was a hot August afternoon. The house smelled of a foul, rotting odor, the source of which Dr. Taff could never ascertain scientifically.

According to Dr. Taff, "I saw a lot of strange things. I saw the fusebox violently ripped out of the wall, candelabras shaking and falling. My team and I began to see little balls of blue-green light. We sealed the house of all sources of light and electricity. The balls of light grew brighter. They zoomed around the house and flew around us. We photographed a great deal, but the results were paradoxical. When we saw something, such as a ball of light, it never showed up on film. But many things we didn't see with our eyes did show up on film. One photo revealed an arc of light over Mrs. B.'s head. I took the photos to the editor of *Popular Photography*. He could find no evidence of fakery or trickery, nor any scientific explanation for the phenomena recorded on film.

"On one occasion, something physically pushed me back. On another occasion, I had taped black posterboard on the ceiling with duct tape in order to seal out light. The posterboard had been violently ripped off the ceiling, along with some of the drywall. I witnessed this myself and saw some of the posterboard violently rip off the ceiling and hit Mrs. B. in the head. All of this activity would come and go. The stench would come and go. The incredible cold would come and go. Finally, after several years, things finally quieted down for her."

Dr. Taff calls this kind of phenomenon *poltergeist activity. Poltergeist* means "noisy ghost," a definition that doesn't really clarify anything for me, so I have chosen the term *psychic attack*. Mrs. B. is a classic case of psychic attack. Spirit possession, in my opinion, is caused by the same entities that cause psychic attack, the only difference being that in spirit possession, one's mind, and not just one's body, seems to come under the control of some outside force. Not only do strange events occur around one, such as fires spontaneously igniting or fuses blowing, but one's mind becomes the target of attack.

Here's a case of spirit possession reported to me by Rosanne, the patient you read about in Chapter 8. During her twenties, Rosanne "fell" under the tutelage of a so-called spiritual teacher, whom I would have to call "evil." This teacher taught Rosanne how to let "entities" enter her, with the stated goal of helping her tap into a higher consciousness. Rosanne learned a method of "making herself (her Self) very small." When her sense of self was as small as the tip of a pin, the entities would enter her body and mind. "I invited them in, and they would actually jump into me. I could see and feel them, and I did whatever they told me to do. My body would spontaneously develop weird movements. My voice radically changed and became that of a man. And my voice had an echo to it as if I were speaking in a large room with marble floors. There were a lot of people around me during this period, dozens of people, including a famous parapsychology researcher from a prestigious Ivy League university. People said that my face was like a chameleon. My face, my eyes would change shape and color. At first I couldn't clearly see the entities. They just had an undefined form and color. But later I could see them clearly. They were so ugly—and scary.

"Through the entities I gained certain paranormal powers. I could put ideas into other people's heads and make them think that the idea actually was their own. This turned really evil when my teacher asked me to use these new powers to help her get the man she wanted. She wanted me to use this power to break up the man's marriage—which I did. The process left me so sick, I nearly died. I was so naïve at the time. I trusted my teacher, and she led me down a very dark and evil path. Once I realized that what I was doing was truly evil, I never did it again. I left my teacher and never invited entities inside again."

Before concluding that Rosanne had been possessed, I had to wonder if she was crazy—but she wasn't. She doesn't hear voices. She doesn't suffer from hysteria, hysterical fits of blindness, amnesia, deafness, or seizures. She doesn't feel that her mind is being controlled by radio or television. She's a survivor of abuse and suffers from mood swings, panic, chaotic relationships, and self-sabotage. I do a great deal of guided imagery work with her, which she works with easily. As a specialist in imagery, I can say with little doubt that the entities she sees are neither fantasy nor imagination.

People who suffer from either psychic attack or spirit possession fit a particular personality profile. According to Dr. Taff, Mrs. B. "fits a typical personality profile of people who experience these phenomena. She was abused as a child by her father. She was very angry, very impulsive, and had a lot of repressed anger. It's like she was wound up and had nowhere to go with her feelings. She also drank a lot, which is very common with this phenomena. The more unstable she was emotionally, the more poltergeist activity."

To me, Mrs. B. sounds like she suffered from child abuse, with subsequent borderline personality. This personality type combined with drinking makes one "psychically open." These people are a metaphysical accident waiting to happen. When you add to this dangerous concoction a lifestyle that includes drugs, alcohol, addiction to sex, and addiction to rage, one's consciousness is lowered to such an extent that "lower" forms of consciousness, such as entities, have an open door through which they can launch a psychic attack.

Spirit possession may sound like mumbo-jumbo to a Western-trained scientist, but we have to acknowledge that possession is recognized in every other culture around the world. It would be foolish to ignore the possibility that possession may be present in any culture, including our own. In spirit possession, psychiatry has the ultimate challenge of trying to understand the underlying biology, the defects in brain metabolism, the psychopathology, the results of child abuse, and the low self-esteem, as well as the cultural and spiritual components.

It is conceivable that our mental hospitals are filled with people who suffer from possession, or a combination of possession and mental illness. Perhaps psychiatry needs to find a way to make psychiatric hospitals more sacred, to make them less inviting for the entities that possess people. Perhaps we need to incorporate devotional singing, meditation, and prayer— and the burning of frankincense—along with appropriate medication. Making our environments more sacred will make us less prone to possession. We need to discover what is polluting our mental environment and our physical environment, then begin to clean up.

The more I have tried to clarify the different mental states, mental illnesses, spiritual states, spiritual illnesses, and strange phenomena—the more subtle and difficult the questions become. There are no easy answers. Nor do I intend to enable people to say to themselves, "I really am not responsible for what happens to me. I'm under psychic attack from an outside force." Rather, I aim to help people take more responsibility for their lives.

Now let's take a minute to see the relevance of entities, psychic attack, and spirit possession for you, the reader. Here are the key points to remember:

1. The chances that you are possessed or suffering psychic attack are incredibly low.

2. Psychic attack, when it does occur, is relatively short-lived.

3. Psychic attack is not truly random. I do not mean to imply that people who suffer from psychic attack are "evil" or that they somehow deserve their fate; nor would I accuse the patient with lung cancer of causing his own demise by smoking all of his life, or the person with colon cancer for eating too much red meat. Yet the way we live has a profound influence on all aspects of our lives—body, mind, and spirit.

4. Apply all the techniques at the end of the following section, "Thought-Forms." Those techniques apply equally well to psychic attack and spirit possession.

5. Each of us can do our part in eliminating the essential precursor to psychic attack and possession—namely, a childhood filled with abuse and/or neglect. As parents, or future parents, it is our duty to raise our children with the utmost love, respect, honesty, consistency, and nonviolence. These are the real preventive medicines. If you were a victim of child abuse, use the techniques in this book to help free yourself from the past, so that the cycle can be broken. Practice the void imagery in Chapter 16. Pray that you will do your children no harm. Do whatever you can to stop the cycle of violence.

6. Parent by example. Don't expect your children to avoid drugs and alcohol if you're abusing them yourself.

## THOUGHT-FORMS

Lisa, a 30-year-old navy lieutenant, was frightened by a vision that she had in a condominium into which she had recently moved. She saw a "two-foot-wide, hideous black cloud with ten sharp hooks around the middle" floating around her bedroom. After the initial shock, Lisa, who had studied metaphysics, realized she had just seen a thought-form. She recognized the cloud with hooks, for she had seen a picture of one in a metaphysics class. From her class she also knew that the color black, when present in a thought-form, represents resentment or malice. The hooks represented a strong sensual craving. She did not feel that her own mind had given rise to the thought-form and was quite sure it "belonged" to someone else.

After collecting herself, Lisa told her landlord, Bill, that she had had a strange experience in her new home. Who had lived there before she moved in? she asked. Bill replied, "My girlfriend, Janet, used to live with me. I asked her to leave three weeks ago. She's an angry alcoholic and was incredibly sexual most of the time. She still calls, leaves messages, and is desperate to get back together with me."

The thought-form that Lisa saw was like those described by Madame Blavatsky, a nineteenth-century founder of the Theosophical Society (a group of "adepts" and spiritual seekers with well-developed *siddhi* powers). According to Madame Blavatsky, thoughts and prayers have power, real consequences, and are visible.[11] (Prayers may not even be as different from ordinary thoughts as we currently believe. The difference may only be one of intention and direction of the thought.)

The Theosophists, including Madame Blavatsky, were able to see thought-forms, and they studied and classified them carefully. The group observed people under a variety of conditions that caused feelings of joy, anger, grief, jealousy, and so on. They observed people praying, worrying, laughing. Each member then drew a picture of the thought-form that hovered over, or nearby, an individual in a specific condition. The results were startling. For any given condition, they all saw the same thing. They were able to draw more than fifty pictures of thought-forms that correspond to specific human conditions.[12]

The Theosophists identified and explored three qualities of thought-forms: color, shape, and clarity. The *color* arises out of the emotion the person is experiencing. The black color of Lisa's vision was due to Janet's anger and intense desire. The *shape* reflected Janet's attachment to Bill— she still had her "mental hooks" in him. The intense *clarity* of the thought-form, the sharpness of the cloud's edges, was produced by the intensity and power of Janet's thought. The more definite the shape of a thought-form, the more time, attention, and power is being given to it.

Because Lisa was educated about thought-forms, the hooked cloud did not affect her. She couldn't make it go away but had only to wait it out. The cloud appeared a couple of more times, although more faintly, and then disappeared for good.

Most of us cannot see thought-forms, yet we know how it feels to enter someone's house when there's been a big argument. We can "feel" the bad vibes, the anger, even if we can't see it. It hangs in the air. If you take the effect of such "vibes" and multiply it by a million, you can imagine a very powerful thought. A very powerful thought, I might add, is what psychics and others with *siddhi* powers see hanging over the Balkan states and the states of the former Soviet Union today.

Thought-forms arise out of the energy we give to them. The more energy we pour into a thought-form, the greater its power. Centuries of negativity gave rise to the former Soviet Union's "dark cloud." (Of course, not all thought-forms are negative or nasty-looking. A purring cat, for example, generates "fuzzy, pink puffs.") When a thought-form gains sufficient energy, it begins to affect our lives. The principle "like attracts like" governs thought-forms. An alcoholic person generates a powerful alcoholic thought-form, and other alcoholic thought-forms are attracted to it.

Some experts believe that alcoholism is a disease, a physical illness—in fact, alcoholism has been proven to have an inherited component. I believe it also has psychological and spiritual causes, and I agree with the philosophy of Alcoholics Anonymous, which brings a powerful spiritual dimension to healing alcoholism. But I also think it can give rise to a powerful thought-form that attracts thought-forms of the same kind.

The world is filled with thought-forms, both positive and negative. After some time, the thought-forms we create develop a life of their own. They feed off of us, and we feed off them. It's a vicious, albeit unconscious cycle. Even when an alcoholic stops drinking, he still has to contend with something that twelve-step programs are not familiar with—the alcoholic thought-form.

If the thought-form is given no further energy, it will wither and disappear. Here are some techniques to help you make sure you don't give energy to a negative thought-form:

1. Practice Mantra Meditation. It will fill your mind with thoughts of God, thereby weakening the influence of negative thoughts.

2. Practice the ABCs of Anger Control. Unbridled anger psychically attracts negative thought-forms, so you'll want to eliminate anger as an energy source.

3. Practice watching your thoughts. When a negative thought repeatedly arises, notice it without trying to push it away. Simply observing the thought will cause it to lose some of its power. After observing the

negative thought, turn (or return) your mind to your mantra, or picture your chosen form of God beside you.

4.  Avoid drugs and alcohol. Their use dramatically increases the power of negative thought-forms.

5.  Consciously lift your thoughts to a higher level. If all you think about, all day long, is drugs, sex, and violence, you will attract those things into your life. Instead, think of ways to be of service—ways to be more peaceful, loving, honest, and nonviolent. The power of these positive thoughts will automatically make negative thought-forms vanish.

6.  Avoid the company of those who bring you down, those who are addicted to negativity. Surround yourself with good people, moral people.

## ARTISTIC HALLUCINATIONS

An artist enters an altered state of consciousness in which she may have all kinds of extraordinary experiences. She may "hallucinate" or have extrasensory perceptions in any sensory modality.

Richard Del Maestro is the producer and composer of several New Age music albums, including *Relax, HeartSpace: Relax II,* and *Language of the Heart.* (The last-named was on the New Age charts for over four years.) He had a fascinating experience while he was composing a film score at the Reuben Fleet Space Theater in San Diego. He was given seven days to score the film, which was about a half-hour long. For about five days, he worked about twenty-three hours a day. After five days he could "see the music pouring out of [his] hands in a spiral formation," as he told me. Yet while he was composing, he had been in such an altered state of consciousness that he later had no recall of the vision. Only after I reminded him of what he had told me did he begin to remember.

Writing music or creating a painting is almost a visionary experience in itself. The composer is hearing music that isn't there. Sometimes the power of that vision can be extraordinary. I myself have composed more than eighteen hundred songs—each with a different melody, lyrics, and style (rock and roll, country-western, reggae, rhythm and blues, chant, devotional-spiritual, and children's music). During one Christmas season, I began to write a spiritual oratorio—or I should say it began to write me. The music would hit me, in a form that was so loud and powerfully emotional, that I would be reduced to tears. I would have to pull over to the side of the road, if I was driving.

I heard the music as if an entire symphony orchestra were inside of me—violins, cellos, trumpets, timpani, clarinets, flutes. A choir was singing the words. Whenever I heard them, I had no choice but to write down the words. Unfortunately, I don't write musical notation very well, so the entire orchestral arrangement is now long forgotten.

Unusual experiences, including artistic hallucinations, are common among painters because they get into a "flow" state while working. A painter often loses all sense of separation between himself, the paintbrush, the canvas, the paint, and the subject he is painting. He may enter a kind of samadhi, or unity consciousness, in which he is one with the painting. It's like being in the zone. In these "flow" states, the artist may "become" the work of art or "become" the process of painting. During such states, time ceases to exist for the artist, boundaries blur between self and others, and a host of paranormal phenomena may occur.

In the case of a great composer like Mozart, one may wonder if he wrote the music or if "the music wrote him." Mozart was able to see and hear an entire symphony in a single moment, and he would write down what he had already seen and heard. The situation with Johann Sebastian Bach is even more mysterious. Musicologists in the twentieth century have calculated that if the world's greatest music transcriber made it his life's work simply to copy Bach's work, note for note, working twenty-four hours a day, it would take over one hundred years to accomplish the task. Not only did Bach accomplish the impossible, he wrote at the level of perfection. Surely Bach could have accomplished this superhuman feat only if he were living and writing in a state of unity consciousness most of the time. Perhaps he was "hallucinating" music all the time.

So close is Bach's music to perfection that for many people he becomes the link to God—the first step that told them that there was something greater than their lower selves. To quote Celedonio Romero, "Bach is the link between man and God."

Of course, the lives of artists are not always blissful. Many of Salvador Dali's paintings were greatly inspired by tormenting visions that he had experienced as a child. Although his were not artistic hallucinations in the strict sense of the word, they shaped his artistic vision. For many people, Dali's ghastly, rotting visions would have caused a life of suffering and insanity. It is the great challenge of the artist to take all experiences, even terrifying hallucinations, and turn them into creative works.

There is great suffering and great joy among artists. Although all of us are born with creative gifts, most of us do not choose to be artists. We should be grateful to those who do walk that often frightening path, for without art, without sculpture, poetry, dance, and music, life would lose its beauty and meaning.


## THE HUMAN AURA

Everybody has an aura, which changes according to one's mood, physical health, and state of consciousness. The physical body, the energy body, the mental body, the intellect, and the soul all have different auras.

The human aura is visible from head to toe. Are those circular halos over the heads of angels, as depicted in Byzantine frescoes, really magnificent bright auras? I think they are.

No other visual phenomenon is equivalent to the human aura, which is as real as the person from which it emanates. It can be any color. It can be extraordinarily beautiful, composed of the most intense, deep blues—or the most exquisite delicate violet that no artist can paint. It is not a fixed light show. When we're angry, red streaks of light permeate our aura. When we're deeply in love, our aura is pink. On two occasions I have seen the most extraordinary one-inch-thick indigo aura hugging the head of a brilliant physicist.

Auras surround not only our heads but the surface of our body. Each internal organ also has its own aura. Nurse-teacher Janet Quinn, R.N., Ph.D., first began to explore auras while attending a workshop on therapeutic touch.[13] The instructor was discussing different aspects of the aura, when one of the students in the class asked, "How does the aura of cancer differ from the aura of an infection?" The class was seated in a circle. The instructor looked around the circle, got out of her chair, and walked over to Dr. Quinn. The instructor placed her hand over her bladder and said, "This is the aura of a bladder infection." Indeed, Dr. Quinn did have a painful, acute bladder infection that day.

Auras have been described as far back as ancient India, Egypt, and Greece. The word *aura* comes from the Greek word for "air" and refers to that "airy" energetic field surrounding all living beings. In Indian and Chinese philosophy, auras are directly connected to prana or chi. The invisible chi—which flows through meridians, is highly concentrated in the chakras, and may erupt violently as kundalini—manifests as the force field surrounding the physical body, as the human aura.

Ancient Egyptian art depicted the human aura. Pre-Christian artists, especially in ancient Persia, drew people with luminous clouds around them. And many paintings of saints show a halo around their heads, clearly depicting the radiant aura of an enlightened being. Modern-day shamans from all cultures are familiar with auras, and those shamans with the most highly developed *siddhi* powers see them easily. In a sense, it is understandable why so many artists have painted auras. Painters have highly developed their sense of sight, both inner and outer. They have also devoted their lives to studying the human form. Seeing auras would be a natural extension of their already highly developed visual acuity and focus on the body.

According to Rosalyn Bruyere, author of *Wheels of Light: A Study of the Chakras,* the meaning of and the colors in the aura vary from one culture to another.[14] Bruyere, who has her own highly developed ability to see auras, says that people in the West display a yellow aura when they are thinking and a blue aura while daydreaming. During a six-hundred-mile journey up the Nile River, she never observed any blue or yellow in the aura of Islamic people. But when she traveled through Israel, she did see yellow auras, which she associates with Western modes of thought.

It strikes me that if people in the East have a different color in their aura from people in the West while thinking, I think it likely that each state of mind, each mood state, and each state of consciousness is associated with a specific auric color. Only insofar as people from different cultures exist at different levels of consciousness, I think, was Bruyere observing auras associated with particular cultures. People in deep meditation display the same characteristic aura, no matter what their culture. People in a fit of rage show the same kind of aura, no matter what their native land. Huge, bright auras, not tightly fitting but oftentimes extending many feet, are typical of enlightened masters from all traditions. Sometimes the aura of an enlightened master will be so vast that one cannot see the edge of it, as if it were merging with the sky.

The main thing to remember, if you're seeing auras, is that it's really no big deal. There's nothing to be afraid of, and it's definitely not a sign of mental instability. Many psychiatrists would call auras hallucinations, but seeing auras is perfectly acceptable and normal and common in all cultures. Some people have a highly developed sense of hearing. Seeing auras is a kind of highly developed sight.

Here are some general guidelines for working with auras:

1. If you see auras, simply regard it as a normal way of perceiving.

2. Remember that, if you're seeing auras, you're probably perceiving the world in ways that are more intuitive and spiritually oriented.

3. All the great spiritual masters tell us to avoid the trap of becoming attached to *siddhi* powers, of which seeing auras is one of the most

common. They advise us not to let our ego get inflated, nor to make a public display of these powers. You should make as little to-do as possible about seeing auras, because overemphasis on siddhi powers will lead you away from the spiritual path and from the ultimate spiritual goal, namely liberation itself.

4. Similarly, avoid the pitfall of thinking there's something special about you if you can see auras. Don't fall into the ego's trap of feeling you are "better" than others.

5. Some people can't help seeing auras. If that is your situation, be discreet about your knowledge and abilities.

6. The ability to see auras can be developed. If you want to develop it, first ask yourself why you want it. Do you want to show off? Do you want to be in the "Spiritual Olympics"? If so, forget it. Don't try to see auras. If, on the other hand, you want to see auras because you think it would make you a better person and would allow you to serve people at a deeper level, then, by all means, develop it.

7. You can find books that will teach you how to see auras, but here's a way to begin. Look at people in "soft focus." Act as if you're looking through them, without focusing your eyes on them sharply. Try to sense the energy around the head. Then try to see a white light surrounding it. After a while, you'll be able to sense a general aura of light around everyone. In time, you'll be able to see specific colors.

8. This ability also has practical applications. Study the color and shape of the auras you see, and notice how a particular aura corresponds to a particular mood. Once you've learned what the aura of an enraged person looks like, you can keep your distance. On the other hand, when you see a shimmering, golden, luminous aura with tinges of pink, you can approach that person, knowing he or she is loving and moral.

9. Remember that in some cultures, trying to see someone's aura is considered an invasion of their personal space. This is the case among some Native American tribes. Therefore, you'll want to ask permission to look at their aura. This is a good rule to follow with everyone, not just Native Americans.

## THE DIVINE WEAVER: A TECHNIQUE FOR INTEGRATING EXPERIENCES
### *Mental Fitness Technique*

For some people, having an unusual experience, such as seeing auras or angels is no big deal. For others, such experiences require a quantum shift in one's belief system in order to integrate the experience into the fabric of one's life. One must not make too much of such experiences, or too little. Here is an imagery technique to help you integrate any experience, whether "unusual," "mystical," or "ordinary."

> *Imagine yourself entering a cave. This is a dark place of great mystery. You go deeper and deeper into the cave, making your way by the light of a candle that you are holding.*
>
> *After navigating several twists and turns in the cave, after squeezing through narrow tunnels and hallways, you suddenly enter a vast opening, a giant room within the cave. In one corner of this vast room is a divine, radiant being, sitting at a loom, weaving a variety of beautiful fabrics and tapestries. After you observe Him weaving these tapestries, you begin to recognize some of them. He is weaving tapestries from your own life, pictures from your childhood, pockets of pain, memories of happy experiences. He has been weaving this tapestry of your life for a long time—forever.*
>
> *You approach this divine being and talk to Him about the experience that you want to have better integrated into your life, for your experience does not yet feel as if it is completely part of you. It still feels separate from you. As you tell this divine being about your experience, all of the feelings, thoughts, sensations, perceptions, images, and states of consciousness flow out of you as if they are a current or a stream. That stream of experience ends up at the feet of this divine weaver. No matter what form that stream of experience takes, the divine weaver quickly picks up part of the stream and continues his weaving. He is now weaving a cloak or coat out of the colors and impressions of your experience. Old experiences, old memories are also woven into this new creation, until finally your new experience becomes a finished work.*

*The divine being stands up, holding up your new multi-colored cloak. Your new experience is symbolically woven into the cloak. The divine being places the cloak around your shoulders. Notice how it fits. Is it too tight? Too loose? If so, ask the divine weaver to make the proper adjustments.*

*Finally, you place your cloak of experience around your shoulders, and you begin to make your way back out of the cave. With each step you take, you notice that your experience no longer seems so separate from you. It has begun to become part of the fabric of your life. As you step out of the cave into the sunlight, you notice that your cloak is even more beautiful and radiant than you had first noticed in the dimly lit cave. Wear this cloak. Walk in the sunlight. Feel the safety and protection that it provides you.*

# 12

# EXTRASENSORY
# PERCEPTION

Extrasensory perceptions may involve any of our five senses. In addition to visual phenomena, ESPs may be heard, smelled, tasted, touched, or sensed.

Like visions, voices, and other paranormal phenomena, ESPs cannot be measured through blood and urine tests, X-rays, CT scans, photographs, radiation detectors, electrical field detectors, direct examination, or physical observation. Nonetheless, we shouldn't pretend that because something can't be measured, it doesn't exist.

## ESP OF SOUND

During psychotic episodes, people often hear voices that are loud and usually menacing. The voices are very real to them, and they experience the voices as coming from outside themselves. Yet they are entirely a projection from their inner subconscious world into the outside world.

Voices of a spiritual nature are referred to as *clairaudience*. I've personally had two clairaudient experiences—here is one of them. When I was chief resident in psychiatry, I had an appointment one morning with a staff member named Joe. We were supposed to meet at eight A.M. Just prior to eight, I was in the back office of the psychiatric ward chatting with the unit secretary, Nancy. At eight I heard Joe's very loud voice calling my name. A few seconds later, one of the staff members, Ron, walked into the back office, looked at me, and prepared to say something. But before he could speak, I said to Ron, "Go ahead and send Joe back here." Ron turned rather pale. "Joe's not here," he said. "He's on the phone. He just called to say he's sick and can't come in today."

Now, hearing one or two voices doesn't make either you or me "crazy." I'm not schizophrenic. Secondly, the voice I heard directly related to a real event that was taking place in the outer world. It was a psychic experience in a real context.

Here's another story of "ESP of voices." Hank, who is now in his forties, heard voices that saved his life when he was in his early twenties. At that time he was in a highly dysfunctional marriage with a disturbed woman. One morning, after spending the night on a couch, Hank was awakened by a loud voice that gave him these instructions: "Wake up! Do not open your eyes. Now slowly roll over. Now open your eyes, just a very tiny bit." Hank had never heard this voice or anything like it before, but he obeyed. Through his barely opened eyes, he saw his wife coming across the room with a rifle aimed at him. She was walking slowly and quietly. Hank pretended to be asleep. When the rifle came within reach, he suddenly grabbed it and took it away from her.

Hank was young, and he needed another miracle or two to get out of that marriage. On a second occasion the same voice loudly woke him. He got out of bed and went into the kitchen, where he found his wife boiling oil that she was about to pour all over him.

He finally got the message, loud and clear. Now he works as an acupuncturist, massage therapist, and teacher, and he doesn't need voices to save his life. Now, if we really wanted to split hairs, we could ask, Who was that voice? Was it the voice of an angel? Was it a dead loved one, voicing a warning from "beyond"? Was it his own telepathy? Neither a schizophrenic nor a borderline will hear a voice only once or twice, then function at a totally normal level for the rest of their lives. Hank's experience wasn't mental illness—it was clairaudience.

Meera hears voices on a regular basis, but she isn't crazy either. When it's time for her husband, Gary, to return from work, she frequently hears him arrive five minutes before he actually does. She hears him pull the car up, close the car door, and whistle. Meera can't tell the difference between Gary's real arrival and the perceived arrival. Because Meera and Gary are so connected to each other, she had the same kind of experience even during a period of marital problems in which they separated. Gary had moved out of their shared house and gone to another city. One night during their separation, Meera awakened to hear Gary screaming her name. A few months later, the two of them worked out their marital problems and got back together. Gary told her that one night during their separation he had been so upset that he had screamed out her name. It was the same night that she had heard his voice.

The voices that a schizophrenic hears often give destructive instructions, such as "jump off a bridge" or "throw yourself in front of a car." The voices that a paranoid schizophrenic hears often confirm his paranoia, such as "watch out, they're reading your mind!" These voices are psychotic and potentially dangerous.

A genuine spiritual or paranormal voice may actually be practical. A female voice said to Meera, "Coffee is the root of all of your problems." Meera had been drinking four or five cups of coffee each morning, which put her on an emotional roller coaster for the day. She was shaky from hypoglycemia, couldn't think straight, and she was exhausted most of the time. After she heard the voice, she gave up coffee, and her symptoms disappeared. "I realized," Meera said, "that coffee is poison for me."

In the West, "hearing the voice of God" is associated with insanity. Yet history is replete with spiritual masters who spoke to God and heard back. Saint Hildegard was so reluctant to speak about her voices and visions that the voice of God said to her, "Oh human weakness. Ashes of ashes. Frailty of frailty. Speak and write what you see and hear. And write it not as it pleases you, but write it after the will of Him who knows all and orders all in the hidden depths of His secret counsel."[1] These certainly are not the kind of words spoken by voices that schizophrenics hear.

Saint Francis of Assisi's life was also radically transformed by voices. Francis, a wealthy man of the world, was heading off to war. He proudly announced to his family and friends that he would return a knight. On the road toward Spoleto, he fell ill with fever and delirium. While in that feverish state, a voice said to him, "Go back to your native town. There it will be made known to you what you shall do." Francis obeyed, without knowing why. Instead of returning as an honored knight, he returned as a defeated laughingstock. Within a short period of time, Francis renounced everything that had been important to him. He took a vow of poverty, gave away all his money and possessions, and proceeded into the hills of Assisi, wearing only the clothes on his back. Initially looked upon as a pitiful, pathetic creature who had ruined his own life, later on he was recognized by the Pope—and the world—as a saint.[2]

A second set of voices gave Francis another life-changing jolt. "Francis," the voice said, "do you not see that my house is in ruins? Go and restore it for me." That message stirred Francis's imagination and led him to found a new religious order within the Catholic Church. Along with a small band of men, he approached the Pope for approval to "restore the church." At first the Pope laughed at Francis, but soon he changed his mind, realizing that he was a sincere, devout person. Francis organized the Franciscan order and helped reinstill the heart of Christianity—love, service, and sacrifice—into the Church.

A "true" voice of guidance can be either the inner voice of conscience or the outer voice of God. Following its directives usually guides one in the direction of one's heart, in the direction of love, peace, and right action. If you've heard the genuine voice of God, fall on your knees and listen. Pray for more guidance to understand the meaning of what was said. When you are clear about the meaning, do everything in your power to follow the divine directive.

## ESP OF SMELL

The first thing you want to determine about a hallucinated smell is whether you can smell it out of both nostrils. If the odor is in only one nostril, a neurological problem might be indicated—possibly a tumor growing along the nerve pathway leading from smell sensors to the brain. A hallucinated smell that is related to a neurological problem will usually be a bad smell.

Millions of normal people hallucinate smell. A psychologist I know perceives coffee periodically when there is absolutely no way for that odor to be present. Odors of a spiritual nature are often fragrant, like jasmine flowers.

Death, too has a smell beyond that of physical decay. I don't know how to describe it, but anyone who has been around death knows the smell. It's not related to the physical body. It's a smell related to a nonphysical plane of existence.

On some occasions, however, death has a sweet fragrance that feels intoxicating. Pepe Romero told me that when Celedonio died, a sweet fragrance, like jasmine or gardenias, poured out of his father's body and filled the air. I believe that the sweet fragrance of his death is directly related to the sweetness with which he lived and died.

According to psychic Shama Smith, a violent death leaves a terrible odor that lingers for months or even years. Shama, on some occasions, has smelled death hours before death occurred. On other occasions she smells death after it has occurred.

During the 1970s I was meditating a lot, having plunged headfirst into my chosen spiritual path. My extrasensory perceptions were heightened, and I was using those heightened abilities to assist in medical diagnosis. In the late 1970s, I was working as a general practitioner in an urgent area clinic. The doctors had a heavy caseload, seeing up to thirty-five patients in four hours. I'd pick up the chart from the slot on a patient's door, close my eyes, and try to sense the patient's problem—without opening the chart. With one chart I experienced a terrible smell. I walked into the room and asked the patient how I could help him. He told me that he was experiencing a terrible odor in one nostril. He had a hallucinated odor that was being caused by a brain tumor. I had smelled the same thing psychically.

A "psychic odor" can also be seen as deep empathy and intuition. You just open yourself up to the other's experience. As a result you feel what they feel, see what they see, and sometimes smell what they smell.

Among devotees of Sathya Sai Baba, the perceived odor of jasmine is common. The fragrance can arise anywhere, and when it does so, one feels almost intoxicated by it. On many occasions many people have perceived jasmine at the same time. On one occasion five people were driving in a car, while an elderly Sai devotee was smoking a cigarette. Suddenly the car filled with the scent of jasmine. Everyone smelled it and marveled at its sweetness, as well as the sense of peace it brought. In addition, the jasmine brought a message to the smoker, who said to the others in the car, "I think Baba is telling me it's time to stop smoking." He never smoked again.

Probably the best-known ESP of smell is that of roses, which often accompanies a vision of Mary, the Mother of Jesus, or indicates her spiritual presence. The bodies of saints are also reported to give off this sweet, uncorrupted smell.

If one has had an extrasensory perception of roses or jasmine, the action steps one should take are:

1. Pray—immediately.
2. Express gratitude for the experience.
3. Stay in the moment, and remain with the feeling of awe. Let the experience carry you further in the direction in which it is taking you.

## ESP OF EMPATHY

We can have extrasensory perceptions through any or all of our senses. We may "know" something is about to happen, or feel someone else's emotional or physical suffering—without really knowing how we know. Every mother has had the experience of knowing when her child was in serious danger or had been injured, whether that child was still in school or in his fifties. The ESP of empathy is simply very deep empathy, an understanding that does not depend on the five senses. It arises out of compassion, love, and empathy, and a desire to lessen others' pain and suffering.

Mary, a nurse who became quite psychic after getting off drugs and alcohol, "perceives" other people's pain. In an elevator she may suddenly be seized by a terrible pain in her leg. She'll look around the elevator and see a man with a leg cast on and know she's experiencing his pain. Or she'll be walking down the street and feel a terrible facial pain. She'll look up and down the street and see someone with a face that has been severely traumatized from an automobile accident. Mary has the experience called *sympathetic suffering,* a kind of ESP of empathy.

The most extraordinary example of ESP-perceived pain is so-called phantom-limb pain. Someone who has had his left leg amputated may continue to experience pain in his left foot—a foot that no longer exists. This is a neurological problem that is poorly understood.

Phantom pain is quite different from so-called imaginary pain. Many people have pain for which their doctors cannot find a physical explanation. The doctor often tells them their pain is imaginary, because he or she can find no reason that explains it. But if you're in pain, you know it's not imaginary. Technically, so-called imaginary pain is neither imaginary nor hallucinated. But it is often debilitating.

Phantom pain has proven to be a puzzle to modern medicine, which found no theory to explain it, nor any treatment that works. I would like to propose a theory, then a treatment. Kirlian photography is a technique for photographing the aura. In Kirlian photographs of a leaf, for example, one sees a colorful halo around the leaf. If a piece of the leaf is cut off, the Kirlian photograph will continue to show the complete leaf. The missing part still exists in the leaf's "auric field."

Perhaps the missing limb of an amputee still exists in the auric field. If it does, perhaps the aura is transmitting information about its still-existing limb to the physical body, which knows the limb is no longer there. The mind may be generating the phantom pain based on the conflicting messages it is receiving from the aura and the physical body. This theory is but one of many possibilities, and I am suggesting it more to raise the question rather than to settle it.

What I can say with certainty is that mental imagery, in combination with energetic medicine (acupuncture, therapeutic touch, huna, reiki) has the potential to reintegrate a person's "multiple bodies," so that all of one's bodies are "in agreement."

I'd like to broaden the topic to include the millions of women who have lost, or fear losing, a breast due to breast cancer. While working with one woman who had had a mastectomy, I asked her, "What did they do with your breast once they removed it?"

"Oh, I don't know. I have no idea."

"Of course you have an idea," I replied.

"All right, I think they probably just tossed it into the Dumpster."

"Yes, they may have, or they may have put it in a jar in formaldehyde. Who knows? It may be sitting on a shelf somewhere. But how do you feel about it?"

"Actually, I think about it a lot. I dream about it. I miss it. I don't feel whole or complete anymore."

"What you need to do," I told her, "is to give your breast a proper burial. We can do that using mental imagery—to begin with."

There has been a kind of secrecy about the whole issue of "missing body parts." A woman doesn't know what happened to her lost breast, so at first she imagines the worst, and then she represses that image and forgets she ever imagined anything in the first place. But she does remember—and suffer.

Here is a simple program that will radically help you with a phantom limb or any other body part that has been permanently removed:

1. Close your eyes. Become aware of your current belief about the missing body part. Where is it? How was it disposed of?

2. How do you feel about how you think it was disposed of?

3. Create a ceremonial burial and memorial service for the body part, using imagery.

> Picture that missing body part and see it "whole" and perfect. Now, you need to bury this part, the same way you'd bury a loved one. Perhaps you'll want to place the body part in the soft, fertile ground of a mountain forest, or on the calm bottom of the Pacific Ocean.
>
> Add rituals to your ceremony. If you are burying the body part, imagine that you are lighting candles. Say a prayer. Perhaps you'll want a rabbi, minister, or priest to assist. Invite your loved ones to the funeral.
>
> Before the actual burial, say good-bye to the body part and thank it for all the years in which it served you well. Now proceed to the conclusion of this memorial service.

4. Mold a symbol of the missing body part—the arm, the leg, the breast—out of clay or whatever substance appeals to you. Take this molded representation and perform an actual memorial service. Actually go to the woods, the beach, the jungle, or the desert, and repeat the ritual you created in the imagery. Of course, you may modify the "actual" burial, depending on how you are feeling, thinking, and imagining at the time. Remember to be bold and creative. Throw your heart and soul into the exercise. You won't recover your breast, but you will recover your soul.

5. Because there is a very good possibility that the human aura "remembers" the missing body part, seek out a practitioner of energetic medicine. See an acupuncturist, an expert in therapeutic touch, or a practitioner of huna (Hawaiian healing).

By using a combination of imagery techniques and energetic techniques, body, mind, and spirit can be healed. When you consciously grieve the lost part, I believe that your mind, body, and auric body will finally come back into alignment. The physical pain will be less, as will the emotional pain.

# MIRACLES

The *Random House Dictionary* defines *miracle* as "(1) an effect or extraordinary event in the physical world which surpasses all known human or natural powers and is ascribed to a supernatural cause. (2) Such an effect or event manifesting or considered as a work of God. (3) A wonder; marvel." I believe that the key words in this definition are *known human powers*. If an experience cannot be explained by known human powers, we call the experience miraculous. Because our understanding of known human powers changes from year to year, so does our idea of what is miraculous.

Not too long ago, the mind and body were considered to be separate and unrelated. Science did not even begin to grasp the power of the mind and its ability to cure the physical body. Now, however, an entire field of science exists, psychoneuroimmunology, that has not only proven that the mind can dramatically affect the body but shown how those changes take place. Hope can cure cancer. Prayer can cure cancer. These cures were once called "miracles," or else "spontaneous remissions."[1] Now science is coming to understand that such healing is part and parcel of normal human powers. What was once believed to be a miracle is now explained in scientific terms.

Until the full human potential is totally understood, there will be a large gap between what actually happens in the world and what we think is possible. When we experience that gap, we call it a miracle. Really, a miracle is an indication of our incomplete knowledge, an indication that we can't explain all phenomena. We will always be ignorant about something, and therefore we will continue to need the word *miracle*.

Many of the stories in this book seem miraculous—the visions of a saint, the healings at a distance, the premonitions of the future. But the experiences in this chapter are even more miraculous. Still, I wonder if they would feel miraculous to a saint or shaman, or if they would just be part of reality as they see it.

We'll explore the miraculous by starting with those experiences that science is beginning to understand, namely mind-body miracles.

## MIND-BODY MIRACLES

Mind-body miracles are healings that make use of mind-body technologies, like meditation and guided imagery. A whole series of books could be written about mind-body miracles, but I will cover only a few examples here, just to give you the flavor.

I once treated a 60-year-old man who had suffered from life-threatening asthma for fifty-five years. Using guided imagery techniques, we were able to cure him in only two sessions! Fifty-five years of asthma cured with two sessions using guided imagery sounds like a miracle—perhaps spiritual healing. But it's not a "real" miracle—it's merely a case of the mind healing the physical body.

Marci, a 20-year-old friend of mine, was in a head-on collision on a San Diego freeway. The combined speed on impact was 140 miles per hour. When I got to the hospital to see her, she was in a lot of pain from fractured vertebrae in her neck. Not even morphine was helping very much. In five minutes, using guided imagery, her pain dropped to zero and stayed at zero for four or five hours.

Many scientific studies have now documented the power of meditation and guided imagery. Using guided imagery, people can raise or lower the platelet count in their blood, or their white blood cell count.[2] Actually, there are many different kinds of white blood cells, but through guided imagery people can raise the count of a specific kind of white blood cell.

The power of the mind is so great that it even holds sway over life and death. Many cancer patients have died "on time" in order to satisfy a doctor who has told them, "You will be dead in three months." Women tend to die after major life events, such as a birthday, Christmas, or an anniversary. Men, on the other hand, tend to die just before such events. This is a kind of miracle—the miracle of the power of the mind.

One of the most remarkable mind-body miracles with which I am familiar took place in the early 1900s. A surgeon was treating a young man who had small bumps all over his body. He was planning to surgically remove them. A friend of the surgeon, a psychiatrist and hypnotherapist, suggested that the surgery be put off because "hypnosis is very successful at eliminating warts." The surgeon agreed to the experiment, but was flabbergasted to discover that afterward all of the small tumors had disappeared. Unbeknownst to the psychiatrist, the boy had not, in fact, been suffering from a case of warts, but rather had had a serious genetic disease that produced skin cancers. There are only two possible explanations for this cure: Either the hypnosis changed the DNA itself, or what is called the genotype; or it changed the phenotype, the expression of the DNA. I think the latter is the more likely explanation. Because the psychiatrist was so hopeful, he was probably able to override the boy's DNA.

These "miraculous" events are miraculous only because we don't fully understand the power of the mind. In time, the mind-body connection will not seem so miraculous at all.


## THE POWER OF PRAYER

Larry Dossey, M.D., in *Healing Words: The Power of Prayer and the Practice of Medicine,* reports on a study done at San Francisco General Hospital by a cardiologist, Dr. Randolph Byrd.[3] The research involved a group of four hundred hospitalized cardiac patients. Prayer groups around the country prayed for individual patients. Half of the patients were prayed for, and half were not. This was a true controlled double-blind study. Neither the patient, the doctor, nor the hospital staff knew who was being prayed for.

The results of the study were so dramatic that if it had been a study of a new drug, it would have been heralded as a major medical breakthrough—a miracle drug. The prayed-for patients were discharged from the hospital sooner than the others, had fewer complications, required less antibiotic treatment, and had less pulmonary edema. Their group had fewer deaths, fewer instances of CPR (cardiopulmonary resuscitation), less need for mechanical ventilation (attachment to breathing machines), and less need for diuretic medication.

Based on the prayer study and other studies, Dr. Dossey concludes that the mind is truly not local. If prayer can have profound, documented results—over great distances—then it is clear that the mind is not confined to the body, let alone to the narrow space between our ears. The prayer study demonstrates what every culture has believed since the beginning of time—that one can reach out, with love and caring, and touch and heal beyond the tyrannical grip of time and space.

What is the difference between the "miracle of prayer" and the "miracle of mind-body healing"? Clearly, the latter can be explained by the power of the mind acting within the body. The power of prayer, by contrast, involves deep reflection. Have we connected with the Absolute, with God, who acts as an intermediary? Does God hear our prayers and then carry out miracles? Or is the power of prayer related to the power of thought, which can have an impact at great distances? I pose these questions without answering them. I can only guess that the "miracle of prayer" sometimes works through the power of our own thought, acting at a distance—and sometimes because God has truly been touched by our yearning and responds in miraculous ways.

Next, we'll see that there are miracles—and there are *miracles,* the grand, absolutely inexplicable wonders that are the signature of God.

## GOD'S INVISIBLE HAND

The true miracles are those that defy the laws of cause and effect, the laws of physics, the laws of time and space, and our general concept of how things normally work in the world. They cannot be explained by mind-body medicine or the power of the mind to act at a distance. They are the handiwork of a Greater Intelligence.

There is no limit to the range, type, or quality of such miraculous events. Miracles often come into our lives at times of birth, death, and crisis. One such miracle occurred before my daughter, Rachel, was born. Several weeks before her birth, I was driving at about 35 miles per hour in Denver. Suddenly, a white dove flew in front of the windshield and hovered in front of it for almost a full block. The dove hovered motionlessly as I continued to drive without slowing down. In other words, somehow the dove was simultaneously hovering in front of my eyes and flying at 35 miles per hour, keeping perfect pace with the car. I knew instantly that the dove was an omen—a sign that everything would be fine with the upcoming birth of my child. And so it was! After a hectic labor, the obstetrician discovered that the umbilical cord had wrapped itself around

Rachel's neck three times. Suddenly she went into a distressed condition. But thanks to the quick, if not somewhat terrified actions of the medical team, Rachel was born some sixty seconds after she went into distress, in "mint condition." That remains as one of the great miracles in my life.

On several occasions Isaac Tigrett, founder of the Hard Rock Café and the House of Blues, has had his life divinely spared. One night he fell asleep at the wheel while driving his Porsche. He woke up as he was flying off a cliff. As he and his car hurtled through space, tumbling, spinning, and slamming into the ground over and over again, his car was torn to pieces. The rollbar and both doors were completely ripped off. There was practically no front or back of the car left, and no windshield.

Nor did Isaac have a seat belt. Certain death was averted by the sudden presence of a divine being who wrapped his arms around Isaac and exerted powerful pressure on his shoulders, as if to keep Isaac firmly in place in the car. Strong, gentle, incredibly powerful hands cradled him, held him so tightly that he couldn't fall out. He walked away untouched from a car that was completely destroyed.

Sometimes miracles bring bad news and come as an omen of impending death. Linda Chavez, head of the civil rights division of the Justice Department under President Reagan, had an unusual experience when she was twelve years old. Her sister Wendy, who was six, suddenly developed a severe kidney ailment. In fact, she got sick on Linda's birthday. Several weeks later, Linda was outside, in the front yard of her family's apartment. She noticed a yellow bird, perhaps a finch or canary, flying around in a somewhat sickly manner. She put her hands out and was able to catch the bird.

She brought it into the house, put it in a shoebox with grass, and poked holes in the box. She thought it might be injured, because it wasn't very active. The bird died after only a day or two. According to Linda, her father was very superstitious and believed the bird's death was a sign of someone about to die. Such, in fact, was the case. A few hours after the bird died, Wendy died of pneumonia and heart failure secondary to her kidney disease.

Linda did not make a big deal of these events. But her father experienced the bird's death as an omen that had come true—a sign from God that something "bad" was about to happen. If the bird's death was a miracle, it may mean that God's invisible signature was present in this family's life, showing the connectedness of life—and the presence of God even in death.

Animals, and pets in particular, have long been associated with the miraculous. My black cat, Leo, now 17 years old, (who has stepped on my computer keyboard far too many times while I've been writing this book) was quite a magical fellow in his youth. On one occasion, Stanley, an out-of-town friend of mine, was visiting. I semijokingly warned him, "By the way, watch out for Leo. He can do some very strange things, like walk through walls and closed doors." The evening of the Fourth of July, Stan and Rachel and I headed out to watch the local fireworks display. I like to keep Leo inside on the Fourth because some people consider black cats to be evil and have been known to attack them on that date (and on Halloween). As we were leaving, I tossed Leo inside the house and quickly slammed the door shut. The three of us turned to leave—but we were stunned to see Leo pop into existence right in front of us. He didn't run out from the house, behind us. He spontaneously appeared. Stanley's eyes got as wide as saucers. "See, I warned you," I said. Rachel was speechless.

Stories abound of cats and dogs that traveled thousands of miles over entire mountain ranges to find their lost owner. No one knows how these animals find their way to an old home or to a location to which they've never been. Perhaps animals have powerful extrasensory perceptions, but I think it all boils down to love. Our pets love us so much that they follow their hearts until they find us.

From time to time, people schedule an appointment with me because they're looking for a real miracle. Very often they are cancer patients. I've never promised a miracle, nor performed one, but miraculous events have occurred in the lives of patients who were under my care. The most amazing of these miracles came into the life of Carmen, a longtime friend whose sister, Anita, had died of ovarian cancer. Anita had been given six months to live from the time she was diagnosed, but she had lived for four years by using a host of traditional and complementary techniques.

When Carmen came to see me as a patient, she had lung cancer so advanced that her doctor had given her only one month to live. She wasn't afraid to die, but couldn't bear the thought of her mother losing her two daughters to cancer. So Carmen got interested in fighting the cancer for her mother's sake.

I taught Carmen Mantra Meditation and some imagery techniques in which she imagined that she was filling up with healing golden light. She imagined the cancer dissolving in the heat of the light. I also suggested that she take a variety of nutritional supplements. During that session we spoke about Sai Baba, and I gave her a bottle of "holy water." It was very rare lingham water, which had been produced by pouring water over a lingham, an egg-shaped stone, that Sai Baba had materialized, or manifested, expressly for the purpose of healing. Even though the water is rare, stories like the one that follows are common when it comes to the miracles surrounding Sathya Sai Baba. I told Carmen that I would stand by her whether she lived or died—and it seemed almost a foregone conclusion that she would soon die.

Carmen was scheduled to have surgery a couple of days after our first appointment. Her surgeon planned to remove her entire right lung, which was full of cancer. But when he opened her chest during surgery, he discovered that the cancer had spread across into her left lung and was wrapped around the great blood vessels—the aorta and the pulmonary artery and veins. The surgeon "closed" Carmen, gave her a single radiation treatment, and sent her home to die.

I didn't hear from Carmen for a few weeks after our session and I feared the worst. But one day I was stunned to hear her sweet, energetic voice. "Dennis," she said, "I have had the weirdest, most amazing experience with Sai Baba. I was meditating a few weeks ago, right after our session. Suddenly I had a vision of Sai Baba. It was as if he were standing right in front of me. He began reaching into my chest, pulling cancer out. I didn't actually see cancer coming out of my body, but I experienced it in this vision. And all day long, even with my eyes open, I could feel him putting his hand inside of me, pulling out the cancer. And you won't believe this. Or maybe you actually will believe this. My cancer has shrunk by 75 percent. My surgeon simply cannot believe it. I believe it, but I don't understand at all why Sai Baba is doing this for me. I don't even know him, and I hardly know anything about him. I was raised a Christian, and I'm still a Christian. Why would he help me? Why would he save my life?"

I've known of many miracles surrounding Sathya Sai Baba, and I've learned not to try to explain them. "Carmen, there is simply no way of knowing why this has happened to you. Perhaps it was your good karma. Perhaps it was because your motivation to live arose from completely unselfish motives. I have no idea. But I am so happy for you." She called me again a few months later to tell me she was continuing to improve. And then she called a year later to say that the cancer had entirely disappeared.

Although most of us believe in miracles, many of us believe that only certain events can take place miraculously and that other events are totally impossible, even through a miracle. We do not realize just how miraculous a miracle can be. Like millions of other devotees of Sathya Sai Baba, I have personally witnessed and experienced some of the most inexplicable, yet commonplace miracles, those of materialization or manifestation.

Sai Baba manifests objects out of thin air. His most common materialization is sacred ash, or *vibhuti*. With a wave, ash pours out of his hand. Sai Baba says that ash is the most sacred of physical objects, for it cannot be further reduced. Everything eventually ends up as ash. *Vibhuti* is a symbol of our mortality and a reminder of that which is immortal and permanent.

As a child of five or six, Sai Baba would sit underneath a tree during his school lunch break, reach up into the tree, and materialize a variety of fruits from all over the world—a mango for one friend, a pineapple for another, an orange for another. He would also materialize pencils for his classmates if they had none. On one occasion, in the third or fourth grade, his teacher instructed him to slap another student in the face, to punish that child for some minor infraction. Sai Baba refused, and as punishment the teacher told him to stand on his chair, which Baba proceeded to do. When the teacher tried to rise from his own chair, he found that he could not separate himself from it. He was stuck to the chair. Another teacher walked by, saw the predicament, and said, "I guess you haven't heard about Sai Baba and his miracles. I suggest you tell him he doesn't have to stand on the chair anymore." The teacher followed that suggestion and immediately discovered that he was no longer stuck to his chair.

During one trip to India, I met a South African fellow named Bharata who shared this incredible story with me:

"After my young wife died of cancer, I was so distraught. The pain, anguish, depression, and despair would not disappear. After six months of this mental torture, I loaded my pistol and held it up to the right side of my head, pressing it against my flesh. I looked at a photo of Sai Baba and, with tears in my eyes, prayed, 'Please forgive me for what I am about to do. I can no longer go on living. After I kill myself, please take care of my two young children.'

"After I finished my prayer, I pressed the barrel of the gun deeper into my skin, then pulled the trigger. There was an enormous bang when the gun fired. Suddenly my children knocked on my bedroom door, shouting, 'Daddy, Daddy, what was that sound?' I thought I was dead and in Heaven. Still, there I was holding the pistol, which was smoking. I quickly hid the gun under the bed and replied to my kids, 'What sound? I didn't hear anything!' My kids entered the room, and something immediately caught their eye. 'Daddy, look! There's a hole in the wall right over Sai Baba's picture. What is that?' "

Bharata couldn't explain to himself or to me how the bullet could have not gone through his own head. He subsequently returned to India, where he had visited before, this time to express his gratitude, for he believed that Sai Baba had somehow prevented him from killing himself.

Bharata continued, "When Baba approached me, he materialized some *vibhuti,* the sacred ash. But rather than the usual way, in which the ash gently pours out of his hands, this time *vibhuti* 'fired' out of his hands and exploded in mine."

I cannot begin to explain these miracles. All I can say for certain is that there is a reason for every one of them. Sai Baba does not perform miracles for the sake of entertainment, nor for power, fame, or money. Each miracle that I have experienced has taught me a spiritual lesson, a lesson in love, faith, or hope. Each miracle has answered some question that I had not yet raised with Sai Baba.

Although I, like millions of others, am inspired by Sai Baba's love and am guided to a higher life through his miracles, I have no desire that the reader follow my chosen path. Follow your own path. Every religious tradition is filled with a rich history of miracles.

Here are some of the greatest miracles, which devotees of one religion regard as fact, and that others regard as fiction. Jesus is said to have raised the dead and materialized large quantities of bread and fish—not to mention restoring sight to the blind. Moses is reported to have parted the Red Sea during the exodus from Egypt. In Hinduism, Krishna is believed to have lifted an entire mountain with one hand, in order to protect his devotees from a monsoon. In the light of "scientific" thought, one could easily dismiss as preposterous these miracles associated with three major world religions. It certainly is easiest to dismiss miracles from someone else's religion.

The Sphinx poses a problem not so easily swept away. Considered perhaps the greatest statue on earth, no one can figure out how it was made. Up until 1985, the Sphinx was believed to be 5,000 to 7,000 years old. Recent research indicates that a more accurate figure may be 10,000 years. In either case, here is the miracle. The Sphinx was made out of individual slabs of limestone (approximately 30 feet by 12 feet by 10 feet), each one weighing 200 tons (400,000 pounds). In the late 1980s a research team attempted to duplicate the feat of lifting a single 200-ton block. The experiment took six months to plan and required twenty men and two of the largest cranes in the world. The boom of the larger crane stood 220 feet high, and a 160-ton weight was necessary to counterbalance it. The team finally succeeded in lifting the one piece 50 feet off the ground—the distance equal to the top of the Sphinx. After lifting one 200-ton block, the engineers and scientists concluded, "We have no way of explaining

how the Sphinx was made." Egyptologists have long claimed that a sophisticated system of ropes and pulleys, and a lot of manpower, made con-
struction of the Sphinx possible. The conclusion of the more recent
research project was that the Egyptians simply did not have anything
close to the technology required to build the Sphinx. But, even with modern technology, modern hydraulic cranes, the team concluded, the task
might still be impossible. I have no idea how the Sphinx was created,
but I suspect that spiritual powers were required, in addition to serious
manpower.

Some modern miracles remain even more mysterious than the
Sphinx. The so-called Shiva caves near Rishikesh in the Himalayas are not
easy to reach but are said to contain an ongoing miracle. For millennia,
and continuing to this day, milk has dripped from the cave ceiling. This
liquid is not the usual water that drips from stalactites in caves all over
the world. It is milk.

Miracles happen every day and to a lot of people. Perhaps some are
a manifestation of our own thoughts, our own spiritual and psychic powers. And perhaps some are God's silent signature on our lives. Perhaps
some of the great miracles are the handiwork of both man and God—
man's human and *siddhi* powers, and God's divine power. They indicate
to us that there is more to our universe than is dreamed of by most of
us, most of the time. These extraordinary divine miracles restore faith,
bring peace and consolation during adversity, and give us the courage to
keep walking toward the Light. They cause us to ponder what we call
"reality."

The effect of the miraculous in our lives is predictable. Miracles, like
angels, make our lives more meaningful. Love is the sign of the miraculous. Miracles lead us to become more loving, more honest, more humble, more dedicated. They build character and help us develop a sense of
unity and community. If a phenomenon does not produce this kind of effect, it most likely is not a miracle. If a voice or hallucinated smell does
not help build character and does not help us become more loving, it most
likely is not a genuine spiritual experience.

Most of all, miracles show us that God loves us. Sai Baba says,
"Miracles are so natural to me that I am amused when you label them miracles." "Love is my highest miracle." "All the ostensible miracles are only
droplets of that Ocean of Love. Do not be dazzled by the droplets." Regarding the limitations of science, Sai Baba says, "Normally the scientist
of the mind looks outside to what can be perceived by the senses in the
world. The scientist of consciousness, on the other hand, always looks inside to that which is beyond the senses or the grasp of the mind."

"One has, therefore, to rise beyond the mind to consciousness to achieve self-realization. To gain the infinite, universal atma (soul), the embodied self must break out of the puny, finite little prison of individuality." "How can science, which is bound to a physical and materialistic outlook, investigate transcendental phenomena beyond its scope, reach, or comprehension? This is a fallacy on the face of it. One belongs to the material and the other to a spiritual plane. Science must confine its inquiry only to things belonging to the human senses, while spiritualism transcends the senses. If you want to understand the nature of spiritual power, you can do so only through the path of spirituality and not science." "That which transcends time and space cannot be explained or understood by modern scientific methods—tools or thought discipline born of the five senses, which are themselves conditioned by the limitations of natural laws governing time and space."

Spiritual inquiry requires an open mind and intellectual courage. Humankind needs to try to comprehend God, miracles, life after death, and the meaning of life. Without this spiritual hunger, this spiritual quest, life lacks purpose. I have seen and experienced miracles beyond a shadow of my doubt, and I hope you too will patiently embrace all of your miracles until your own spiritual path is clear. After you have done your own research and lived your own life, you must be the judge of your own experience. Please do not wait for science to prove to you that miracles exist or that God exists.

Science cannot even begin to explain the experience of love, which is more common than miracles. We can search for the next thousand years to find "love in a bottle," but we will never isolate it or find it in a part of the brain. We may find that neuropeptide levels increase in the brain and in the blood when we experience love—but we must not confuse those neuropeptides with love itself. If even this most universal of experiences cannot be explained, confined, limited, defined, or put in a bottle, how can we begin to intellectually understand the infinite, the miraculous? The intellect can only point us in the direction of the infinite, of God. But the infinite cannot be grasped by the finite. The indescribable cannot be put into words.

Good medicine can be described with one word—*practical*. Combining science and spirituality is the practical thing to do. Simply put, it's what works. It's what relieves suffering. It's what preserves health. It's what helps prevent illness. It's what gives meaning, purpose, understanding, and hope to suffering and to life.

Being practical means giving a hungry person lunch. Hungry people don't need preaching—they need food. Being practical also means providing the spiritually hungry with soul food. A doctor needs to be able to say, "I don't know the answer, but I have some strong hunches. I think part of your long-term depression can be directly attributed to your childhood, to your parents giving your brothers more attention—to your teachers telling you that girls aren't smart enough to excel at math or science. I am almost certain that your brain chemistry is out of balance. But I also believe that your sense of distance, fear, and estrangement from God is at least as important as the mental, physical, and social factors." I have arrived at this conclusion after twenty years as a physician—through trial and error, through reason and intuition—through consultation with specialists in psychopharmacology; with priests, rabbis, and holy men; with my patients, who have been Christians, Jews, Muslims, Hindus, Buddhists, non-Christian Native Americans; and with my friends, who are all of the above religions as well as Sikhs and Zoroastrians.

Having explored the world of paranormal phenomena, altered states of consciousness, and miracles, let's take a linear approach to this most nonlinear phenomenon—miracles:

1.  When you've had an experience that seems miraculous, suspend judgment. Don't come to any immediate conclusion. The power of saying, "I don't know the answer, but I'm willing to tolerate the uncertainty of the situation" is powerful.

2.  Compare your miracle with those reported by the world's major religions. If your miracle is in keeping with them, you are on safe ground in considering the possibility of a legitimate miracle.

3.  If you decide the experience was not miraculous, try to find another explanation, but do not pigeonhole the experience, so that you can bury it in the recesses of your mind.

4.  If you decide it was a genuine miracle, pray and meditate that you can fully benefit from it. The possibility that God showers miracles doesn't mean that all of us make the best use of them. If you know you've experienced a miracle, yet do not allow the experience to change you, the miracle will have been wasted.

5.  Seek the deeper meaning of the miracle. What is the lesson in it for you? How are you supposed to change? Does the experience call on you to be more loving, honest, peaceful, nonviolent, or moral?

6.  Here is a potentially frightening suggestion: If you are sure you've witnessed a miracle, allow your current reality to be shattered. That's

what miracles do—they shatter the mind's tight grip on our reality. You can dismiss the miracle and say to yourself, "The miracle actually didn't happen. Reality is the same as I've always believed it to be." Or you can say, "My current understanding of life is incomplete. I'm going to tolerate this shaky uncertainty and keep soul-searching until I understand what the saints and sages have been teaching. I know the experience was real. I just have no way of explaining it."

7.  After you have "diagnosed" your miracle and integrated the experience into your belief system, remember the words of the roshi: "Don't worry, the experience will pass." In other words, don't get hung up on miracles. Don't get hung up on angels, auras, or prophetic dreams. Experience them. Learn from them, and then move on.

8.  In order to look for the miracle behind the miracle, you may want to make a conscious effort to make direct contact with the Source. Here is a simple yet powerful technique called "Practicing the Presence," also called "Visualizing the Divine Form," that helps us feel closer to God, and to experience his presence more frequently. This technique draws you closer to God, to Higher Consciousness, and fosters the feeling of devotion, the highest, purest kind of love.

## PRACTICING THE PRESENCE
### *Mental Fitness Technique*

*Each day, upon arising from bed, think of your chosen form of God, and then "carve" Him out of thin air as if you were a sculptor. Fill in the details from head to toe.*

*Imagine you reach out and hold His hand as He lifts you out of bed. Continue to picture Him beside you throughout the day, sitting in the car with you, walking with you, sitting beside you at business meetings.*

*If you like, "ask" God to wait outside the bathroom when you need to use the facilities.*

These steps are the way I approach the miraculous in my practice. If I don't understand a patient's miraculous story, I'll say, "I don't know right off the top of my head what to call this experience. Let's look at this together." Out of that pregnant unknowing, that willingness to tolerate uncertainty, that hunger to know the truth, both doctor and patient can set aside the "supposed-to-be's"—and have a deep, honest, profoundly healing discussion.

People are afraid and embarrassed that someone might say, "You're crazy for talking about entities, nirvana, possession, clairvoyance, past-life memories, and life after death." Let us remember that what was once held as pure nonsense, unreality, and superstition often later becomes accepted as scientific fact. Old scientific explanations are only partial truths. And to that I must add that this book is only another small partial truth.

Just as Abraham Lincoln, Gandhi, and Martin Luther King, Jr., fought the delusion of racial superiority and the immorality of racism and oppression, the times now are asking us to fight the delusion of scientific superiority and spiritual inferiority. We must overturn the false idea that spirit doesn't matter. Today, despite extraordinary technological advances, it's clear that something is desperately wrong with our society. It's time to shed false beliefs, look at new realities, and take courageous steps into the future.

The times are also desperately calling us to take a new look at psychiatry and medicine. By incorporating the wisdom of the ages into modern science, psychiatry can actually help both the manic and the mystic. Doctors must treat all patients with knowledge, wisdom, and compassion. Certainly we must not glorify psychotic experience—we must treat psychotic people with great compassion and with appropriate medication. But we should also not treat the mystic with Thorazine. And we should not treat the schizophrenic with a strong dose of yoga and meditation.

It's time to admit that spirit counts, that angels fly (or walk), and that some people can read minds. It's time to try to figure out the difference between schizophrenic hallucinations and spirit possession—between ghostly hauntings and the visions of alcohol withdrawal—between mania and kundalini. It's time for medicine to fully embrace the idea that spiritual experience is—real!

# PART IV

*Tools for*
*Transformation:*
*Making Your*
*Own Miracles*

# 14

## SPIRITUAL FIRST AID

As the artificial walls between body, mind, spirit, and energy have begun to crumble, people today are facing new questions. "How do I know if the angel I saw was a genuine spiritual experience or a sign of insanity?" "How do I cope with kundalini energy once it's been unleashed?" "How do I know if I'm hearing the 'real' inner voice or if it's just my imagination?" "How can I overcome a crisis in faith?" Medicine of the twenty-first century must help with these tough problems, rather than pretend they don't exist. The times are calling for medicine to help us heal the split.

Lacking medical assistance, people in such dilemmas are still on their own. Several steps can help us better handle our spiritual emergencies.

1. Begin to recognize the inner voice more clearly. In so doing, you will be more certain about what to call your experience and what to do about it.

2. Learn to evaluate your own experience by expanding the limited vocabulary of consciousness, expanding your awareness of "awareness," and discovering ways to systematically diagnose yourself.

3. Develop specific strategies for each particular kind of spiritual emergency.

Reactions to spiritual experience range from mild distractions to genuine emergencies—from mild anxiety to overwhelming panic. Because of the range and diversity of these responses, a different approach must be used for each kind of response, reaction, or spiritual emergency.[1]

## HOW TO RECOGNIZE THE REAL INNER VOICE

The more clear, the more silent your mind is, the easier it is to recognize the real inner voice, the voice of conscience or, sometimes, of God. Meditation, by quieting the mind, makes it easier to recognize the inner voice. The better able you are at recognizing that voice, the easier right action or moral conduct will become, and the easier it will be for you to turn spiritual experience into an opportunity for transformation. Here are some guidelines to help you determine if the voice you hear or heard is real:

1. Does the voice give advice that is in keeping with the five core human values? Did it suggest you do something that would lead to more peace, love, truth, nonviolence, or right action? If so, it's probably the real inner voice.

If, on the other hand, the inner (or outer) voice told you to kill yourself or somebody else, it definitely was not the real inner voice. Rather it was the voice of psychosis, imagination, or a racing mind. The only instance in which violence may be the dharmic, the correct thing to do is when one is defending one's nation, city, family, or oneself against an obvious unprovoked attack.

2. Does the voice provide a consistent message? Let's say you're considering quitting your current job but aren't sure yet if it's the right thing to do. You quiet your mind and ask for guidance. Your inner voice says, "Quit your job." But five minutes later you ask again, and your inner voice says, "Stay at this job." Five minutes later, your inner voice says, "Move to Ohio."

When the inner voice provides a high moral message that remains consistent over time, it is likely that it is the real inner voice.

3. Does the voice prompt action that is for the highest good of all concerned, that promotes unity rather than separation? If so, that's the voice of conscience, the real inner voice. If the voice is directing you to take violent or divisive action, what you are hearing is not your real inner voice.

Practice listening to your inner voice. After a while, you'll develop a sense for what is the real inner voice and what is simply mental clutter.

Over the years, it has become easier for me to "hear" the voice of Sai Baba inside myself. His answers are almost always one word, such as, "Come," "Done," "Yes," or "Wait." When I ask the same question, I get the same answer on a repeated basis. Therefore, I have come to trust that voice. But when the voice says one thing one minute and something else the next, I know that my mind is fooling me and that I can't rely on that inner voice.

## HOW TO DIAGNOSE YOUR OWN MIRACLES

If you've had an unusual experience that you suspect may be a genuine spiritual experience, but you're still not sure, follow these steps in order to gain greater clarity and peace of mind. After you've read each question, answer, yes or no.

### 1.   IS YOUR BRAIN OKAY?

You want to make sure that the unusual experience was not caused by a problem with your brain. Let's say you had an experience that you believe was samadhi, or unity consciousness.

During or after the experience, did you notice any problems that were more prevalent on one side of your body than another? For example, did you become weak on your left side? Did you develop numbness in your lower right leg? Such one-sided physical problems may indicate a brain problem.

Have you had problems remembering things since the experience? Have you, in particular, had problems remembering things that happened recently? If so, you may have a brain problem.

Was your experience accompanied by severe mental confusion, so severe that you didn't know if it was day or night? If so, you might have been experiencing a delirium, a disorder of brain chemistry.

If any of these symptoms rings a bell for you, you should see a neurologist to make sure your brain is okay.

Is your brain okay? _____ Yes _____ No

### 2.   IS YOUR MIND OKAY?

If in doubt, review the chapters in Part II to find out if your experience was really a case of mania, schizophrenia, depression, anxiety, or borderline personality.

Is your mind okay? _____ Yes _____ No

### 3.    CAN YOU NAME YOUR OWN SPIRITUAL EXPERIENCE?

If you think you experienced samadhi, review Chapter 10. See if you can find a description of your altered state of consciousness there.

If your strange experience was a visual phenomenon, review Chapter 11 to discover what to call it.

Can you name your own spiritual experience? _____ Yes _____No
What is the name of your experience? _____

### 4.    DID THE EXPERIENCE IMPROVE YOUR LIFE?

Did your experience leave you feeling uplifted, more peaceful, or more loving? Do you now feel closer to Nature and to your fellow men and women? If so, you probably had a genuine spiritual experience.

If, on the other hand, you are more frightened or even paranoid, find it harder to interact with others, have become increasingly anxious, or have been staying home from work, it is less likely that you had a genuine spiritual experience.

Did the experience improve your life? _____ Yes _____ No

### 5.    DOES YOUR EXPERIENCE STAND THE TEST OF TIME?

Is your experience consistent with the teachings of the Vedas, the Bible, or the Koran? If so, you probably had a genuine spiritual experience. Some religions have gone into greater detail in describing spiritual experience than others, even though all teach the core principles of right living. You may want to explore some of the more esoteric, mystical writings from your religion in order to have a more complete picture.

Does your experience stand the test of time? _____ Yes _____ No

Now, simply add up number of times you answered yes.

Total Yes _____ This number is your score.

If you scored 0, you did not have a genuine spiritual experience.
If you scored 1, you probably did not have a genuine spiritual experience.
If you scored 2, you may have had a genuine spiritual experience.
If you scored 3, you probably had a genuine spiritual experience.

If you scored 4, you almost certainly had a genuine spiritual experience.

If you scored 5, you definitely had a genuine spiritual experience.

Before proceeding to the actual management of spiritual emergencies, let's review some general steps and some general principles.

## General Steps for Managing Spiritual Emergencies

1. What is the name of your spiritual experience?

2. What is your *main concern* regarding the spiritual experience?

3. How do you *feel* emotionally about your main concern?

4. How does your main concern affect your *belief system* or sense of meaning in life?

5. Talk about your experience with someone. Powerful spiritual experiences can unleash intense emotion, sometimes emotion that has been held inside for a lifetime. If you know you're not crazy but your friend, spouse, priest, rabbi, or psychiatrist is trying to convince you that you are, keep looking until you find a sympathetic ear. Yes, it is possible that all of those people are wrong and that you are right.

6. If the one nearest and dearest to you can't stand to hear you utter a word about your angel sighting or near-death experience, please ask them to read this book. You've got to feel heard, not just tolerantly listened to.

## Goals of Dealing with Spiritual Emergencies

1. Move away from the idea that everything about your health you don't yet understand is a disease. Modern medicine looks at just about everything through the disease model—even childbirth. With spiritual experience, you need to give birth to a new kind of process, a new way of thinking, feeling, perceiving, and believing. But first you need to get rid of the idea that spiritual experience is a sign of disease.

2. Strive to find the healing potential within your spiritual experience, and realize that a spiritual emergency is your "inner wisdom's" way of forcing you to grow.

3. Realize that spiritual growth and ego death go hand in hand. The more intense the spiritual emergency, the greater the loss of your false

safety net. Spiritual experience may nudge you in the direction of giving up arrogant self-aggrandizement, or angry, righteous indignation. Learn to grieve the small ego deaths while you are giving birth to your new, truer Higher Self.

4. Keep going. Don't give up. Even if your spiritual emergency is impending death, keep going. You're alive until you're dead, so use each spiritual experience to bring you closer to love, truth, and God.

## COMMUNICATING WITH YOUR MAIN CONCERN
### *Mental Fitness Technique*

*Human values fostered by this technique: Truth, Right Action, Peace, Love, Nonviolence*

In this technique, you'll go deeper by working with symbols.

Not only is mental imagery the language of the imagination and the unconscious, it is the language by which the mind and body communicate with each other. The use of imagery to cure warts is a good example—visualizing warts disappearing often makes them disappear.

Carl Jung was the first of the modern psychologists to work extensively with symbols. Later on, Roberto Assagioli, M.D., developed a complete healing system, called psychosynthesis, that is based on mental imagery. Oncologist O. Carl Simonton, M.D., was the first to use imagery with cancer patients.[2] Over the past twenty years, a number of people have helped systematize imagery work, so that symbols could be more easily accessed and used for personal growth and healing: they include Martin Rossman, M.D. (codirector of the Academy for Guided Imagery and author of *Healing Yourself: A Step-by-Step Program for Better Health Through Imagery*[3]), David Bresler, Ph.D. (codirector of the Academy for Guided Imagery), and Rachel Naomi Remen, M.D. This script is a modification of one developed by Dr. Rossman, and Dr. Remen.

This technique can help you develop each of the human values. You may use it to assist you with your main concern. (If necessary, use the PSA to refresh your memory about what your main concern is.) Now, here's how to proceed.

*Close your eyes, take a few deep breaths, and just let yourself let go and relax. Get in touch with all the thoughts, feelings, and sensations associated with your main concern.*

*Imagine that you have a volume control like one on a radio or television. Turn up the volume on the entire experience of your main concern.*

*Now, allow an image to emerge that represents your main concern. That image may be anything—a person, animal, plant, rock—any object outside yourself. It may be made of any material, or it may be as fine as a mist. Notice the color and texture of the image.*

*You'll want to bring all your senses into play. What sights, sounds, smells, and sensations are associated with your image? If you are a kinesthetic person, you may not "see" the image but feel or sense it.*

*The image that appears to you may seem silly at first, but try not to judge it. Your unconscious mind automatically provides you with the right image.*

*Observe the qualities of the image. Is it powerful, gentle, frightening, soothing?*

*Now, imagine that the image has a voice. You're using your imagination, so you can give anything a voice, even a rock. Tell the image how you feel about it. You can speak silently, not necessarily out loud. If you want the image to go away, tell it that. If you're angry with it, tell it that. Whatever you're feeling about the image, tell it.*

*Now that you've experienced and expressed your initial feelings, see if you have any deeper feelings. Share those.*

*Ask the image what it wants from you. Give it time to answer. Then ask what it needs from you. Why does it need that? Is the image protecting you from anything? Ask it if it has anything it wants to teach you.*

*Now, imagine that you switch places with the image. You are the image, looking back at yourself through the eyes of the image. How does it feel to be the image? How does the "real" you look through its eyes?*

*Switch places again so that you're looking directly at the image. Notice if anything has changed about it. Is there anything you hadn't noticed before?*

*You may wish that the image would just leave you alone and disappear forever, but asking it to leave is not likely to help. You need to "negotiate a settlement" with it. You want something from the image (perhaps to lighten up on a symptom or problem)—and it wants something from you.*

*Ask the image what you need to do to meet its need. If
you meet that need, will it meet you halfway and let up
on your symptom or problem? Keep talking to the image
until you have a satisfactory negotiation.*

If you're tape-recording this imagery script, take a break for a
minute, so that I can explain a little more about the process of negotiation. Let's say your main concern is chronic headaches. In your negotia-
tions your image of pain has "told" you that it feels neglected and would
like you to check in with it for a few minutes every day. If you're comfortable with that, you're close to "closing the deal." But if you feel that
daily visits are too frequent, perhaps you'll offer three visits a week. Keep
negotiating in this way until both you and your image are satisfied.

Make the negotiation as clear as possible, so that you could actually
write out a contract with a series of three or four points. Here's an example of how a negotiated contract might look:

1.   I will check in with you, the image, every other day for five minutes
     before I go to sleep.

2.   You will lighten up on my symptom or problem.

3.   If I fail to live up to my end of the agreement, you, the image, have
     the right to increase my symptom or problem.

4.   If you, the image, do not let up on my symptom or problem, I will
     renegotiate with you and have the right not to visit you so frequently.

In your notebook, draw a picture of your image, using paint,
crayons, pencils, or whatever you like. But please don't be shy. Getting it
down on paper is a powerful step. Write down your negotiation as well
as your thoughts and feelings about this imagery experience.

If this kind of work is new to you, please try to suspend judgment.
It is extremely likely to help you with any problem imaginable. Sometimes
the results are truly miraculous, as they were for the man who was cured
of fifty-five years of asthma after two imagery sessions, or the young lady
who was cured of severe PMS after one session.

By communicating with your symptom, you begin to break up old
habit patterns. Let's say you have chronic pain. That pain has become a
complex habit. By now it's woven into the fabric of your life. You eat,
sleep, walk, and talk pain. After a while, it becomes difficult to separate

the pain from yourself. Working with the image of your pain can help you break up these longstanding habit patterns.

And here's one more benefit: Because symbolic imagery works on so many levels, it will open up parts of your life that you weren't even focusing on. Even if your main concern is pain, you may find that suddenly you're calmer, sleeping better, feeling more connected to God, and more comfortable in all of your relationships.

Here's a brief story that illustrates the power of communicating with your symptom. I was asked to see Edie, a 73-year-old woman, six days before she was scheduled for major back surgery. Although she had had a whole host of medical problems over the years, she didn't seem able to cope with this one. Her oncologist asked me to see her because her fear was overwhelming.

Indeed, overwhelming fear was what Edie spoke to me about. She had a strong feeling that she would die during surgery, she told me. Ventilating her fear didn't help her, so I asked her to picture her fear. She pictured her fear as "a bum named Jim. I detest him. He doesn't care for himself. But I do feel sorry for him." Then I helped her communicate with the bum. She negotiated an agreement with him: She was to give him sympathy by checking in with him every day. He, in turn, was to give her understanding and let up on her fear.

Despite the depth and power of this imagery experience, I remained deeply concerned about Edie. I called her surgeon and found out that he too was scared about whether she was really ready for the operation.

The following morning I reviewed Edie's hospital chart. Her surgeon's note read: "Patient amazingly clearer today. She fully understands options and risks of surgery and wants to proceed." Not only was her fear 90 percent gone, but she had said, "Today is the first day in six months that that dark black cloud of despair has lifted."

During the remaining three visits before the surgery, I asked Edie to continue listening to Jim. On the second day, Jim needed some help from her and "required" a place to take a bath. The next day "Jim had moved off the streets and had a place to live."

As a result of this imagery work, Edie did a full 180-degree turn, shifting from terror and despair to hope, tranquillity, and faith in the surgical treatment ahead. The surgery went well.

## PROFOUND SELF-ACCEPTANCE/EMBRACING
## OVERWHELMING PAIN AND FEAR
### *Mental Fitness Technique*

*Human value fostered by this technique: Peace*

Sometimes our suffering is so great that imagery work alone doesn't make a dent. The pain or the fear goes on and on, even after utilizing symptomatic kinds of treatments, after meditating, after communicating with your main concern, after examining your resistance.

This technique is inspired by the work of Stephen Levine, author of *Who Dies* and *Meetings at the Edge*.[4] For several years Stephen and Ondrea Levine offered free twenty-four-hour-a-day counseling by telephone for those with terminal illness.

It is human nature to try to push away pain and fear and hold on to pleasure. But sometimes you need to fully embrace pain, rather than diminish it. This imagery script is perhaps the most powerful of all the tools of transformation at my disposal. It helps one overcome any overwhelming experience, emotion, or sensation:

> *Begin by getting in touch with the variety of bodily sensations you have . . . the feeling of your body on the chair, couch, bed, or floor . . . the feeling of your clothing on your skin . . . the temperature of the air . . . the rising and falling of your diaphragm. Notice areas of comfort and areas of discomfort.*
>
> *Allow all these different physical sensations to arise . . . and dissolve. As you bring your awareness to these sensations, you will see that they change. Even the pain or fear sensations will arise, change, and dissolve when you bring your awareness to it.*
>
> *Most of us have a way of closing around the pain. Imagine that there is a fist closed around the pain or fear. Examine the fist, and then begin to allow the fingers to open one at a time until the pain is resting in the palm of that hand . . . until you are really down to the original pain. The body reacts to pain. Muscles cramp around it. But now allow yourself to feel the original pain, the original fear, the one at the center before you tightened around it.*
>
> *And allow those sensations to arise, change, and dis-*

*solve. Simply observe. Make no effort to make the pain go away. As the pain sensations arise and dissolve, notice the thoughts, feelings, and images that pass through your consciousness. Observe them also in the same way. Your awareness is simply penetrating and exploring the pain.*

*After a while the pain or fear may just seem to float or take on a new characteristic. Continue to observe the sensations. Imagine that you are opening to the pain over and over again.*

*Now become aware that pain or fear has two qualities: discomfort and energy. Yes, pain is a form of energy. Allow the energy of the pain to move up into your head as if it is charging the batteries of your mind or spirit. Continue to observe it. Continue to let the energy part of the pain rise out of it. Notice how you may want to utilize this pain energy. Perhaps you can use it to sharpen your concentration or to take you into a deep meditation.*

One might call Embracing Overwhelming Pain and Fear a "non-technique technique." Nonetheless, it is quite powerful. The pain or fear will almost always change. And observing pain in this way may cause a whole barrage of feelings to arise. Many people fear when they have pain, that it will never stop—that it will ruin their lives—that they will end up helpless invalids. This technique is ideal for people with cancer who have survived the first round of treatment and are now experiencing the overwhelming fear of recurrence.

I have used a variety of techniques to alleviate fear in cancer patients. But the fear is often so enormous that it transcends techniques. Cancer and AIDS trigger enormous, even overwhelming fear when the initial diagnosis is made. But even after the person has been treated and the cancer is gone, a deep fear of recurrence is often present.

So in the case of overwhelming fear, I ask people to simply observe it without trying to push it away. Let your mind explore the fear.

*Where is the fear in your body? What are the fearful thoughts and images? Just observe, allowing the fear to arise, change, and dissolve. Let the fear float. Let it break free from the clutches of your mind. Let yourself be fully immersed in the fear. Embrace the fear. Breathe in and out of the fear, allowing your breath to gently massage the fear.*

The results are powerful. Sometimes the fear seems to float out of the body or gradually disperse. But the experience of embracing the fear, immersing oneself in the fear, allows for transformation of the fear. Even the fear of death can be alleviated using this approach. Regardless of what is feared, embracing the pain is a powerful tool that everyone should be aware of. It is part of the treatment program for many spiritual emergencies.

## LETTING GO OF THE PAST
### Mental Fitness Technique

*Human values fostered by this technique: Love, Peace, and Nonviolence*

Most of us have a difficult time living in the moment. We repeatedly have thoughts such as "I feel so guilty about . . . ," "I'll never forgive her for leaving me," and "I keep thinking about my ex, and it makes me sad." If your mind works like that, you tend toward depression. You need to work on releasing guilt, letting go of resentment, and practicing forgiveness. All of these qualities keep us anchored in the past and prevent us from living more fully in the moment.

Let's start with an imagery script that helps release guilt. The Temple of Forgiveness Imagery was developed by Mary Jayne Carlson, Ph.D.,[5] and is immensely powerful:

### Releasing Guilt

*The burden of guilt you are carrying is very heavy, and you struggle step by step up the path, looking for the Temple of Forgiveness. You see ahead a large wall covered with ivy, and you know that behind the wall is the place you have been seeking. A massive gate is the entrance. The guard of the Temple steps forward to greet you. To enter, you must truly desire forgiveness. Search your heart for this desire.*

*The guard nods and opens the gate. You struggle through. Looking up, you see the Temple—simple, yet an impressive sight. You are very aware of how heavy your burden of guilt is. Stepping through the opening of the Temple, you feel the sacredness of this holy place. Look around and listen.*

*You sit in the back, feeling the peace and comfort of this holy place. You have with you a plain wooden box. Into the box you place your guilt and shame, all that you wish to be forgiven for. And now you take your plain wooden box to the altar. On the altar is a very large and beautiful open container on which there are many symbols of release and forgiveness. You place your box inside the container. Taking one of the candles, you light the box. Kneeling, you pray for your guilt to be replaced with forgiveness. Watch the box burn, noticing any feelings you might have. Watch until only ashes are left.*

*As you rise, leaving the Temple to go into the sun with the ashes, you notice how light you feel, relieved of your burden, free. Finally, forgiven. Joyfully, you draw a circle on the ground, then mix the ashes with the dirt. Everything seems bright and new. The colors are brighter, the sounds crisper and more soothing. When the soil is prepared, plant the seeds of the new ideas, attitudes, and direction. Then water what you have planted. When you are finished, someone will appear who will watch over your planting while you aren't there. This will be a caretaker who will water, weed, and protect the new growth.*

### Letting Go of Resentment

Letting go of resentment is no small task. It seems easier to continue to blame and feel resentful. Before we go into a specific technique, here are a few guidelines:

1. Understand that fear lies buried underneath your anger and resentment.

2. Realize that underneath the fear is pure, raw pain. When you reach raw pain, you can fully experience it, let go of it, and begin to live more fully in the present. Blame is a cover-up for pure pain.

3. You can't pretend to be free of resentment. You can't fake it. You have to go through the hard work of honest soul-searching, examining what may seem ugly within yourself.

4. In your notebook, write down all the things you resent about a particular person. After you've done that, picture that person in your mind, as if she were in the room with you, and read out loud those words of resentment you've just written down.

5. If you believe you can speak directly to the person in question without hurting her, without seeking revenge, speak to her face-to-face or on the phone. Avoid blaming her. Try using phrases like, "I know there is another side to this, but I'd like to tell you how I felt when you did such-and-such. I'm still angry and hurting because of that incident, that remark."

6. Remember that the brutal, honest truth is not always the best policy. If the "brutal" truth will destroy a relationship that you want to foster, choose your truthful words carefully.

7. It's never too late to clear the air, even if you're dealing with a parent who abused you fifty years ago.

8. Once you have expressed your anger, hurt, and resentment, don't wallow in it. There is a time to express negativity, and there is a time to let go.

Now cut the ties to any person, event, or symbol from the past to which you are still bound, using the following imagery script:

> Imagine there is an actual physical bond connecting your body to her body. This bond symbolizes the negative aspects of your attachment to that person. The bond may be made of any substance—ropes or chains, ribbon or string, wood or metal, tar or taffy, smoke or light—and may run from any part of her body to any part of yours. Look closer. There may be more than one bond.
>
> How does the bond feel? How does energy flow in and out of the bond? What energy do you send in to the bond? What kind of energy does she send into the bond?
>
> Using whatever tools are needed (scissors, saws, power tools, explosives, anything that works), remove the negative bond between you and the other person. When you have removed it, dispose of it. Burn it, bury it, or throw it into a deep canyon, but get rid of it.
>
> By removing the bond, you are not necessarily ending the relationship. Removing the negative part of attachment makes room for a relationship in which both of you are independent beings. Cutting the ties that bind makes room for love to move back into a relationship.

This "cutting the ties" technique was thoroughly developed by Phyllis Krystal. She has written about it in her books *Cutting the Ties that Bind* and *Cutting More Ties that Bind*.[6] My extremely abbreviated version is not intended as even a close translation of her work, and I would strongly encourage anyone doing this work to study Krystal's technique. There are books, tapes, and Cutting the Ties groups all over the world.


## PRACTICING FORGIVENESS

You can't begin to forgive until you've gotten in touch with your anger and resentment, expressed it, and finally cut the ties. Once you've done all this, proceed with these steps:

1. In your notebook, review your list of resentments. In your mind's eye, forgive that person for each and every "offense." Say the forgiving words out loud.

2. When you're ready, speak to that person face-to-face and forgive her, one item at a time.

3. Finally, you'll want to ask her for forgiveness. That's right. The person whom you have seen as your abuser, your tormentor, is the person you now need to forgive. If the thought of forgiving her shocks you, you're still stuck in resentment. You may want to ask her forgiveness for never having fully understood her side of the story, or for having reacted to her only with anger and blame.

4. If you're having trouble forgiving, pray that you may forgive.

5. Practice all the Developing Love techniques in the Mental Fitness Program (see Chapter 5). Once you've weeded the garden of your mind and rid it of negativity, sow the seeds of love. Love needs help in order to grow. The more you develop love, the further resentment will recede into the past, and the more you will become free from the past and able to live in the moment.


## LETTING GO OF THE FUTURE
### *Mental Fitness Technique*

*Human value fostered by this technique: Peace*

Those of us who aren't stuck in the past may well be stuck in the future. If you're one of these people, your mind has thousands of thoughts a day that go something like this: "I'm so worried about . . . ," "What if I don't have time to finish work, pick up the kids, and then fix dinner?" "I'm going to get killed by the IRS at tax time next year." If your mind works this way, you're stuck in the future. From a spiritual standpoint, you need to work on faith, trust, and surrender. Once you have complete faith in God, you will have absolutely no anxieties or worries. You will deeply trust that your life is "handled." That doesn't mean that you don't have to take action to make things happen. You still have to take action, even though you may believe that everything is a sign of God's grace and will.

There are two paths to faith. By taking the first path, the spiritual seeker explores, looks for evidence, is finally convinced, and then has faith. By taking the second path, the seeker jumps into the unknown, making that leap of faith, then discovers that that leap brings more faith.

If you're living in the future, practice the Crisis in Faith as Spiritual Emergency techniques. Anything that inspires faith in you will, in turn, decrease your worry and anxiety and will keep you anchored in the present. Here are a couple of starting points to keep you out of the future:

1. Remember that worry is the most common kind of mental activity. All day long many of us are picturing bad things that may or may not happen to us. Observe how your mind worries about the future. You're probably having more than 10,000 thoughts a day, and 5,000 of them are worries. Once you're aware of the fact, you may want to do something about it.

2. Practice your mantra every time you find yourself worrying.

3. Every time you imagine something bad happening to you or to a loved one, mentally rehearse the same scene, only with a happy ending. If you're imagining coming home from work and having an unpleasant argument with your husband, tell your mind, "Stop." Now, close your eyes, have that conversation with your husband in your head, and make it a good conversation. Forget about "how it's always been." Picture the two of you working out your differences with sweetness and tolerance.

    Practice Mental Rehearsal every time you worry about anything. The fact is that the more you imagine yourself fighting with your husband, the more likely it is that the fight will go exactly as you've mentally rehearsed it, exactly the way you feared it would turn out.

4. Practice "already-thereness," a concept that Jack Hawley writes about in *Reawakening the Spirit in Work: The Power of Dharmic Management*.[7] Many of us are strivers, always trying to get "there." When

we get "there," we start up the hill to get somewhere else. "Already-thereness" means that you're already okay as you are right now. "Already-thereness" is not an excuse for inaction—one needs goals. When we can love and accept ourselves as we are, we are already there. Forget the idea that if you work for the next ten years toward your ultimate goal, you will finally be happy. Be happy now, but still work toward your goal.

5.  Practice "instantaneousness," another of Jack Hawley's concepts. Instantaneousness means that we are capable of radical change immediately. Traditional psychiatry teaches that change is slow, that it takes ten, twenty, or thirty years. If you expect your transformation to take thirty years, it will—and you will "live" in the future. But through my years as a psychiatrist, practicing the techniques you've read about in this book, I have witnessed a nearly instantaneous transformation about once a month. In the 1980s I worked a lot with children and adolescents, often very disturbed kids who required treatment in a psychiatric hospital. After I had worked there for many years, the head nurse approached me and said, "Dr. Gersten, it's amazing, but every one of your kids here gets better." "Betty," I replied, "I thought they were *supposed* to get better."

    That's the truth. I honestly thought they were supposed to get better. If they weren't improving, I assumed that I was doing something wrong, or that the right technique or approach simply hadn't been invented yet. I'm telling you the same thing. You are supposed to get better—and I know you can change. Now.

6.  Close your eyes and say to yourself, "I can change right now, this moment." Be assured that there is always a way to change, a way to be transformed, and even to be radically transformed immediately. It requires a lot of courage, but practicing the techniques you've just read will help you live in the moment and not be a prisoner of the future.

Surrender is the other major lesson that all of us, but especially worriers, need to learn. It's difficult to surrender if your faith is shaky—and if you have no faith at all, it is impossible. Surrendering does not mean turning over our power to someone else but becoming more of who we really are.

In Eastern spiritual practice, there really is no one to surrender to. In early stages we pray and meditate to God. When we become enlightened, or experience nirvana or samadhi, we have the experience of being one with everything, even with God. At that point, there is no God to surrender to, and there is no self left to surrender. This divine state is reached when one's own inner voice, one's own will, becomes so fully imbued with truth, right action, peace, love, and nonviolence that the voice of our conscience is the same as God's voice.

Here's how to surrender:

1.  Surrender to the truth of a given situation. Discover for yourself what is the truth and the Truth.

2.  Once you know the truth of a situation, muster the courage to carry out the dharma, the correct action for that situation.

3.  If you don't know what the correct action is, pray for fifteen minutes, asking for guidance. If you've kept your mind still for fifteen minutes, you will almost certainly hear your true inner voice clearly and will know what to do.

4.  Once you are certain about the truth of a situation and the correct course of action, take that course of action.

5.  Make a vow to yourself this very moment that you will always strive to know the truth of every situation and that you will muster the courage to take the right course of action.

By following these steps, you surrender to right action. You do what you must do, no matter what anyone else thinks about you. People may praise you for your "courage" or blame you or your "stupidity," depending on their vantage point. But once you have made this commitment, you have surrendered to a powerful path. You no longer need to worry about the future, for you realize that you will do what is right, no matter what. The "no matter what" is important, for if you qualify your decisions and your actions and make "small" compromises in the human values, you will never conquer fear and worry, and you will always live in the future, rather than in the present. Make the bold, courageous decision this very moment, so that you don't spend the rest of your life worrying about whether you're going to be courageous in a particular situation.

The ultimate example of such courageous surrender is the crucifixion of Jesus. Jesus knew ahead of time how his physical life would end. He knew he would be betrayed. And he knew that the betrayal was a necessary part of the drama, without which his lesson could not be taught.

Surely the enlightened Jesus could have disappeared into thin air, vanished from the jail, or used any of the miraculous powers that were at his wish and command. But the lesson for him was not about using his miraculous powers. It was about surrendering to the moment and to right action. Because he knew that the crucifixion was God's will, and because he was one with God's will, his final challenge was to muster the immense courage to do what was right. It wasn't fancy, and it wasn't pretty. It was painfully agonizing. People have explored the meaning of the crucifixion in many ways. For now, consider that Jesus taught us how to live in the moment, how to steer free from worry and anxiety simply by deciding to know the truth and by courageously following right action. If we can muster a small fraction of that kind of courage in our day-to-day affairs, we will become free from the future, for in fact the future only exists in our imaginations. Only the moment is here—now.

# 15

# SPIRITUAL EMERGENCY:
# OPENING THE DOOR
# TO CHANGE

In this chapter you'll read about ways of managing feelings. This chapter focuses on emotions that are specifically triggered by spiritual experiences.

I encourage you to embrace spiritual "emergencies" as blessings in disguise, as opportunities for change. In Chinese, the pictogram for "crisis" is made up of the ones for "danger" and "opportunity." Your genuine spiritual experience may seem dangerous to you—it may shake the foundation of your beliefs. It may make you depressed or anxious or overwhelm you with panic. But side by side with that danger lies the opportunity. Spiritual emergencies are really "transitions," times of evolution. Life is not static. If an angel has gotten your attention, it's a good thing. In fact, it's a great thing. It's a gift, a blessing, and a wake-up call for change and perhaps even radical transformation.

## ANXIETY AS SPIRITUAL EMERGENCY
### *Mental Fitness Technique*

*Human values fostered by this technique: Love and Peace*
   1. Practice this one-minute anxiety ritual four times a day.

STEP 1   RELAXATION AND MENTAL CLEARING   15 SECONDS

Close your eyes. Take three deep breaths, and allow yourself to let go of tension with each breath. Imagine that, with each breath, a wave of relaxation spreads from your head to your toes.

Silently recite your mantra along with each breath you take. Allow yourself to sink into the peaceful stillness of your own mind. By so doing, you center yourself and temporarily withdraw from life's distractions.

STEP 2   REGULATE ENERGY WITH THE BREATH   15 SECONDS

**A.** Inhale to the count of four.

**B.** Hold your breath to the count of four.

**C.** Exhale to the count of eight.

STEP 3   SPECIFIC IMAGERY: THE WAVE   25 SECONDS

*Do you get so rushed and stressed out at work that you don't have the luxury of relaxing? Not even a break to let go of stress? The wave imagery innovated by Phyllis Krystal was designed for you.*[1] *Once you learn how to "ride" the wave, you can teach yourself to relax in just a minute.*

*Imagine you are at the beach, lying on the warm sand. The waves are rolling in, and each one comes closer and closer to you . . . until the waves are starting to wash over your body before they roll back out. As each wave falls away from you and returns to the sea, tension, anxiety, and stress are removed. With each wave you feel a little more relaxed. Just feel the wave gently pulling tension out of you.*

STEP 4   COMING BACK   5 SECONDS

Take one more long, deep breath, and completely bring yourself back to normal consciousness.

2. Develop your inner voice. Ask yourself what the anxiety is about and why it's being triggered by your spiritual experience.

3. Communicate with your anxiety, allowing an image to emerge that represents it.

4. Practice Mantra Meditation throughout the day in order to become calmer and to slow down the mind.

## DEPRESSION AS SPIRITUAL EMERGENCY
### *Mental Fitness Technique*

*Human values fostered by this technique: Peace, Nonviolence, and Right Action*

1.  Ask yourself what the meaning of your depression is.

2.  Exercise—a lot. Jog, swim, or bike thirty minutes a day, five days a week. Not only will this lift your depression, but if anger is buried beneath the depression, exercise will help mobilize the anger.

3.  If you get in touch with buried anger and it starts to erupt, practice the ABCs of Anger Control.

4.  A host of nutritional supplements and herbs may assist you. The amino acids tyrosine and L-tryptophan (now legal again) can be powerful antidepressants.

5.  Make your diet "lighter." Lighten up on the heavy stuff like red meat and cheese and shift toward a vegetarian diet.

6.  Practice the energizing breath technique:

    A.  Inhale to the count of two.

    B.  Hold your breath to the count of two.

    C.  Exhale to the count of one.

7.  Use this imagery technique to help not only with depression but with other painful emotions if they arise:

    > *Imagine that you're walking in your favorite setting in nature. You come across a hole in the ground, about eight inches wide, that goes clear down to the center of the earth.*
    > *Get in touch with all the thoughts, feelings, sensations, and images related to the depression, and dump them down the hole in the ground. Just let the depression flow out of you.*

8.  Communicate with a symbol of depression.

## PAIN AS SPIRITUAL EMERGENCY
### *Mental Fitness Technique*

*Human value fostered by this technique: Peace*

1. Practice the pain one-minute imagery ritual four times a day.

STEP 1   RELAXATION AND MENTAL CLEARING   15 SECONDS
Close your eyes. Take three deep breaths, and allow yourself to let go of tension with each breath. Imagine that a wave of relaxation spreads from your head to your toes with each breath.

Silently recite your mantra along with each breath you take. Allow yourself to sink into the peaceful stillness of your own mind. By so doing, you center yourself and temporarily withdraw from life's distractions.

STEP 2   REGULATE ENERGY WITH THE BREATH   15 SECONDS

A. Inhale to the count of four.

B. Hold your breath to the count of four.

C. Exhale to the count of eight.

STEP 3   SPECIFIC IMAGERY: PAIN TECHNIQUE   25 SECONDS

A. *Focus your attention on your pain or discomfort. Imagine your pain has a certain size, shape, and color. What does it feel like? Is it rough or smooth? Does it stay in one place or move around?*

B. *Allow the pain to turn to liquid. It has the same size, shape, and color as before, but now it's liquid.*

C. *Roll that liquid down to the nearest arm or leg, and let it flow out of your fingertips or toes. Watch it as it flows out of the room, out of the house (or hospital), down the street. Just watch it and see where it goes. Maybe it flows all the way down to the ocean. If your pain was a 100 percent before this exercise, what percent is it now?*

STEP 4   COMING BACK   5 SECONDS
Take one more long, deep breath, and completely bring yourself back to normal consciousness.

2. Practice the technique "Profound Self-Acceptance: Embracing Overwhelming Pain and Fear," in Chapter 14; every day for thirty to sixty minutes.

3. If your physical pain is the result of a kundalini process, you'll want to look at the technique for Redirecting Obstructed Energy and see if blocked energy is producing your pain.

## MARITAL PROBLEMS AS SPIRITUAL EMERGENCY
### *Mental Fitness Technique*

*Human values fostered by this technique: Love, Truth, and Peace*

When one partner has had an unusual spiritual experience and the other hasn't, marital problems frequently arise. Suddenly, the two people are on different wavelengths, thinking, feeling, and believing differently. If you're the one who had the spiritual experience, you may not even be able to put it into words, thereby widening the gap between you and your spouse.

Most likely, the "normal" spouse will want everything to quickly return to normal. She may think you're crazy and may push you hard to "pull yourself together." You're left feeling alone, misunderstood, and frightened. Your spouse may not understand that you love her as much as before, maybe even more. She may interpret your spiritual experience as an attempt to pull away from her. With these basic problems in mind, here's how to proceed:

1. Communicate. Sit down face-to-face and share all the details of your spiritual experience with your partner. Ask her to listen, without judging, until you have completely finished.

2. If you are the partner who did not have the spiritual experience, the best thing you can do is reassure your partner how much you love her. Keep listening. Keep loving. The more space you provide for your partner to air her feelings, the quicker she will move through the spiritual emergency.

3. Ask your partner to read this book. If she thinks you're crazy, review Part II together, so that you can reassure her that you do not have a genuine mental illness.

4. Be patient. Remember that a spiritual emergency is a transformative process that almost always leaves you better off. It will pass, so don't act in haste. You may feel the desire to spare your partner the suffering you may be experiencing. Maybe you feel that a divorce would be the best thing for her. You're probably wrong. Hang in there as a team.

5.  Don't try to convert your spouse to your newfound spiritual insights. Expect her to listen, but don't demand that she follow your path.

6.  If no one else understands you, remember that God does. If you are questioning that, dive into the techniques in Crisis in Faith, later in this chapter.

## CONFUSION AND PANIC AS SPIRITUAL EMERGENCY
### *Mental Fitness Technique*

*Human value fostered by this technique: Peace*

If your spiritual experience is producing a feeling of confusion or panic, you're in a serious spiritual emergency. First, realize that the reason for your confusion is that your old belief system has been overwhelmed. You have no context within which to understand your new spiritual experience. Your beliefs are no longer in sync with what you now know to be genuine spiritual experience. And yet because you can't explain it, you feel overwhelmed or panicky. Here's what to do:

1.  Clarify, one more time, the name of your spiritual experience. You need to do this in order to reassure yourself that you're not losing your mind.

2.  In order to bring your belief system up to speed with your new experience, practice a symbolic imagery. It will help you discover the meaning of the experience:

> *Get in touch with your feelings of panic or confusion.*
> *Ask yourself, "What is the meaning of the experience?"*
> *Allow an image to emerge that represents the meaning of the experience.*

After you've gotten in touch with the image of "meaning," you can work with it in several ways:

A.  Use the Communicating with Your Main Concern technique.

B.  Picture your chosen form of God next to the image of "meaning." Ask God what the image means and what you should think, feel, or do about it.

C. Oftentimes, the meaning of an image, a symbol, automatically becomes apparent as soon as you visualize it. Here's an example: I asked a patient of mine, a young man with a chronic sleep disorder, to allow an image to emerge representing the problem of insomnia. He immediately "saw" a Scotsman tossing heavy fifty-pound weights, which were attached to three-foot chains. My patient knew that his insomnia was like that fifty-pound weight. He'd had the problem for so long, he felt as if he simply couldn't make any progress. He couldn't lift the heavy weight, but he knew he had to.

Immediately, in his imagination, he began picking up the weights and chain. At first, they felt so heavy he could barely lift them off the ground. He continued to practice in his mind until he could swing a weight and chain around and around, finally letting go and tossing it forty or fifty feet. By so doing, he was able to "move" his sleep problem and make headway.

D. If you're feeling overwhelmed with confusion, chances are you're really frightened. Don't try to bury the fear or chase it away. Rather, embrace it with the technique Profound Self-Acceptance: Embracing Overwhelming Pain and Fear.

## CRISIS IN FAITH AS SPIRITUAL EMERGENCY
### Mental Fitness Technique

*Human values fostered by this technique: Peace, Love, Right Action*

Although usually our faith is relatively stable, almost all of us experience a crisis in faith from time to time. If you're having a spiritual emergency of a crisis in faith, you may suddenly feel as if God has totally abandoned you. Or you may feel like you're "going to hell" because "Christians don't have past-life memories." Don't panic. Rather, practice this extensive program to restore faith.

1.  Practice connecting with God using this imagery technique:

*Picture your chosen form of God in front of you. Imagine that a hollow tube connects your heart to God's heart.*

*Imagine that divine love flows through that tube into you.*
*Allow it to continue flowing until you are filled with love.*

2. Increase your practice of Mantra Meditation (reciting the name of God) and visualizing your chosen form of God. These two techniques make each moment more sacred and make the Divine more of a living presence in your life, rather than an intellectual abstraction.

3. Pray—a lot. If you've lost all faith, pray that your faith be restored.

4. Explore the void.

5. Go to church or synagogue more often.

6. Speak to your rabbi, minister, priest, or guru, and ask the tough questions. If their answers don't satisfy you or quench your spiritual thirst, keep looking.

7. Practice a deeper level of surrender by using this prayer: "Lord, I know that everything is your will." A crisis in faith arises when you ask yourself, "How can this be happening to me?" If you're asking this question, it means that what you believe is not in harmony with what is happening in your life. Pray that you can surrender at a deeper level.

8. Examine an image of "resistance to faith."

9. Reassess whether your religion is the right one for you. Does it answer the tough questions?

10. If, through reassessment, you decide that your current religion is still the right one for you, don't retreat from the spiritual practices it recommends. Rather, double your efforts.

11. Have faith that the spiritual practices of the world's great religions have withstood the test of time. Even if they don't make you feel better in the short run, trust that the long-term benefits are worth the effort.

# 16

## FACING THE VOID:
## HOW PROFOUND EMPTINESS
## IS CURED

Few of us grew up under ideal circumstances, and many of us suffered some degree of abuse or neglect, whether physical or psychological, while we were growing up. Those who did, know how hard it is to leave the past behind. You may have gone to therapy for twenty years, joined twelve-step programs, and practiced meditation, guided imagery, emotional release work, or even shamanic healing. Yet you still may not yet feel whole, for psychological damage in our early years leaves an incredibly deep wound.

Inner child work is aimed at reparenting that part of ourselves that was wounded as a child. But most people do not yet know that inner child work doesn't fully heal a heart that was broken in childhood. For almost two decades, I have worked extensively with the abused and have identified several persistent inner states that are invariably associated with abuse and neglect. The "wounded inner child" is one such inner state. The other states are the "inner abuser," the "inner battlefield," and the "void."

To "diagnose" your own condition, if you were abused or neglected as a child, try this exercise:

> *Close your eyes. Notice if you feel as if you are standing at the edge of a great void—a great chasm or canyon. If you are, notice how far across it extends and how deep it goes. Notice how you feel standing at the edge of it. Then open your eyes.*

The void is the huge psycho-spiritual gap that is created within us when our trust is radically shaken as a child. The void can be healed, but do not attempt to do it on your own. It is much too dangerous. And do not begin to explore the "inner abuser" until you have sought out professional help and are beginning to heal the void. The void is present not only in people who were severely abused or neglected but also in people who, as adults, are in the middle of an existential crisis—whose world has just fallen apart. Maybe they've just been diagnosed with cancer. Maybe they just got divorced, or fired from work. Maybe they're experiencing a radical shift in their worldview, in what they consider to be important or real. Maybe they are wondering about the meaning of life—or if their life has meaning at all. Maybe they are having a crisis in faith, a dark night of the soul, or a good old-fashioned "midlife crisis." These problems can also be transformed immensely by exploring the void.

## FACING THE VOID
### *Mental Fitness Technique*

*Human values fostered by this technique: Peace, Love, Nonviolence, Right Action*

In the Appendix of this book, you will find a way to locate an imagery specialist in your area. What follows is an imagery protocol for healing the void. Do not do this work on your own. Find a good imagery therapist, one who has experience with abuse. (Work on the void has thus far only been published in *Atlantis: The Imagery Newsletter,* so most psychotherapists do not yet know how to work with it and the "inner abuser.") Bring him or her the following script, and ask for guidance through it:

## EXPLORING THE VOID

The void is a terrifying place. You'll need a good deal of guidance to make the descent.

> *Close your eyes. If you feel an inner void, picture that*
> *void now. Stand back from the edge. Gaze across the void*
> *and see how far across it stretches. How deep is it?*

People who were abused as children usually have similar experiences of the void. It is often described as "wider than the Grand Canyon" and "deeper than anything imaginable." It is almost always a bottomless pit. Many people live at the edge of the void every day of their life. Once you have pictured it, you need to prepare for the leap of faith into it.

> *Imagine you have a parachute on your back. It's one of those high-tech parachutes that gives you lots of control. You'll be able to turn right or left as you choose. Picture your parachute, and feel it on your back. Are you ready to jump into the void?*
>
> *If you're still too frightened to jump, imagine you have a jet-pack on your back. You can fly up, down, or sideways using your jet-pack. Why don't you practice using it? Fly over a tree or a small hill.*

## DIVINE ASSISTANCE

By now you are ready to "jump," but one more element of the imagery needs to be introduced at this point—the spiritual dimension.

> *Imagine that a Divine Being joins you at the top of the void, a being full of light and love, a being you can fully trust. This Divine Being may be male or female, both or neither. Make contact with this being in any way you like. Hold His hands. Look into His eyes.*
>
> *Now I'd like you to carry one more thing with you. Imagine you're carrying a powerful flashlight.*
>
> *When you feel ready, jump off the edge into the void. Feel yourself slowly drifting down. Pull on the strings of your parachute, guiding yourself this way and that.*

At this point, I generally suggest that people fall or drift into the void uninterrupted for five or ten minutes. Then I ask them to describe their experience. I ask them to shine their flashlight on the walls of the void, in order to see what it looks like. I may ask them to touch the sides of the void, in order to know what it feels like. By visualizing the sides of the void in this way, they can observe differences. They can observe changes in the walls—perhaps from hard rock to sandstone. They begin to feel differences in the weather, changes in temperature. The void begins to differentiate. It is no longer one giant bottomless pit.

> *Continue to feel the presence of the Divine Being beside you, making your journey safe.*

Without the Divine Being, no patient of mine has ever successfully traversed the void, reached the bottom, and made it back to the top. Years of parachuting with my patients have taught me the necessity of introducing the Divine Being during every phase of traversing the void.

Toward the end of the first void session, I ask my patient to look for the bottom. Almost invariably they reply, "There is no bottom. It just goes on forever." There are ways to bring the bottom of the void into view, but at this point I suggest:

> *Imagine that there is a ledge jutting out from the side of the void. Land on the ledge and rest for a while.*

Usually this is as far as I take people on their first exploration of the void. At this point I bring them back to the top of the void, with the assistance of the Divine Being and their jet-pack. During our next session, I have them jump and quickly find their way to the ledge. From there they jump again and are shown how to bring the bottom of the void into focus—and how to reach the bottom.

## REACHING THE BOTTOM OF THE VOID

During the second session, after you've jumped back into the void and have landed on the precipice, rest for a minute, gain your bearings—and then jump again. In most cases the bottom of the void will not come into focus without some further imagery work:

> *Continue your descent with the Divine Being by your side, with your parachute catching the wind. Now take your flashlight and shine it on the walls of the void. Notice the texture, color, and hardness.*
> *Now shine your flashlight directly below. What do you see?*

At this point, most people begin to see the bottom of the void. Before they first jumped in, their fear was so great that the void felt like a bottomless pit, ever waiting to swallow them up. After a couple of jumps, however, the fear dramatically decreases. The void is no longer one giant problem. It has now been explored safely and has been examined with curiosity. Finally, as fear diminishes, the bottom comes into view. Sometimes people will see the void narrowing before they reach the bottom.

On rare occasions, if my patient is unable to see the bottom, I make further suggestions. I may say something like, "Imagine that the void is narrowing. The air is changing—becoming different colors, and different temperatures. Below you the void bottom *will soon be* coming into view."

At last they reach the bottom. But the work is not over. In fact, it's just begun. In most cases the bottom is not a pretty place. It must be transformed. It must be made solid and safe. For one woman, the bottom of the void was "an awful oily tar that goes really deep." And so we must solidify the bottom.

## TRANSFORMING THE BOTTOM OF THE VOID

> Be aware of the Divine Being who accompanies you into
> the void—your angel, or God. You also have a magic wand
> in your hand. Become aware of how deep the muck is.
> Maybe you'll throw a stone into it to see how far down
> it goes. Now it's time to transform the muck. Ask your
> angel for advice as to how to transform it, or use your
> magic wand.

In most cases the murky depths turn into crystal-clear water. In one situation, a woman patient had been struggling to see the bottom below the oily muck. It just seemed to go on forever. I asked her if the void came to a point, and in response she began to sob uncontrollably. "Yes, it does. It does come to a point. I thought it went on forever. And—and there's a huge glowing diamond at the bottom of the void. The diamond turned the oil into clear water."

At the moment when the murky depths are transformed, radical shifts in both mind and body take place. People say, "I can breathe again. The air is so clear." And the quality of their breath changes. One woman experienced the water as a healing spring full of energy or prana. "I feel heat rising up my spine. I feel oxygen entering every cell in my body. It's as if my cells have never been able to fully let oxygen in. This is the kundalini energy. It's rising up my spine. I am in total peace and bliss."

> *After you have stood in the muck and transformed it, set up an altar at the bottom of the void. Put whatever you like on the altar—photographs, candles, incense, a crucifix, a Star of David—whatever you like. Bring your angel to the altar with you.*
>
> *Sit at your altar, and pray or meditate. As you become more and more peaceful, the void is no longer the place you once feared you would fall into and never return. Paradoxically, the bottom of the void has become a place of total safety and comfort, a place far away from the worries of the world—a place where you have finally conquered your worst fear and discovered that your enemy is actually your vehicle for transformation.*

Among my different patients, several images appear at the bottom of the void over and over again. Images of creation and destruction are common. One woman saw molten lava pouring out of the earth, a burning dangerous lava that gave birth to new land as soon as it cooled down. The molten lava was at the very center of the bottom of the void, and around that was water—a second image that is usually present.

Circular imagery is also common—a ring of fire at the bottom, or a ring of angels. One lady, a devotee of Sathya Sai Baba, "saw" a ring of Babas around herself. The most common universal symbols present at the bottom of the void are water, fire, and a circle.

Once people have transformed the void, I ask them to return to the top and then to come back to normal consciousness. Now they are finally ready to explore the void on their own, at home, without a guide. They have gone through the crucible of transformation, almost like a shaman's initiation ritual. They have been burned by the fire, immersed in the nothingness. They have gotten stuck in the quicksand at the bottom and almost suffocated. And at last they have begun to heal.

Sometimes "transforming the bottom" is so powerful that people are physically ill for several days afterward. One woman was sick to her stomach, had dry heaves for days, and developed hives. Many people report that their breathing changed the day after this experience. One patient told me, "I noticed today that my breathing has become much more regular and deeper. I also realized for the first time that whenever I get stressed out, I hold my breath and stop breathing. But now, I recognize that I'm doing that, and I resume breathing." This same patient, who suffers from chronic fatigue syndrome, reported that her physical energy went way up.

It is truly difficult to convey in words the power of the experiences I have witnessed with my patients. Although I have had no intention of taking them through a "birth" experience, their physical and emotional reactions are not unlike the process of birth. When they complain that they are stuck in the muck, that they feel that they're suffocating, and that suddenly oxygen rushes into their body when the bottom of the void is finally transformed—it sounds similar to the birth process.

In time the void slowly closes. It fills in on its own, but the process takes years. Years of traveling to the bottom of the void, setting up the altar, and meditating or praying. There is no need to fill the void, for once it is no longer feared, it becomes a place of personal discovery, a true inner treasure, like a vein of gold.

## THE INNER ABUSER

He's lurking in the shadows, lurking in the depths of the void. He's been stalking people from the inside of their minds all their lives, sabotaging them.

The inner abuser should lie undisturbed until you have thoroughly explored and transformed the void. Only then, and with caution, should you tackle the inner abuser, who continues to terrorize you, continues to sabotage your best plans, hopes, and dreams, continues to set you back a step every time you take one step forward. But now the ground is fertile for healing. The void is no longer a place of death, fear, and despair. Fear has been conquered, and the void has become a place of refuge and safety.

After you have clearly and definitely transformed the bottom of the void, the inner abuser will usually spontaneously present himself or herself. The inner abuser "lives" in the void. It's his home, and he wants to keep it that way. He doesn't like having his home disturbed, and he often becomes menacing after the void is transformed.

Once the inner abuser has been visualized, all the tools available to the imagery therapist must be called on, for this is a very difficult condition to modify. The damage of early child abuse is so deep that it is as if the abuse is recorded or programmed completely into every cell in the body-mind. People who are survivors of childhood abuse often suffer from compromised immune systems and are much more prone to chronic fatigue syndrome than are the general public. You must be very patient with this work and be prepared to be quite inventive.

You will want to use an inner adviser or a Divine Being to help you interact with the inner abuser. Once you've identified the inner abuser, use Communicating with Your Main Concern to begin to come to terms with it.

Critical to this process, I have found, is the recognition of the void and the inner abuser's relationship to it. As the void is transformed, the inner abuser is transformed and vice versa. This is dangerous work, for the inner abuser carries an immense charge. He carries the fear, the rage, and the destructive urges. If these urges are unleashed prematurely or in a chaotic fashion, the person is likely to get worse, not better.

Here is an overview of the steps required to recover from abuse or neglect. No matter what phase of healing you are undertaking, always bring in a spiritual component. Always imagine that God is by your side, and visualize Him:

1. Work with the wounded inner child, providing it comfort, safety, and nurturing.

2. Explore and transform the void.

3. Transform the inner abuser by dialoguing with this image, keeping in mind that it "lives" in the void.

4. Do whatever work is necessary to clear up feelings about the people who committed the abuse. Cut the ties to everyone who was abusive.

5. Use the "cutting the ties" technique (part of Letting Go of the Past) to cut the tie to the symbol of abuse.

6. Reenact the abuse scene in imagery.

7. Do everything in your power to bring more love into your life. The void came into existence due to a failure of love. Exploring the void and working with the inner abuser will remove the major part of your shadow side. You will have let go of the darkness. Now you need to fill that void with love. Dive into the moment, seeking love in every interaction, absorbing the beauty of every flower you see. Practice all the techniques from Chapter 5, "Your Mental Fitness Program."

Finally, strive to deepen your spiritual connection, for it is only through the purest, most unconditional love that the deepest wounds can be fully healed.

> "Life is a game, play it.
> Life is a dream, realize it.
> Life is love, enjoy it.
> Life is a challenge, meet it."
>
> —SATHYA SAI BABA

# Appendix A: Mental Fitness Techniques

## MFT LISTING

| TECHNIQUE | PAGE |
|---|---|
| Anger Control, ABCs of | 171 |
| Anger, Taking the Lid Off | 173 |
| Anxiety as Spiritual Emergency | 266 |
| Breath, Regulating Energy with | 38 |
| Ceiling on Desires | 76 |
| Communicating with Your Main Concern | 252 |
| Connecting to God's Love | 78 |
| Confusion and Panic as Spiritual Emergency | 271 |
| Crisis in Faith as Spiritual Emergency | 272 |
| Decision-Making | 174 |
| Deep Breathing | 64 |
| Depression as Spiritual Emergency | 268 |
| The Divine Weaver: A Technique for Integrating Experiences | 221 |
| Facing Up to Self-Lies | 60 |
| Facing the Void | 275 |
| Human Values, Visualizing Symbols of | 44 |
| Human Values for Personal Growth, Working on | 47 |
| Judgment Review | 95 |
| Learning to Relax | 163 |
| Letting Go of the Future | 261 |
| Letting Go of the Past | 258 |
| Love Is Ice Cream | 75 |

Magic Box                                                              37
Mantra Meditation                                                      31
Marital Problems as Spiritual Emergency                               270
Mood Words                                                             54
One-Minute Imagery Rituals                                             79
Pain as Spiritual Emergency                                           269
The Power of Paradox                                                   72
Practicing the Presence                                               243
Profound Self-Acceptance/Embracing Overwhelming Pain and Fear         256
Psycho-Spiritual Assessment                                            49
Redirecting Obstructed Energy                                         115
Resistance, Overcoming                                                 69
Resistance to Love                                                     77
Smiling Buddha                                                        158
Thought Watch                                                          28
"Who Am I?" Meditation                                                103

# MFT BY HUMAN VALUES

*Some of the techniques foster more than one human value.*

### Techniques That Foster Love

| TECHNIQUE | PAGE |
|---|---|
| Ceiling on Desires | 76 |
| Connecting to God's Love | 78 |
| Love Is Ice Cream | 75 |
| Practicing the Presence | 243 |
| Profound Self-Acceptance/Embracing Overwhelming Pain and Fear | 256 |
| Resistance to Love | 77 |
| Smiling Buddha | 158 |

### Techniques That Foster Peace

| Deep Breathing | 64 |
|---|---|
| Magic Box | 37 |
| Mantra Meditation | 31 |
| Mood Words | 54 |
| Redirecting Obstructed Energy | 115 |
| Regulating Energy with Breath | 38 |
| Smiling Buddha | 158 |

### Techniques That Foster Truth

| Facing Up to Self-Lies | 60 |
|---|---|
| Mood Words | 54 |

Psycho-Spiritual Assessment 49
"Who Am I?" Meditation 103

### Techniques That Foster Nonviolence
ABCs of Anger Control 171
Judgment Review 95
Profound Self-Acceptance/Embracing Overwhelming Pain and Fear 256
Taking the Lid Off Anger

### Techniques That Foster Right Action
Decision-Making 174
Mood Words 54
Psycho-Spiritual Assessment 49
Regulating Energy with Breath 38

### Techniques That Foster All Five Core Human Values
Communicating with Your Main Concern 252
The Divine Weaver: A Technique for Integrating Experiences 221
Facing the Void 275
Overcoming Resistance 69
The Power of Paradox 72
Visualizing Symbols of Human Values 44
Working on Human Values for Personal Growth 47

# *Appendix B: Resources*

## RECOMMENDED READING

### *Mental Imagery*

Achterberg, Jeanne, Ph.D. *Imagery in Healing: Shamanism and Modern Medicine.* Boston: New Science Library/Shambala, 1985.

Assagioli, Roberto, M.D. *Psychosynthesis.* New York: Viking Press, 1971.

Bresler, David, Ph.D. *Free Yourself from Pain.* New York: Simon and Schuster, 1979.

Dossey, Barbara, R.N., M.S., Jeanne Achterberg, Ph.D., and Leslie Kolkmeier, R.N., M.Ed. *Rituals of Healing: Using Imagery for Health and Wellness.* New York: Bantam Books, 1994.

Gallegos, Eligio-Stephen, and Teresa Rennick. *Inner Journeys: Visualization in Growth and Therapy.* Wellingborough, Northamptonshire: Turnstone Press Limited, 1984.

Jaffe, Dennis, Ph.D. *Healing from Within.* New York: Alfred A. Knopf, 1980.

Jensen, Peter, Ph.D. *The Inside Edge: High Performance Through Mental Fitness.* Toronto: Macmillan Canada, 1992.

Krystal, Phyllis. *Cutting the Ties That Bind: Growing Up and Moving On.* York Beach, ME: Samuel Weiser, Inc., 1993.

———. *Cutting More Ties That Bind.* Longmead, Great Britain: Element Books, 1990.

Progoff, Ira. *At a Journal Workshop.* New York: Dialogue House Library, 1975.

Remen, Rachel Naomi, M.D. *The Human Patient*. New York: Anchor Press/Doubleday, 1980.

Rossman, M.D. *Healing Yourself: A Step-by-Step Program for Better Health Through Imagery*. New York: Walker and Company, 1987.

Samuels, Mike, M.D., and Nancy Samuels. *Seeing with the Mind's Eye*. New York: Random House, 1975.

Simonton, O. Carl, M.D., Stephanie Matthews-Simonton, and James Creighton. *Getting Well Again: A Step-by-Step, Self-Help Guide to Overcoming Cancer for Patients and Their Families*. New York: Bantam Books, 1978.

### Mind-Body Medicine

Barasch, Marc Ian. *The Healing Path: A Soul Approach to Illness*. New York: Penguin Books, 1995.

Benson, Herbert, M.D. *The Relaxation Response*. New York: Avon Books, 1976.

Borysenko, Joan, Ph.D. *Minding the Body, Mending the Mind*. Reading, MA: Addison-Wesley, 1987.

Chopra, Deepak, M.D. *Quantum Healing: Exploring the Frontiers of Mind/Body Medicine*. New York: Bantam Books, 1989.

Cousins, Norman. *Anatomy of an Illness*. New York: Norton, 1979.

Dossey, Larry, M.D. *Meaning and Medicine: A Doctor's Tales of Breakthrough and Healing*. New York: Bantam Books, 1991.

Frank, Jerome. *Persuasion and Healing*. New York: Schocken Books, 1974.

Jampolsky, Gerald, M.D. *Love Is Letting Go of Fear*. Millbrae, CA: Celestial Art, 1979.

LeShan, Lawrence. *The Mechanic and the Gardener*. New York: Holt, Rhinehart, and Winston, 1982.

Locke, Steven, M.D., and Douglas Colligan. *The Healer Within: The New Medicine of Mind and Body*. New York: E.F. Dutton, 1986.

Ornish, Dean, M.D. *Stress, Diet, and Your Health*. New York: Holt, Rinehart, and Winston, 1982.

Pelletier, Kenneth. *Mind as Healer, Mind as Slayer*. New York: Dell Publishing Company, 1977.

Ryan, Regina Sara, and John Travis, M.D. *Wellness Workbook*. Berkeley: Ten Speed Press, 1981.

Siegel, Bernard, M.D. *Love, Medicine, and Miracles*. New York: Harper and Row, 1986.

Weil, Andrew, M.D. *Spontaneous Healing: How to Discover and Enhance Your Body's Natural Ability to Maintain and Heal Itself*. New York: Alfred A. Knopf, 1995.

### Consciousness, Spirituality, and Health

Benor, Daniel, M.D. *Healing Research: Holistic Energy Medicine and Spirituality*. Deddington, Oxfordshire, Great Britain: Helix Editions Ltd., 1993.

Borysenko, Joan, Ph.D. *Fire in the Soul: A New Psychology of Spiritual Optimism.* New York: Warner Books, 1993.

Dossey, Larry, M.D. *Healing Words: the Power of Prayer and the Practice of Medicine.* San Francisco: Harper San Francisco, 1993.

Evans, Hilary. *Alternate States of Consciousness: Unself, Otherself, and Superself.* Wellingborough, Great Britain: The Aquarian Press, 1989.

Grof, Stanislov, M.D., and Christina Grof (editors). *Spiritual Emergency: When Personal Transformation Becomes a Crisis.* Los Angeles: Jeremy Tarcher, Inc., 1989.

James, William. *The Varieties of Religious Experience.* New York: Macmillan Publishing Company, 1985.

Krishna, Gopi. *Kundalini: The Evolutionary Energy in Man.* Berkeley: Shambhala, 1971.

Levine, Stephen. *Healing into Life and Death.* Garden City, NY: Anchor Press/Doubleday, 1987.

Morse, Melvin, M.D. *Closer to the Light: Learning from the Near-Death Experiences of Children.* New York: Villard Books, 1990.

Nelson, John, M.D. *Healing the Split: Integrating Spirit into Our Understanding of the Mentally Ill.* New York: State University of New York Press, 1994.

Peck, Scott, M.D. *The Road Less Traveled: A New Psychology of Love, Traditional Values and Spiritual Growth.* New York: Simon and Schuster, 1978.

Sandweiss, Samuel, M.D. *Spirit and the Mind.* San Diego: Birth Day Publishing Company, 1985.

Sannella, Lee, M.D. *The Kundalini Experience: Psychosis or Transcendence?* Lower Lake, CA: Integral Publishing, 1992.

Tart, Charles. *Altered States of Consciousness.* New York: John Wiley and Sons, Inc., 1969.

White, John. *Kundalini: Evolution and Enlightenment.* New York: Paragon House, 1990.

Wilbur, Ken. *The Spectrum of Consciousness.* Wheaton, IL: The Theosophical Publishing House, 1977.

### Sathya Sai Baba

Hislop, John. *My Baba and I.* San Diego: Birth Day Publishing, 1985.

Sandweiss, Samuel, M.D. *Sai Baba: The Holy Man and the Psychiatrist.* San Diego: Birth Day Publishing, 1975.

For more information about books, videos, and audiocassettes regarding Sathya Sai Baba, contact the Sathya Sai Book Center of America, 305 West First St., Tustin, CA 92680. Tel.: (714) 669-0522.

# CUTTING THE TIES: THE WORK OF PHYLLIS KRYSTAL

Because the imagery work of Phyllis Krystal is so important, especially in helping us free ourselves from past relationships, a special section on her work is included here.

## Books

Krystal, Phyllis. *Cutting the Ties That Bind: Growing Up and Moving On.* York Beach, ME: Samuel Weiser, Inc., 1993.

Krystal, Phyllis. *Cutting More Ties That Bind.* Longmead, Great Britain: Element Books, 1990.

Krystal, Phyllis. *Workbook for Use with Cutting the Ties that Bind.* Los Angeles, 1992.

Contact for Workbook:
Peggy Lenney
12785 Newhope St.
Garden Grove, CA 92640
(714) 638-1650

## Videos

Stephen Moffitt
611 North Blanche St.
Ojai, CA 93203
(805) 646-3228

## Locating a "Cutting the Ties" Practitioner

To locate a practitioner of the "Cutting the Ties" technique, please use the Internet and visit *Atlantis: The Imagery Newsletter* at: www.imagerynet.com/atlantis

Practitioners are listed by state and by country. There are a number of "Cutting the Ties" groups, which operate at no charge, in addition to psychotherapists who utilize these techniques as part of their clinical practice.


# ACADEMY FOR GUIDED IMAGERY (AGI)

Academy for Guided Imagery
P.O. Box 2070
Mill Valley, CA 94942
(800) 726-2070
(415) 389-9324
Internet: www.healthy.com/agi

Codirectors of AGI: Martin Rossman, M.D., and David Bresler, Ph.D.

**Books, Tapes, Videos**

The Academy for Guided Imagery offers a wide variety of books, tapes, videos, and seminars in mental imagery. They offer the only certification program for mental imagery in the United States as well as a home-study program.

**Locating an Imagery Practitioner**

Mental imagery practitioners certified through the AGI may be located either by calling the AGI or through their Internet Web site.

## ATLANTIS: THE IMAGERY NEWSLETTER

Dennis Gersten, M.D., Publisher
125 North Acacia Ave. Suite 110
Solana Beach, CA 92075

*Atlantis* is a how-to-do-it, practical newsletter, published quarterly. Order or call for more information at: (800) 546-6707.

*Atlantis*'s Internet Web site address: www.imagerynet.com
*Atlantis* on-line contains more than 150 pages of imagery techniques.

# Notes

## INTRODUCTION

1. Giorgio Papasogli, *Saint Theresa of Ávila* (Boston: St. Paul Books and Media, 1990).

2. Marilyn Ferguson, *Marilyn Ferguson's Book of PragMagic,* adapted and updated by Wim Coleman and Pat Perrin (New York: Pocket Books, 1990); also reported in *Brain/Mind Bulletin* (August 1990).

## CHAPTER 1: OPENING TO THE POSSIBILITIES

1. See Samuel Sandweiss, *Sai Baba: The Holy Man and the Psychiatrist* (San Diego, CA: Birth Day Publishing Co., 1975).

## CHAPTER 2: TWENTY-FIVE SPIRITUAL QUESTIONS PSYCHIATRISTS ARE AFRAID TO ASK

1. Richard Del Maestro, personal communication, 1996.

2. Pema Chodron, *The Wisdom of No Escape: And the Path of Loving-Kindness* (Boston: Shambhala, 1991).

## CHAPTER 4: THE HEALING POWERS OF HUMAN VALUES

1. Archie Bahm, *Yoga Sutras of Patanjali* (Berkeley: Asian Humanities Press, 1993).

2. *The Path Divine.* For Sri Sathya Sai Bal Vikas Group III. Education in Human Values Series (Prasanthi Nilayam, India: Sri Sathya Sai Bal Vikas Education Trust, 1981).

3. Stephen Levine, *Healing into Life and Death* (New York: Anchor Press/Doubleday, 1987).

## CHAPTER 5: YOUR MENTAL FITNESS PROGRAM

1. Norman Cousins, *Head First: The Biology of Hope* (New York: E.P. Dutton, 1989).

2. Peter Jensen, Ph.D., *The Inside Edge: High Performance Through Mental Fitness* (Toronto: Macmillan Canada, 1992).

## CHAPTER 6: BELIEF MEDICINE

1. Bobette Perrone, Henrietta Stockel, and Victoria Krueger, *Medicine Women, Curanderas, and Women Doctors* (Norman and London: University of Oklahoma Press, 1989); and Ari Kiev, M.D., *Curanderismo: Mexican-American Folk Psychiatry* (New York: Free Press, 1968).

2. Personal communication with Raymond Woo, M.D., D.O.M. (Doctor of Oriental Medicine), 1996.

3. Deepak Chopra, M.D., *Quantum Healing: Exploring the Frontiers of Mind/Body Medicine* (New York: Bantam Books, 1989).

4. Dr. Vasant Lad, *Ayurveda: The Science of Self-Healing* (Santa Fe, NM: Lotus Press, 1984).

5. Frank Lawlis, Ph.D., "Unity in Diversity: Cross-Cultural Perspectives," *Atlantis: The Imagery Newsletter* (June 1989).

6. David Reilly. "Is Evidence of Homeopathy Reproducible?" *Lancet* 344 (8937) (Oct. 1994), pp. 1601–6, and in *Brain/Mind Bulletin* (Feb. 1995).

7. Horace Miner, "Body Ritual of the Nacirema," *American Anthropologist*, vol. 58, no. 3 (1956), pp. 173–78.

8. Princeton Religion Research Center, *Religion in America* (Princeton University Press, 1994).

9. O. Pfister, *Psychoanalysis and Faith: The Letters of Sigmund Freud and Oskar Pfister*. (New York: Basic Books, 1963).

10. David Larson, M.D., M.S.P.H., and Susan Larson, M.A.T., *The Forgotten Factor in Physical and Mental Health: What Does the Research Show?* (Rockville, MD: National Institute for Healthcare Research, 1994).

11. Ibid.

12. G. W. Comstock and K. B. Partridge, "Church Attendance and Health," *Journal of Chronic Disease*, 25 (1972): 665–72.

13. S. Stack, "The Effect of Religious Commitment on Suicide: A Cross-National Analysis." *Journal of Health and Social Behavior.* 1983b. 24: 362–74.

14. D. Larson, M.D., and W. Wilson, "Religious Life of Alcoholics," *Southern Medical Journal*, vol. 73, no. 6 (1980): 723–27.

15. Carol Tavris and Susan Sadd, *The Redbook Report on Female Sexuality: 100,000 Married Women Disclose the Good News About Sex* (New York: Delacorte Press, 1977).

16. Comstock and Partridge, "Church Attendance."

17. D. Zuckerman, S. Kasl, and A. Ostfeld, "Psychosocial Predictors of Morality Among the Elderly Poor," *American Journal of Epidemiology*, 118 (1984): 410–23.

18. Jeffrey Levin, Ph.D., and H. Vanderpool, "Is Religion Therapeutically Significant for Hypertension?" *Social Science Medicine,* vol. 29, no. 1 (1989): 69–78.

19. L. Propst et al., "Religious Values in Psychotherapy and Mental Health: Empirical Findings and Issues," *Journal of Consulting and Clinical Psychology,* in press.

## CHAPTER 7: GETTING CONSCIOUS ABOUT CONSCIOUSNESS

1. Interview with Jeanne Achterberg, Ph.D., "Woman as Healer," *Atlantis: The Imagery Newsletter* (Dec. 1990).

2. R. D. Laing, *The Politics of Experience* (New York: Pantheon Books, 1967).

3. Homer Youngs, *Translations by Baba,* a Sanskrit-English dictionary (Tustin, CA: Sri Sathya Sai Book Center of America, 1975).

4. Gopi Krishna, *Kundalini: The Evolutionary Energy in Man* (Berkeley: Shambhala, 1971).

5. Lee Sannella, M.D., *The Kundalini Experience: Psychosis or Transcendence?* (Lower Lake, CA: Integral Publishing, 1992).

6. John White, *Kundalini: Evolution and Enlightenment* (New York: Paragon House, 1990).

7. Ajit Mookerjee, *Kundalini: The Arousal of the Inner Energy* (New York: Destiny Books, 1982).

8. *The Gospel of Paramahansa Ramakrishna,* originally recorded in Bengali by M., a disciple of Ramakrishna; translated into English by Swami Nikhilananda (New York: Ramakrishna-Vivekananda Center, 1942).

9. *Diagnostic and Statistical Manual of Mental Disorders,* or *DSM-III* (Washington, D.C.: American Psychiatric Association, 1980).

## CHAPTER 8: WHAT IS THE MIND?

1. Fred Plum, M.D., and Jerome Posner, M.D., *The Diagnosis of Stupor and Coma* (Philadelphia: F. A. Davis Co., 1972).

2. Joanne Greenberg, *I Never Promised You a Rose Garden* (New York: New American Library, 1964).

3. Anne Gordon, *A Book of Saints: True Stories of How They Touch Our Lives* (New York: Bantam Books, 1994).

## CHAPTER 9: WHEN THE SPIRIT CAN HELP THE MIND

1. David Bresler, Ph.D., "The Clock Imagery," *Atlantis: The Imagery Newsletter* (Feb. 1992).

2. The idea that "standing outside the fire" symbolizes neurosis is inspired by the song "Standing Outside the Fire" (words and music by Jenny Yates and Garth Brooks).

## CHAPTER 10: HIGHER STATES OF CONSCIOUSNESS

1. Raymond Moody, M.D., *Life After Life: An Investigation of a Phenomenon—Survival of Bodily Death* (New York: Bantam, 1975); and Melvin Morse, M.D.,

*Closer to the Light: Learning from the Near-Death Experiences of Children* (New York: Villard Books, 1990).

2. Melvin Morse, M.D., *Transformed by the Light: The Powerful Effect of Near-Death Experiences on People's Lives* (New York: Ivy Books, 1992).

3. William James, *The Varieties of Religious Experience* (New York: Collier Books/Macmillan, 1961).

## CHAPTER 11: VISUAL PARANORMAL EXPERIENCES

1. Alfred Kazin, ed. *The Portable Blake* (New York: Penguin Books, 1946).

2. See Hilary Evans, *Alternate States of Consciousness: Unself, Otherself, and Superself* (Wellingborough, Great Britain: Aquarian Press, 1989).

3. Anne Gordon, *A Book of Saints: True Stories of How They Touch Our Lives* (New York: Bantam Books, 1994).

4. René Fulop-Miller, *The Saints That Moved the World* (Salem, NH: Ayer Company, 1945).

5. See Jay Haley, *Uncommon Therapy: The Psychiatric Techniques of Milton H. Erickson, M.D.* (New York: Norton and Company, 1973). See also Jay Haley, *Strategies of Psychotherapy* (New York: Grune and Stratton, 1963).

6. Gersten, Dennis, M.D., "Psychotherapy of Visual Hallucinations: A Paradoxical Intervention." *Journal of Strategic and Systemic Therapies* (JSST). Volume 7, Number 4, Winter 1988. London and Ontario, Canada.

7. Sophy Burnham, *A Book of Angels* (New York: Ballantine, 1995); and Sophy Burnham, *Angel Letters* (New York: Ballantine, 1991).

8. Scott Sparrow, Ed.D., *Blessed Among Women: Encounters with Mary and Her Message* (New York: Harmony Books, 1997).

9. Jeanne Achterberg, Ph.D., *Woman as Healer: A Panoramic Survey of the Healing Activities of Women from Prehistoric Times to the Present* (Boston: Shambhala, 1991).

10. Barry Taff, Ph.D., personal communication, 1996.

11. *The Collected works of Madam Blavatsky*, 14 vols., compiled by Boris de Zirkoff and Dara Eklund (Pasadena, CA: Theosophical University Press, 1981).

12. Annie Besant and C. W. Leadbetter, *Thought Forms* (Madras, India: Theosophical Publishing House, 1901).

13. Janet Quinn, R.N., Ph.D., "AIDS, Hope and Healing," *Atlantis: The Imagery Newsletter* (Dec. 1991).

14. Rosalyn Bruyere, *Wheels of Light: A Study of the Chakras* (Sierra Madre, CA: Bon Productions, 1989).

## CHAPTER 12: EXTRASENSORY PERCEPTION

1. René Fulop-Miller, *The Saints That Moved the World* (Salem, NH: Ayer Company, 1945).

2. Ibid.

## CHAPTER 13: MIRACLES

1. Andrew Weil, M.D., *Spontaneous Healing* (New York: Alfred A. Knopf, 1995).

2. Janet Quinn, R.N., Ph.D., "The Effect of Imagery on Platelets," *Atlantis: The Imagery Newsletter* (Dec. 1991).

3. Larry Dossey, M.D., *Healing Words: The Power of Prayer and the Practice of Medicine* (San Francisco: HarperSanFrancisco, 1993).

## CHAPTER 14: SPIRITUAL FIRST AID

1. Stanislav Grof, M.D., and Christina Grof, *Spiritual Emergency: When Personal Transformation Becomes a Crisis* (Los Angeles: Jeremy Tarcher, 1989).

2. O. Carl Simonton, M.D., Stephanie Matthews-Simonton, and James Creighton, *Getting Well Again: A Step-by-Step Self-Help Guide to Overcoming Cancer for Patients and Their Families* (New York: Bantam Books, 1978).

3. Martin Rossman, M.D., *Healing Yourself: A Step-by-Step Program for Better Health Through Imagery* (New York: Walker and Company, 1987).

4. Stephen Levine, *Who Dies: An Investigation of Conscious Living and Conscious Dying* (New York: Anchor Books, 1982).

5. Mary Jayne Carlson, Ph.D., "Temple of Forgiveness Imagery," in *Atlantis: The Imagery Newsletter* (Oct. 1989).

6. Phyllis Krystal, *Cutting the Ties That Bind: Growing Up and Moving On* (York Beach, ME: Samuel Weiser, 1993); and Phyllis Krystal, *Cutting More Ties That Bind* (Longmead, England: Element Books, 1990).

7. Jack Hawley, *Reawakening the Spirit in Work: The Power of Dharmic Management* (San Francisco: Berrett-Koehler Publishers, 1993).

## CHAPTER 15: SPIRITUAL EMERGENCY: OPENING THE DOOR TO CHANGE

1. Phyllis Krystal, personal communication (1992).

# Index

## A

Achterberg, Dr. Jeanne, 106, 201
Action. *See* Right action
Acupuncture, 90, 91, 93, 153
Adams, Dennis, 102
AIDS, 110, 121, 257
Alcoholics Anonymous (AA), 99, 215
Alcoholism, 99, 215
Allah, 12
"Already-thereness" concept, 262–63
Alzheimer's disease, 126
American Indians, 187
American medicine men, 93, 94–95
Amino acids, 37, 153, 268
Amphetamines, 128, 135
*Angel Letters* (Burnham), 198
Angels, 51, 144, 191, 197–202, 204
  vs. hallucinations, 198, 202
Anger
  controlling, 76, 171–74, 215, 268
  dealing with, 169, 170–71
  nipping in bud, 173–74
  responsibility for, 172–73
  roots of, 172–73
  spiritual approaches to, 174
  Taking Lid Off, 173–74

Antipsychotic medications, 134
  and schizophrenia, 129–30
Anxiety, 110, 123
  as spiritual emergency, 266–67
Anxiety disorders, 158–64
  and faith, crisis in, 161
  and fear, handling, 162
  relaxation techniques for, 163–64
Artistic hallucinations, 216–18
*Asana*, 42
Assagioli, Dr. Roberto, 252
*Atharva Veda* (Hindu text), 91
Aura, 218–20, 228, 230
Awareness, 47, 108
  *See also* Sacred awareness
  and consciousness, 103
Ayurveda (medical system), 91

## B

Bach, Johann Sebastian, 217
Balinese, 86–87, 94
Bate de Agala (Eagle's Leg), 89
Belief, importance of, 87–101, 251
  American medicine men, 93, 94–95
  Eastern healing systems, 90–92
  healing, mixed messages about, 97–100

Belief, importance of (*cont'd.*)
　　healing principles, universal, 92–93
　　Judgment Review, 95–97
　　shamanism and sorcery, 87–90
Bharata, 238–39
Bird, Larry, 103
Birth process, 109, 280
Blake, William, 192
Blavatsky, Madame, 214
Body, physical, 44
Body-awareness, 103
Boleyn, Anne, 209
*Book of Angels, A* (Burnham), 198
Borderline personality disorder, 123,
　　124, 126, 129, 138–46, 188
　　vs. depression, 139
　　hallucinations in, 139, 193
　　and multiple personality disorder, 146,
　　150
　　vs. neurosis, 165
　　vs. schizophrenia, 139, 140
　　"split personality" in, 129, 140, 141,
　　193
　　and trust, 142–43
Borley Rectory (England), 209
Brahma, 20
Brain, 249
　　*See also* Organic brain syndrome
　　and depression, 152–53, 155, 157
　　left vs. right, 108
　　vs. mind, 130, 161
　　overdrive of, 133–38
Breath, energizing, 38–39, 65, 80, 267,
　　268, 269
Breathing, deep, 64–65, 117
Breathwork, 58, 64–65
Bresler, Dr. David, 163, 252
Brown Lady of Raynham Hall (ghost), 209
Bruyere, Rosalyn, 219
Buddha, 158, 167, 180, 195
Buddhism, 19, 21, 32, 111
Bull, Rev. H. D. D., 209
Burma, customs in, 91
Burnham, Sophy, 198
Byrd, Dr. Randolph, 233

## C

Campbell, Joseph, 166
Cancer, 100, 182, 197, 231, 236–37, 257
　　vs. infection, 218

Carlson, Dr. Mary Jayne, 258
Chakras, 111–12, 218
Change, actively resisting, 72–73
Character building, 82
Chavez, Linda, 235
Cheating, 21
Cherokee tribe, 94
*Chi* (energy), 7, 44, 90–91, 111, 112,
　　218
Child abuse, 213
　　*See also* Inner abuser; Inner child
Chinese medicine/philosophy, 7, 90–91,
　　108, 111, 201, 218, 266
Chodron, Pema, 22
Chopra, Dr. Deepak, 91
Chronic fatigue syndrome (CFS), 12–15,
　　110
Church attendance, 98–100
Clairaudience, 223–24
Clarity, of thought-forms, 214
Claustrophobia, 158, 160
Clock imagery technique, 163
*Closer to the Light* (Morse), 182
Color, of thought-forms, 214
Commitment, religious, 98–100
Communicating with main concern, 58,
　　62, 66–68, 252–55, 271, 281
Compassion, 43
Complex OBE, 180
Concentration, 42
Concern. *See* Main concern
Confidence, 54
Confusion, as spiritual emergency,
　　271–72
Consciousness
　　*See also* Higher consciousness; Unity
　　consciousness
　　altered states of, 101–3, 105, 108–11,
　　112, 114, 179–80, 198, 201, 206–7
　　and awareness, 103
　　evolution of, 110
　　expansion of, 109
　　four dimensions of, 101–2
　　and grief, 102–3
　　group state of, 106
　　language of, 108–10
　　"lower" forms of, 212
　　male, 107
　　masters of, 107
　　and mental illness, 109
　　mob, 106
　　"money," 108

"normal," 102, 105, 106–7, 108
and pain, 102–3
"shock," 105
"sliding states of," 140
social, 106
and space, 102
television, 109
and time, 102, 106, 107
Crawford, Dr. Don, 174
Crisis in faith
and anxiety disorders, 161
as spiritual emergency, 262, 272–73
Cultural belief, 92–93
Culture shock, 105
*Curanderas*, 88, 89
*Cutting More Ties that Bind* (Krystal),
260
"Cutting the Ties" technique, 260–61,
281
*Cutting the Ties that Bind* (Krystal), 260

### D

Dalai Lama, 19
Dali, Salvador, 217
Dass, Ram, 18
David, statue of (Michelangelo), 5
Death, 49, 184, 204, 206, 208
and near-death experiences, 182–83
smell of, 226
and visions, 192
voodoo, 95
Deathbed experiences (DBEs), 183–84
Decision-Making technique, 174–75
Delirium, 126, 127, 193, 249
Del Maestro, Richard, 17, 216
Delusions, in schizophrenia, 130
Dementia, 126
Departed, visions of, 202–4
Depression, 109, 122, 123, 151–58, 242
vs. borderline personality disorder, 139
and brain chemistry, 152–53, 155, 157
and ego deflation, 155–56
vs. mania, 137–38
as spiritual emergency, 268
spiritual technique for, 157–58
Desires, ceiling on, 76
Detachment, 25
Devi, Indra, 111
Dharma, 166, 167, 168
Diana (goddess), 201

Diego, Juan, 200
Diet, 116, 268
"Dissociation," 181
Divine assistance, and the void, 276–77
Divine visitations, 201
Divine Weaver Technique, for Integrating
Experiences, 221–22
DNA, 233
*Doshas*, 91
Dossey, Dr. Larry, 233–34
Drug abuse, 99
Dying, and living, 184

### E

Eastern healing systems, 44, 90–92
Eastern philosophy, 107, 123
Eastern religions, 19, 108, 263
ECT (electroconvulsive therapy), 153
Ego, 166, 169
boundaries, 140
death, 251–52
deflation vs. hyperinflation, 137–38
and depression, 155–56
Egypt (ancient), 218, 239, 240
Eightfold path to enlightenment, 42
Empathy, ESP of, 227–30
Encephalitis, 110
Energy
*See also* Breath, energizing
redirecting obstructed, 115–17
spiritual, 4–8
Enlightenment
eightfold path to, 42
and extrasensory perception,
223–30
and higher consciousness, 179–90
and miracles, 231–44
overpowering quality of, 179
and perpetual peace, 180
transformation by, 183
and visual paranormal experience,
191–222
Entities, 211–12
vs. ghosts, 205, 208
Erikson, Milton, 196
Eskimos, 108
Exercise, 116, 268
Exorcism, 205
Experiences, 50, 57
technique for integrating, 221–22

Extrasensory perception (ESP), 9–10,
    223–230
  of empathy, 227–30
  of smell, 226–27
  of sound, 223–26

## F

Faith, 97–100
  *See also* Crisis in faith
  two paths to, 262
Fasting, 116
Fatima, miracle of, 200, 201
Fear
  and anxiety disorders, 162
  embracing overwhelming, 69, 256–58,
    269, 272
Feather imagery technique, 163
Feelings, importance of, 145, 155, 198,
    251
Fight-or-flight response, 161
"Figure eight" technique, 144–45
"Force-field," creating, 144
Forgiveness, 76, 261
Francis of Assisi, St., 225–26
Freeze, Dr., 127, 128
Freud, Sigmund, 98, 165, 166, 167, 169
  influence of, 23
Frieder, Dr. Glenn, 141–42
Future, letting go of, 261–65

## G

Gabriel (angel), 200
Gandhi, Mohandas, 244
Ghosts, 191, 204–9, 244
  vs. entities, 205, 208
Goals, importance of, 50, 52
God
  belief in, 22
  connecting with, 19, 78, 156,
    272–73
  direct experience of, 198
  faith in, 262
  as force, 18
  grace of, 20
  "holding hand of," 145
  imagining, 26–27, 158
  invisible hand of, 234–43
  love of, 78
  and mantras, 32, 160
  presence of, 16, 114–15
  questions about, 23–24
  seeing, 34–35
  talking to, 41
  time of, 107
  trust in, 159–60, 161
  voice of, 264
  will of, 265
  worship of, 201
Goddess, 18
  worship of, 201
Godzilla, 193
Greeks (ancient), 20, 218
Grief, 166, 192
  and consciousness, 102–3
  and visions of departed, 203–4
Guadalupe, Our Lady of, 200
Guillain-Barré syndrome, 90
Guilt, releasing, 258–59

## H

Hallucinations, 3, 219
  vs. angels, 198, 202
  artistic, 216–18
  auditory and visual, 126
  in borderline personality disorder, 139,
    193
  definition of, 191
  vs. illusion, 193–94
  and schizophrenia, 192–94, 244
  vs. vision, 192–94, 195
Happiness, 84
Haraldsson, Erlunder, 192
Hauntings, 204–9, 244
Hausa tribe (Nigeria), 88
Hawaii, 64, 87, 89, 209
Hawley, Jack, 262–63
Healing
  Eastern systems, 44, 90–92
  mixed messages about, 97–100
  universal principles of, 92–93
*Healing Words: The Power of Prayer and
    the Practice of Medicine* (Dossey),
    233
*Healing Yourself: A Step-by-Step
    Program for Better Health Through
    Imagery* (Rossman), 252
*HeartSpace: RelaxII* (Del Maestro), 216
Henry VIII, King, 209

Higher consciousness, 179–90
  *See also* Nirvana
  deathbed experiences, 183–84
  identity transformations, 187–88
  and Judgment Review technique,
    95–97
  near-death experiences, 182–83
  out-of-body experiences, 180–83
  trances, healing, 184–86
Hildegard of Bingen, St., 194, 225
Hinduism, 7, 20, 21, 38, 91, 111, 239
  mantras, 32
Homeopathy, 93
Hope, importance of, 92, 121–22
Hopi tribe, 86, 202
Human values
  deficiencies in, 44, 103
  healing power of, 42–55
  integrating, 82
  as mantras, 32
  and mood words, 54–55
  and personal growth, 47–48
  prioritizing, 82
  and Psycho-Spiritual Assessment,
    48–54
  and visualizing symbols of, 44–45, 82
Hyperthyroidism, 113
Hypnosis, 109


I

Ibo tribe (Nigeria), 88, 89, 93, 96
Id, function of, 166
Identity transformation, 187–88
  vs. possession, 187
Illusion, 126
  vs. hallucinations, 193–94
Image, of meaning, 271–72
Imagery, 268, 269
  guided, 37–38
  Rituals, One-Minute, 58, 79–80, 83,
    84
  symbolic, 252–55
  Temple of Forgiveness, 258–59
  wave, 267
Imagery techniques
  clock, 163
  feather, 163
  peaceful place, 164
  stress, footprints of, 164
Immune system, 141

India, 218
  consciousness in, 105–6, 108
  healing systems in, 90, 91
  yogis and gurus in, 87
"I-ness," 103
*I Never Promised You a Rose Garden*
    (Greenberg), 129
Inner abuser, and the void, 280–81
Inner child, 274, 281
Inner voice, recognizing, 248–49
"Instantaneousness," 263
Intellect, 44, 123
  vs. intuition, 108–09
Iroquois tribe, 7
Ishtar (goddess), 201
Islam, 32, 200, 219
Ituri tribe, 7


J

James the Apostle, 200
Japanese, 86, 108
Jesus, 16, 153, 158, 180
  crucifixion of, 264–65
  forgiveness of, 208
  love of, 12
  miracles of, 239
  mother of, 200, 227
  teachings of, 7
  worship of, 194
Jewish mantras, 32
Joan of Arc, St., 143
John the Evangelist, St., 200
Jones, Carla, 199
Jordan, Michael, 103, 107
Joseph, St., 200
Judgment Review technique, 68, 69,
    95–97
Jung, Carl, 252
Jungians, 23


K

Kabbalah, 7
Kahunas (Hawaii), 89
Kali (Hindu divine mother), 195
Kidney, 90
King, Martin Luther, Jr., 244
Kirlian photography, 228
Knock, miracle at, 200

Krishna, Gopi, 110, 112, 115, 158, 239
Krystal, Phyllis, 260–61, 267
*Kundalini: The Evolutionary Energy in Man* (Krishna), 110
Kundalini energy, 4, 6, 110–15, 121, 135, 192, 218, 244, 270
   management of, 115–17
*Kundalini Experience, The: Psychosis or Transcendence?*, (Sannella), 110
Kung fu technique, 112

## L

Laing, R.D., 107, 129
Language of consciousness, 108–10
*Language of the Heart* (Del Maestro), 216
Larson, Dr. David, 98
Latipso ceremonies, 95
Lawlis, Dr. Frank, 92
"Layer of bliss," 44
Levine, Ondrea, 256
Levine, Stephen, 256
Life
   meaning of, 104
   mission in, 105
   as teacher, 85
*Life After Life* (Moody), 182
Life-force, 44, 90–91, 111, 112
*Life Is a Challenge, Meet It* (Thomas), 189
*Life Is a Dream, Realize It* (Thomas), 189
*Life Is a Game, Play It* (Thomas), 189
Lincoln, Abraham, 244
Lithium, 134, 135, 138
Liver, problems of, 90
Living
   and dying, 184
   fully in moment, 76–77
*Loka Samastha Sukino Bhavantu,* 41
Long-Term Mental Fitness Plan, 58, 81–84
Lourdes, miracle at, 200, 201
Love
   conveying fully in moment, 77–78
   developing, 58, 75–78
   encouraging expansion of, 77
   as goal of spiritual practice, 18, 21
   God's connecting to, 78
   as human value, 43, 45, 48, 49, 52, 69, 75, 103, 158, 252, 258, 266, 270, 272, 275
   as ice cream, 75
   as invisible, 22
   as kundalini energy, 110, 115
   making, 109
   and miracles, 240, 241
   obstructions to, 76
   resistance to, 77
   seeking, 281–82
*Love, Medicine, and Miracles* (Siegel), 122
LSD, 3–4, 128
Lying, 21
   *See also* Self-lies

## M

Magic Box technique, 37–38
Magnetism, and kundalini energy, 111
Main concern, 66, 145, 155, 157, 251
   clarifying, 198
   communicating with, 58, 66, 67–68, 252–55, 271, 281
   identifying, 50–51, 54–55
   naming, 62
   prioritizing, 62
   stop working on, 72
   and visualizing symbol, 63
Maintenance Program, for Mental Fitness Program, 83
Mania, 113, 123, 124, 126, 133–38, 244
   vs. depression, 137–38
   mind of, 138
   vs. nirvana, 190
   vs. schizophrenia, 137
   vs. spiritual person, 138
Manic-depressive illness, 90
Mantra(s)
   Buddhist, 32
   Christian, 32
   defined, 31
   Gayatri, 27, 40–41
   God the Father, 160
   Hindu, 32
   Islamic, 32
   Jesus Christ, 153
   Jewish, 32
   Meditation, 31–34, 49, 57, 59, 60, 62–65, 66–70, 72, 75, 79, 83, 84, 161, 163, 267, 273

names of, 32
"*Om Sai Ram*," 27, 41
purposes of, 33–34
repetition of, 27
Zoroastrian, 32
Marital Problems, as Spiritual Emergency, 270–71
Mary (Mother of Jesus), 192
visions of, 200–201, 227
Meaning, 145, 154–55, 198
image of, 271–72
of life, 104
Meditation, 26, 42, 202, 219, 248
all-day mindfulness, 115, 161
"lost," 105
Mantra, 31–34, 49, 57, 59, 60, 62–64, 66–70, 73, 76, 79, 84, 85, 161, 163, 215, 267, 273
"Who Am I," 60, 82, 103–7
Medjugorje, miracle at, 200, 201
*Meetings at the Edge* (Levine), 256
Mental clearing technique, 79–80, 267, 269
Mental Fitness Program, 56–85
happiness, 84
life as teacher, 85
weeks 1-12, 59–83
Mental Fitness Techniques, 28–34, 37–39, 44, 47, 49, 54, 60, 64, 69–70, 72–73, 75–80, 95, 103, 115, 158, 163, 171, 173, 174, 221, 243, 252, 256, 258, 261, 266, 268–72, 275
Mental illness, 90, 121–24
and consciousness, 109
Mental Rehearsal, 262
Merton, Thomas, 19
Mind
body and spirit, 44
vs. brain, 130, 161
as home base, 34
losing, 123–24
and LSD, 3–4
manic vs. spiritual, 138
normal vs. manic, 138
okaying, 249
positive work for, 33–34
quieting, 58, 59
slowing down, 33
unconscious, 140, 175–76
witnessing, 39–40
Mind-awareness, 103
Mind-body connection, 157

Mind-body miracles, 232–33
Miner, Horace, 93–95
Miracles, 231–44
definition of, 231
diagnosing, 249–52
God, invisible hand of, 234–43
linear approach to, 242–43
mind-body, 232–33
and Practicing the Presence technique, 243–44
prayer, power of, 233–34
Mohammed (Prophet), 200
Montana, Joe, 6, 39, 101
Mood words, 54–55
Moody, Dr. Raymond, 182
Moral conduct. *See* Right action
Moral illness, 45–47
Morse, Dr. Melvin, 182–83
Moses (Jewish leader), 6–7, 239
Mother Teresa, 22
Mozart, Wolfgang Amadeus, 217
Multiple personality disorder (MPD), 123, 146–50
and borderline personality disorder, 146, 150
subpersonalities in, 146–47
Mystical experiences, vs. schizophrenia, 131–32

## N

Nacirema, 93–95
Native Americans, 20, 27, 89, 92, 220
Nature mantras, 32
Nature worship, 87
Near-death experiences (NDEs), 182–83
Negotiation technique, 253–54
Neurosis
vs. borderline personality disorder, 165
definition of, 166–67
examples of, 167–69
obsessive-compulsive, 168–69
and separateness, 167, 170
and spiritual ignorance, 167, 169–70
spiritual perspective vs. psychoanalytic view, 167
and suffering, 166, 167, 170
symptoms of, 169
Nigeria, 88, 89, 93

Nirvana, 42, 109, 188–90
  *See also* Samadhi
  vs. mania, 190
Nonviolence
  as human value, 43, 45, 48, 49, 69,
    95, 103, 157, 171, 173, 252, 258,
    268, 275
  in thought, 95
Nutrition, 268


# O

Obsessive-compulsive neurosis, 168–69
Organic brain syndrome (OBS), 123,
  125–27, 129
Osis, Karlis, 192
Out-of-body experiences (OBEs), 180–83
  vs. near-death experiences (NDEs),
    182–83


# P

Pain, 51
  and consciousness, 102
  embracing overwhelming, 68, 256–58,
    269, 272
  imaginary, 228
  phantom-limb, 228–30
  as spiritual emergency, 269–70
Panic, as spiritual emergency, 271–72
  *See also* Anxiety disorders
Pantheism, 20
Paradox
  definition of, 71
  power of, 58, 71–73
Paranoid schizophrenia, 43–44, 129,
  132, 137, 225
Past, letting go of, 258–61
  guilt, releasing, 258–59
  resentment, letting go of, 259–61
Patanjali (Indian yogi), 42
Peace
  as human value, 43, 45, 48, 49, 54,
    64, 69, 72, 76, 103, 115, 158, 163,
    171, 252, 256, 258, 261, 266,
    268–72, 275
  symbol for, 116
Peaceful place imagery technique, 164
Pélé (Goddess of volcanoes), 87
Penicillin, 92

Perception, 191
Persia (ancient), 218
Personal growth, and human values,
  47–48
Pfister, Rev. Oskar, 98
Phantom-limb pain, 228–30
Pheochromocytoma, 113, 134
Phobia, social, 113–14
*Politics of Experience, The* (Laing), 107
Poltergeist activity, 210, 212
Possession, spirit, 205, 209–13, 244
  vs. identity transformation, 187
Practicing the Presence technique, 27,
  69–71, 74
  for miracles, 243–44
Prana, 7, 44, 92, 111, 112, 218
*Pranayama*, 38, 42
*Pratyahara*, 42
Prayer, power of, 214, 233–34
Problem, 49–50, 52
Pseudo-spirituality, 124
Psychiatrists, shortcomings of, 22–23
Psychiatry, traditional vs. spiritual, 40
Psychic attack, 205, 209–13
Psychics, 204–8
Psychoneuroimmunology, 231
Psycho-Spiritual Assessment (PSA),
  48–54, 55, 57, 58, 60, 61, 100,
  144–45, 155, 157, 198, 252
  first question of, 179
Psychosynthesis, 252
Psychotic episodes, in schizophrenia,
  130–31


# Q

Quinn, Dr. Janet, 218


# R

Rage. *See* Anger
Ramakrishna, Paramahansa, 112, 115,
  194–95
Reagan, Ronald, 10
*Reawakening the Spirit in Work: The
  Power of Dharmic Management*
  (Hawley), 262
*Relax* (Del Maestro), 216
Relaxation, 267, 269
  techniques for, 79–80, 163–64

Religion, 167, 273
  *See also* Eastern religions; Faith
  and spirituality, 24
Remen, Dr. Rachel Naomi, 252
Renée, Capt. Frederick, 209
Resentment, letting go of, 259–61
Resistance
  exploring, 58, 69
  overcoming, 69–70
Reyes, Dr. Benito, 180–81
Right action
  as human value, 43, 45, 48, 49, 54,
    69, 103, 252, 268, 272, 275
  and neurosis, 166–67
Rituals, One-Minute Imagery, 58, 79–80,
    83, 84
Romero, Angelita, 184
Romero, Celedonio, 183–84, 203, 217,
    226
Romero, Celin, 183
Romero, Pepe, 6, 102, 156, 184, 189–90,
    203, 226
Rossman, Dr. Martin, 252


# S

Sacred awareness, 17–19, 22
  and spirituality, 167, 170
Sacred vision, 22
Sai Baba, Sathya, 11–12, 26, 34, 43, 74,
    124, 169, 227, 236–39, 240, 249,
    279, 282
Saints, visions of, 194–95
Samadhi, 7, 42, 43, 140, 188, 249
  *See also* Nirvana
Sandweiss, Dr. Samuel, 11
Sannella, Dr. Lee, 110
Sanskrit, 108, 109, 166, 190
  mantras, 32
Sarita, Hermana, 88–89
Sathya Sai Education in Human Values
    (Sathya Sai EHV) system, 43
Schizophrenia, 88, 90, 92-93, 109, 123,
    124, 125, 126, 127–33, 161, 187
  and antipsychotic medications, 129–30
  vs. borderline personality disorder,
    139, 140
  chemical imbalance in, 132
  delusions in, 130
  and hallucinations, 192–94, 244
  vs. mania, 137

mind vs. brain in, 130
  vs. mystical experiences, 131–32
  paranoid, 43–44, 129, 132, 137,
    225
  psychotic episodes in, 130–31
Science, vs. spirituality, 241
Scientific medicine, 98
Self-acceptance, profound, 58, 68,
    256–58, 269, 272
Self-lies, facing up to, 60–61
Separateness, and neurosis, 167, 170
"Serpent fire." *See* Kundalini energy
Shamans, 87–90, 109, 187, 219
Shape, of thought-forms, 214
Shintoism, 198
Shiva, 195
  caves, 240
*Siddhi* powers, 87, 214, 215, 219–20,
    240
Siegel, Dr. Bernie, 122
Simonton, Dr. O. Carl, 252
Simpson, O.J., 200
Sleep deprivation, 116
Smell, ESP of, 226–27
Smiling Buddha technique, 158
Smith, Shama, 187, 188, 204–8,
    226
Social phobia, 113–14
Sorcerers, 87–90
Soubirous, Bernadette, 200
Soul
  awareness, 103, 107
  difficulty of contacting, 123
  as eternal, 124
  as ineffable, 179
Sound, ESP of, 223–26
Space, and consciousness, 102
Sphinx, making of, 239–40
Spirit, nature of, 44
Spiritual approaches, to controlling
    anger, 174
Spiritual beliefs, 86–87
Spiritual emergency
  anxiety as, 266–67
  confusion and panic as, 271–72
  crisis in faith as, 272–73
  depression as, 268
  goals of dealing with, 251–52
  handling, 247–48
  managing, 251
  marital problems as, 270–71
  pain as, 269–70

Spiritual energy, 4–8

Spiritual experience, 123, 144
  genuineness of, 250–51
  naming, 250

Spiritual ignorance, and neurosis, 167, 169–70

Spirituality, 14, 182
  defining, 17–18, 21–22
  and human values, 19–20
  and religion, 24
  and sacred awareness, 167, 170
  vs. science, 241

Spiritual person, vs. manic, 138

Spiritual practices, 17–18, 21
  deepening, 58, 67

Spiritual psychiatry, workings of, 25–28, 43, 44

Spiritual qualities, importance of, 18–19

Spiritual questions, twenty-five, 23–24, 81

Spiritual technique, for depression, 157–58

Spleen, problems of, 90

"Split personality," in borderline personality disorder, 129, 140, 141, 193

Stress
  footprints of, imagery technique, 164
  handling, 161–62
  metabolic imbalances caused by, 36

Subpersonalities, in multiple personality disorder, 146–47

Suffering
  and neurosis, 166, 167, 170
  sympathetic, 228

Sufis, 7

Sundowning, 126

Superego, function of, 166

Surrender, 117
  in Eastern spiritual practice, 263–64
  guidelines for, 264
  meaning of, 14
  prayers of, 27, 273

Suzuki-roshi (teacher), 195

Symbols
  and imagery, 252–55
  nature of, 108
  using, 175–76

visualizing, of human values, 44–45, 82
  visualizing, and main concern, 63

Sympathetic suffering, 228

Symptom, as main concern, 49–50

Syphilis, 110


## T

Taff, Dr. Barry, 210, 212

Taoism, 111

Temple of Delphi, lessons of, 172

Temple of Forgiveness Imagery, 258–59

Theosophical Society, 214

Therapy, as moment, 35–36

Theresa of Avila, St., 194

Thomas, Joy, 189

Thomas, Rev., 202–3

Thought, Eastern vs. Western, 108, 109

Thought-forms, 213–16
  negative, 215–16

Thought Watch Mental Fitness Technique, 28–31, 57, 60

Tigrett, Isaac, 235

Time
  and consciousness, 102, 106, 107
  perception of, 102

Tolerance, importance of, 43

Tomlin, Lily, 16

Tower of London, hauntings in, 209

Trances, healing, 184–86

Transformation, 43
  *See also* Identity transformation

Transformational Program, for Mental Fitness Program, 84

*Transformed by the Light* (Morse), 182

"True nature," 3

Trust, 92
  and borderline personality disorder, 142–43
  in God, 159–60, 161
  value of, 43–44

Truth
  as essential, 21
  as human value, 43, 45, 48, 49, 54, 60, 69, 103, 252, 270

Twilight state, 198

## U

Unconscious mind, 140, 175–76
Unity consciousness. *See* Nirvana;
     Samadhi
Universal intelligence, 32

## V

Values. *See* Human values
Vedanta theory, about anger, 172
Vedas, 21, 38, 97
Vibhuti (sacred ash), 238, 239
Vision(s)
     and death, 192
     definition of, 191
     of departed, 202–4
     vs. hallucination, 192–94, 195
     sacred, 22
     of saints, 194–95
     and visitation, 195–97
Vision Quest, 94
Visitation, and vision, 195–97
"Visualizing the Divine Form" technique,
     243
Visualizing symbols
     of human values, 44–45, 82
     and main concern, 63
Visual paranormal experiences, 191–222
     angels, 51, 144, 191, 197–202, 204
     artistic hallucinations, 216–18
     aura, 218–20, 228, 230
     Divine Weaver Technique, 221–22
     ghosts, 191, 204–9, 244
     hauntings, 204–9, 244
     possession, spirit, 187, 205, 209–13,
          244
     psychic attack, 205, 209–13
     thought-forms, 213–16

visions of departed, 202–4
visions vs. hallucinations, 192–94, 195
Vital capacity, 10
Vitamins, 37
Voice, inner, 248–49
Void, the, 274–82
     dealing with, 142, 145–46
     and divine assistance, 276–77
     exploring, 275–76
     facing, 275
     and inner abuser, 280–81
     reaching bottom of, 277–78
     transforming bottom of, 278–80
Voodoo death, 95

## W

War, nature of, 107
Wave imagery, 267
*Wheels of Light: A Study of the Chakras*
     (Bruyere), 219
"Who Am I" meditation, 60, 81, 103–5
*Who Dies* (Levine), 256
*Wisdom of No Escape, The* (Chodron),
     22
*Woman as Healer* (Achterberg), 106,
     201
Work, as worship, 34
Worry, 262, 264–65

## Y

Yin and yang, 201
Yoga, 42
     kriya, 110
     postures, 112, 116
Yogis, 3–4, 87, 109
Yoruba tribe (Nigeria), 8

# ACKNOWLEDGMENTS

I am profoundly grateful to so many people. To Larry Dossey, for his encouragement, advice, and belief in the book. To Kitty Farmer, half of my agent team, who fell in love with the book and shepherded it through to completion. To Ned Leavitt, the other half of my agent team, for uncommon wisdom, for his phenomenal ability to point out weaknesses and clarify solutions.

To my editor, Leslie Meredith, whose enormous time, energy, and unflagging spirit were priceless. I am especially thankful for her brilliant and scholarly eye that helped guide the book. My thanks also to Laura Wood, Associate Editor, who worked tirelessly and enthusiastically, and who was always available to lend a hand. To Janet Biehl I am indebted for her extraordinary skills in copy editing. And to Andrew Stuart, who helped coordinate the logistics at Harmony Books. My agents and the staff at Harmony have been a dream team.

I am indebted to my good friend Richard Del Maestro, who kept me grounded. I wrote the first draft of this book in six weeks and thought it was complete. Richard simply responded, "Yeah, right," and then proceeded to refuse to read the book for five more years so that his mind would be fresh when he felt he could truly be of help. I am grateful for his brainstorming, his hours of consultation, and his insistence that I never settle for even a single line that was not the absolute best I could give. Thank you to Gregory Wright, who critiqued and edited the book when it was still in its infancy.

To Shama Smith I am grateful for her support and faith in the project, her wealth of stories which appear within these pages, and her brilliance in helping clarify some of the tough questions about consciousness and paranormal phenomena.

I am indebted to so many friends who shared their magical, mystical experiences with me—to Pepe and Celedonio Romero, Stephanie O'Rielly, Dian Kerr, Joy Thomas, Sherrill Stoner, Raymond Woo—and to Samuel Sandweiss, M.D., the first doctor I met who believed in the importance of integrating spirituality with medicine and who began to open me up to the possibilities.

To each and every friend who has contributed in so many ways—Shanti Del Maestro, Connie Fox, Madeline Gershwin, Sharon Purcell, Barbie Dossey, Marilyn Ferguson, Tory Pryor, Daniel Benor, Ted Kahn, Mahri Kintz, Sid Jordan, Sid and Elizabeth Stave, Linda Carol, Barbara Morse, John Raatz, the entire Romero family, the Sandweiss family.

To my mother, who gave me this birth and a love for creativity.

A special thanks to my daughter, Rachel, who came to learn that dad often worked seven days a week, and who came to laugh at my statement, "The book is done!" Thank you for your love and patience and for being so wise and loving.

Most of all I am indebted to my patients who have had the courage to share the secrets of their souls, who have demonstrated how it is possible to survive the worst nightmares conceivable and still embrace their dreams and miracles. They have taught me more than any teacher or any school. They are my real instructors in the University of Life.

## ABOUT THE AUTHOR

Dennis Gersten, M.D., has been practicing psychiatry in San Diego since 1978, specializing in mind-body techniques, mental imagery, and metabolic medicine. He publishes *Atlantis: the Imagery Newsletter* and has served as an imagery consultant to Rodale Press/*Prevention Magazine* for eight of their most recent books. He authored *The POW Survival Guide* dedicated to the Allied troops of Operation Desert Storm.

Because of his integrated body-mind-energy-spirit approach, he works with traditional psychiatric problems such as anxiety and depression, as well as with peak performance; cancer, AIDS, and other chronic and serious illnesses; and spiritual emergencies.